**HENRY
HOLT**

Batsford Chess Library

Winning With the Dragon

Chris Ward

An Owl Book
Henry Holt and Company
New York

To the memory of my Grandfather, George W. Rea,
without whom I would never even have played chess.

Henry Holt and Company, Inc.
Publishers since 1866
115 West 18th Street
New York, New York 10011

Henry Holt® is a registered
trademark of Henry Holt and Company, Inc.

First published in the United States in 1994 by
Henry Holt and Company, Inc.
Published in Great Britain in 1994 by B. T. Batsford Ltd.

Library of Congress Catalog Card Number: 94—075547

ISBN 0-8050-3287-8 (An Owl Book: pbk.)

First American Edition—1994

Printed in the United Kingdom
All first editions are printed on acid-free paper. ∞

10 9 8 7 6 5 4 3 2 1

Adviser: R. D. Keene, GM, OBE
Technical Editor: Graham Burgess

Contents

Bibliography

Laszlo Sapi and Attila Schneider, *Sicilian Dragon Yugoslav 9 ♗c4* (Batsford, 1989)
Laszlo Sapi and Attila Schneider, *Sicilian Dragon: Classical and Levenfish Variations* (Batsford, 1990)
David Levy, *The Sicilian Dragon* (Batsford, 1972)
David Levy, *Sicilian Dragon: Classical and Levenfish Variations* (Batsford, 1981)
Tony Miles and Eric Moskow, *Sicilian Dragon: Yugoslav Attack* (Batsford, 1979)
Eric Schiller and Jonathan Goldman, *The Sicilian Dragon Yugoslav Attack* (Chess Enterprises, 1987)
Andrew Soltis, *Sicilian Dragon For Black* (Chess Digest Incorporated, 1983)
Eduard Gufeld, *Sizilianisch Drachen-System* (Schachverlag Rudi Schmaus, 1985)
Fabio Lotti and Angelo Picardi, *The Italian Dragon* (ASIGC, 1990)
Chris Ward and Bob Wade, *Developments in the Sicilian: Dragon* (Quadrant Marketing Ltd, 1988)
Bruno Carlier, *Trends in the Sicilian Dragon Yugoslav Attack* (Trends Publications, 1991)
Nigel Davies, *Trends in the Sicilian Dragon* (Trends Publications, 1993)
John Nunn, *Beating the Sicilian* (Batsford, 1984)
John Nunn, *Beating the Sicilian 2* (Batsford, 1990)
Anatoly Karpov, *The Semi-Open Game In Action* (Batsford, 1988)
Alexander Matanovic (ed.), *Encyclopedia of Chess Openings B* second edition (Sahovski Informator, 1984)
Informator volumes 10-57 (Sahovski Informator)
New in Chess Yearbooks 1-29 (Interchess BV)

Preface

If you are reading this, then you either want to become a Dragon player or else wish to improve your fire breathing skills. A wise move, but take heed! The Sicilian Dragon is the most hotly debated opening known to chess theory. Characterized by its razor-sharp variations; to be successful using this lethal weapon, you often need guts and nerves of steel.

If you have never before played the Dragon, then believe me, you have been missing out. In this book, I have attempted to develop the reader's understanding of this riveting opening, by frequently relating my own learning experiences. Join me on the road of discovery and you will find out that there is nothing more satisfying than winning with the Dragon! Certainly your chess will never be quite the same again.

Good luck!

Chris Ward
Kent, January 1994

Symbols

+	Check
++	Double check
#	Checkmate
$\pm$ ($\mp$)	Slight advantage to White (Black)
$\pm$ ($\mp$)	Clear advantage to White (Black)
+- (-+)	Winning position to White (Black)
=	Level position
!	Good move
?	Bad move
!!	Outstanding move
??	Blunder
!?	Interesting move
?!	Dubious move
Δ	Intending
OL	Olympiad
Ch	Championship
Wch	World Championship
Z	Zonal
IZ	Interzonal
Ct	Candidates
Corr.	Postal game

1   Introducing the Dragon

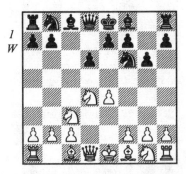

Above is the most common starting position of the Sicilian Dragon. It is rumoured to have been named so because Black's pawn structure resembles the shape of the legendary beast. Personally I find the link rather tenuous to say the least, but who cares, the title 'Dragon' sounds cool! Besides, bearing in mind the fierce battles that may lie ahead, being known as the 'Pelikan' or 'Kan' (like other Sicilian counterparts), would hardly portray the appropriate macho image.

From the moment White trades his d-pawn for Black's c-pawn (recapturing on d4 with his knight), the game becomes an 'Open Sicilian', and Black can initiate the Dragon variation with ...g6. After 1 e4 c5, although many believe that White should be forced into playing the Open Sicilian (to make things exciting), sadly this is yet to be written into the Laws of Chess!

Therefore White has other options available, which Black needs to be aware of. Strictly speaking, these options are out of this book's scope, and so I shall refer to them as early deviations, before the early deviations! Based on my experiences, I have listed below, in descending order of popularity, these alternatives:

Sicilian 2 c3

Closed Sicilian

Grand Prix Attack

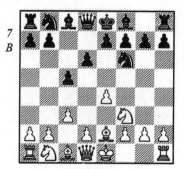

St George (Basman) System

Sicilian 3 ♗b5+

Kopec System (with 4 ♗d3 or 4 h3)

Morra Gambit

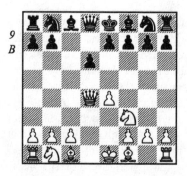

Sicilian 4 ♕xd4

Sicilian 2 g3 (or 2 d3)

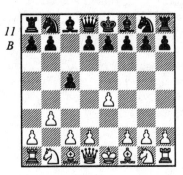

Sicilian 2 b3

Some of these, and others such as the Wing Gambit 2 b4 (and Deferred Wing Gambit 2 ♘f3 followed by 3 b4) may be known elsewhere by different names (and collectively as Anti-Sicilian systems), but none of them are particularly worrying. Nevertheless, at least a brief knowledge of them (in conjunction with an understanding of this book) completes a defensive repertoire to 1 e4.

The reader will observe, simply by looking at the bibliography, that there already exists an extraordinary amount of Dragon textbooks. Many will imply that such books are pointless as new games and analysis always crop up, constantly questioning and even refuting the summations in previous works. Indeed there is some logic to this argument, but I have tried to make this book different. Sure, I have often used recent games, and yes, perhaps reflecting the trends in the variations. However my main aim has been to supply the reader with a variety of concepts and ideas.

John Nunn once said that there is no room for principles in the Dragon, and that it is all about moves. With the loss and gain of even one tempo often being the decisive factor in the more 'cutthroat' lines, at top flight in particular, it is easy to see what he means. Nevertheless, having played the Dragon all of my life, I would have to disagree. My intention has been to produce a handbook of guidelines that I wish had been around when I was learning the opening. Memorising variation C21368 is all very well, but what of the moves that aren't in the books?! i.e. those played rarely by Grandmasters and International Masters, but frequently by club players. Hopefully these 'principles' will save the reader unnecessary defeats, and go some way to making him/her understand why the textbook theory is what it is.

Although I don't think that I have ever read a chess book from the beginning to the end, this is exactly what I am suggesting should be done here. Young juniors including it as bedtime reading, may need to have a dictionary handy (I certainly had to!).

In trying to make this book appealing to a broad spectrum of chessplayers, I realize that it is possible that I have bitten off more than I can chew. For the strong player, some parts may appear rather basic. To compensate, for the keen theoreticians, I have divulged a number of what were opening secrets, and I can guarantee that there are plenty of 'innova-tive' juicy morsels to be found. The widespread games collection, ranges from common club player continuations, to recent Grandmaster clashes. With regards to the interest in 'raw moves', I am realistic. I accept that in the future, developments may take place which will supersede some individual variations. However the ideas will remain forever, it is merely the specifics that may occasionally need rethinking. One final tip from me to help you get under way, is that in the Dragon it often pays to be optimistic. I have had no problems with this book's title as the Dragon is after all, all about winning! I have tried to be user-friendly, let's hope you're a friendly user!

2 Important Dragon Concepts

The Power of the Dragon Bishop

The 'Dragon bishop' is a term I hear a lot and funnily enough not only in discussions about the Sicilian Dragon. The term usually refers to a fianchettoed black king's bishop which sits at home on g7 and yet cuts like a laser across the board. When playing the Dragon, you will notice how, even with a knight on f6, the bishop exerts latent pressure on White's d4-knight which then transfers onto the c3-knight, when the former moves away. Clearly with both of White's knights removed from the diagonal, the b2 pawn comes under scrutiny and plentiful attacking possibilities follow. Below is a rather unsubtle display of the Dragon bishop's attacking power.

Rea-Ward
Simul, Wimbledon 1990

See diagram next column

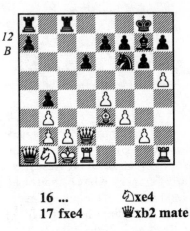

12
B

| 16 ... | ♘xe4 |
| 17 fxe4 | ♛xb2 mate |

However something that is often underestimated, without good reason, are the Dragon bishop's defensive qualities. Should White ever get both a queen and rook aligned on the h-file, having sacrificed the h-pawn, his first task is to remove the f6-knight which defends h7. Attempts to do this by advancing the g-pawn up to g5 will only result in the knight blocking the h-file after ...♘h5. From here it will be able to rejoin the game via g3 or f4, when the threats to the king have subsided.

Therefore, and as you will later discover, White's best method of removing this knight is to achieve ♘d5 (△ ♘xf6). However a common mistake is to concede the dark-squared bishop for it.

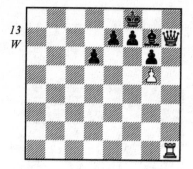

*13
W*

With no control over the dark squares around Black's king, White can make no progress (note the difference a white bishop on h6 would make!). Trebling the major pieces, intending the pretty finish ♕h8+ ♗xh8, ♖xh8+ ♔g7, ♖1h7 mate, is easily refuted by ...e6, creating another escape square for Black's king. Besides, while 19 'points' of fire-power are being thwarted by the Dragon bishop, Black ought to be able to undertake something constructive on the other side of the board!

Clearly the easiest way to neutralize both the attacking and defensive possibilities that the Dragon bishop offers, is for White to exchange it for his own dark-squared bishop. This means that White must defend against Black's attempts to exchange this piece for a knight, usually through either ...♘g4 or ...♘c4. Given the choice, in order to safeguard this key piece, White will often prefer to concede his light-squared bishop.

It should not be assumed that the Dragon bishop is only of use in stormy mating attacks, when White has castled on the queenside. Indeed it is equally pcwerful in the more quiet variations with castling on the same side. There, in contrast to the dark-squared King's Indian bishop, often hemmed in by pawns on d6, e5 and f4, it may lend long-distance assistance to a queenside minority attack. Finally, of course, a bishop is a bishop, and in an Open Sicilian ending, it's bound to be quite useful anyway!

The Exchange Sacrifice

As I was informed of the famous 'Dragon exchange sacrifice' at an early age, I am well aware of the difficulty that less experienced players may have in coming to terms with this concept. Nowadays I will confidently donate the exchange with as many people as possible watching! However I do nonetheless recall when I would get all materialistic and wonder why on Earth I had just given up a whole rook for a measly knight! Truth be told, invariably the exchange sacrifice involves ...♖xc3 (a move particularly characteristic of the Dragon but also frequently played in other Sicilian variations) and while it is often played with Black already a pawn to the good, the pawn now on c3 (after bxc3) is sometimes won. Even if it is not, White's queenside pawns are shattered beyond repair, whilst Black's pawn structure remains impeccable.

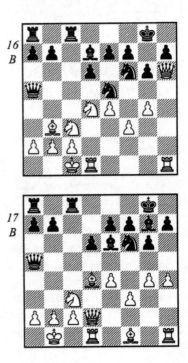

Note how even with a 3:2 majority, White will be unable to make any queenside progress without both a miraculous king penetration and a return exchange sacrifice.

Whilst theory correctly dictates that sometimes Black must make an exchange sacrifice in order to 'stay alive', more often than not this 'staying alive' involves Black obtaining a very good position! Therefore the exchange sacrifice

on c3 can be both positional, ruining White's queenside structure and weakening his e4-pawn, and tactical, in decelerating any White attack (whilst probably accelerating Black's attack). However c3 is not the only location for potential exchange sacrifices. Bearing in mind the value of the Dragon bishop, an exchange sacrifice may well involve a black rook for White's dark-squared bishop (say ...♖(c4)xd4), removing White's main 'neutralizer'!

For the time being though I will give a sample of positions (detailed later) in which ...♖xc3 is deserving of at least one '!'.

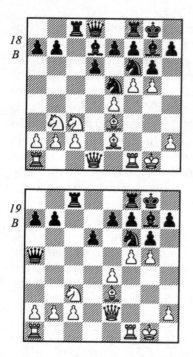

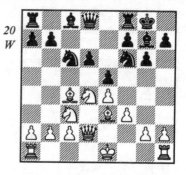

played, often leading to such positional weaknesses as shown below.

The Role Of the e7-Pawn

As previously mentioned, one of the beautiful aspects of the Sicilian Dragon, especially by comparison with other Sicilian variations, is the lack of weaknesses in Black's pawn structure. The d6-pawn, which often becomes a liability in, for example, the Najdorf, Pelikan and Scheveningen variations, is adequately defended in the Dragon by the e7-pawn. This of course has not had to move to allow the king's bishop to develop. Indeed, I cringe when I see the horrible move ...e5

By playing this move, Black has made three dreadful concessions:

(A) The d6-pawn is now backward and therefore extremely weak. There are few pieces available to defend it, especially with the bishop on g7 instead of e7. Meanwhile White may easily attack it with ♖d1 (or 0-0-0) and ♘b5.

(B) Black has turned the d5-square into an outpost for White. Previously White may have wanted to place a knight there, but may have been concerned about it being menaced by ...e6. Now though he has no such worries as the pawn on e5 cannot go backwards! In addition, the scope of White's light-squared bishop has just increased because it will never find resistance along the a2-g8 diagonal.

(C) Finally, and perhaps the worst sin of all, Black has severely reduced the scope of his Dragon bishop. The attacking potential of the bishop is now limited and White may do well to refrain from trying to exchange it off. ♗h6 should probably be withheld as in comparison to the g7-bishop, the e3-bishop is also effective on the queenside.

In playing ...e6, only the former of the above concessions really applies, although also now the scope of Black's light-squared bishop is somewhat reduced.

With this in mind, I wouldn't blame any readers who now decide that their e7-pawn is not going anywhere and indeed I more or less let it be for the earlier part of my Dragon 'career' too. However it should be brought to your attention that there are some circumstances under which the e-pawn can prove to be of great use, even when weighed up against our list of created concessions. The following positions (snapshots from the book's main body) have been reached following the move ...e6!.

21
W

Black removes the intruder from d5, without the pressure on e7 and the blocking of the b7-bishop that ...♞xd5 would have allowed. Now after ♞xf6+ ♞xf6, White's e4-pawn is as weak as Black's d6-pawn. Besides, Black will soon be able to break with the 'thematic' ...d5, eliminating the last weakness and attempting to open up the position completely for his 'raking' bishops.

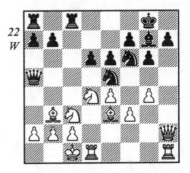

22
W

With 15 ♕h2, White threatened the simple 16 ♞d5, in order to get at the h7-square with a winning attack. On the face of it, it looks as though Black has just squandered his chance of 15...♖xc3!?, the 'thematic' exchange sacrifice. However while this would obviously have prevented 16 ♞d5, White can take the exchange and keep his queenside pawns intact with 16 ♗d2!. After 15...e6!, Black is a pawn up and White not only has difficulty maintaining an attack, but he is also unable to exploit the weakened d6-pawn.

The following positions show ...e5! in a good light. The first example is a purely tactical ...e5, temporarily blocking in the Dragon bishop, but removing White's dark-squared bishop from the solid d4-square. This will then allow consecutive sacrifices on g4 and c3 (see chapter 5).

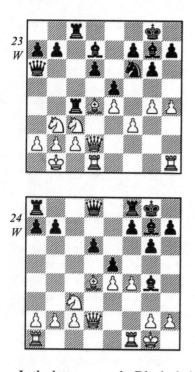

In the latter example, Black challenges White's central space advantage, seeking to obtain a long-term foothold on e5 (an excellent square for either a bishop or a knight). He can be safe in the knowledge that not only will the g7-bishop blockage be temporary, but also the weak d6-pawn will be counter-balanced by White's weak e4-pawn.

The Use of the c-file

After White plays d4 and Black ...cxd4, thus making an 'Open' Sicilian, Black has an entry into the game for his rooks that should not be neglected. Of course, rooks love open files and seventh ranks, but half-open files are not to be sniffed at and Black has one at his immediate disposal.

Then from the moment a black rook appears on the c-file, White must attempt to guard against the previously-mentioned thematic ...♖xc3 exchange sacrifice, as well as having to worry about a more obvious problem. Whether White castles kingside or queenside, there is always the danger that his c2-pawn will come under attack. Depending upon the urgency of the position, Black can double or even treble his major pieces on the c-file, and remove the flimsy cover of the white c3 knight with ...b5-b4. In fact, even if the knight manages to move with c2-c3 being put up as a barrier, still such a 'minority attack' is likely to result in a devastating attack or a favourable endgame.

To facilitate ...♖c8, Black must first move his light-squared bishop. I have known ...♗xg4 (a pawn) to be its first move, but more likely is ...♗e6, with no white knight on d4, or ...♗d7 otherwise. In some of the 'quieter' (i.e. those that don't involve do-or-die attacks) lines, sometimes the c8-bishop can also perform well on b7.

With the black queen out of the way (usually on a5), the rooks are connected and ready, if required, to double up. The most common way of achieving this 'doubling up' involves the ...♘c6-e5(a5)-c4 manoeuvre, after which White is likely to exchange his light-squared bishop for it. This is because not only will he probably want to preserve his more important dark-squared bishop (assuming that it is on e3), but also the b2 pawn will be a problem for him. Note even if it is protected, the chances are that there will be a combination involving ...♘xb2, for example undermining the defence of the white c3 knight.

After ♗xc4 ♖xc4, the black rook will be hard to remove, with b3 rarely being a viable option for White.

...♖c8-c7, to prepare doubling, is hardly ever used as it tends to walk into annoying ♘b5 or ♘d5 moves, but ...♖c8-c5 often fulfils a useful purpose. Here it defends the queen along the fourth rank, though of course when placing it here, Black must be sure that is safe from the white knight on d4 or White's dark-squared bishop. Finally,

while the c-file is obviously a very useful asset for Black, the d-file is of significantly less value to White as it is headed by the 'Rock of Gibraltar' on d6.

The Endgame and Assorted Tips

Although endgames arising from an exchange sacrifice will be discussed later, there are a few words to be said about endgames with equal material.

Generally speaking these are at least equal for Black, even if his Dragon bishop has been traded off. As previously mentioned, with or without queens, the c-file is of more use to Black than the d-file is to White, and White is also worse off if he has advanced his kingside pawns in a failed attack. As you will discover later, Black is usually encouraged to attack with 'pieces rather than pawns'. This means that his queenside pawns will probably not be similarly weakened, although even if they have been advanced, they are generally less accessible to the enemy king than White's. In addition, while Black may have to worry about his a- and b-pawns in endgames following opposite-side castling, White must secure his e-, f-, g- and h-pawns, especially in view of a possible Black ...♔g8-g7-f6-e5-f4 manoeuvre.

In the following nice example from **Burgalat-Trifunović**, Mar del Plata 1953, White has just prevented the aforementioned king intrusion with 18 g5.

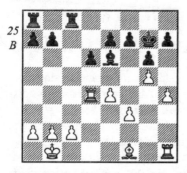

25
B

18...h6! 19 &h3 &xh3 20 &xh3 hg 21 hg &h8 22 &xh8 23 a4 &h5 Black has gained control of the only open file and now goes hunting for pawns **24 &c4** Activating the rook, but with his king so far away, Black will always win a pawn race. Clearly 24 f4 would have failed to 24...&h4 **24...&xg5 25 &c7 &g3 26 &xb7 &xf3 27 &xa7 g5 28 &a5 &f6** Both 28...f6 and 28...f5 also look promising **29 &a8 &g7 30 &a2 g4 31 &a5 f5! 32 &d5 g3 33 &d1 f4 34 a5 g2 0-1**

Finally a few helpful tips for you to commit to memory:

(A) If White eventually gets around to playing &d5, although it controls several useful squares, try to avoid the reflex response of ...&xd5. It could well be that this is the best reply, but at least consider

the awkward pressure that might arise down the e-file after exd5. Alternatives might be to capture the white knight at some stage with the light-squared bishop, chase it away with ...e6, or play around it until you are ready to take it, and then round up the d5-pawn.

Indeed &d5 is a White possibility that should always be on Black's mind. So long as it is, then you will never fall for the following fairly common trap. Black has just played 12...&ac8?.

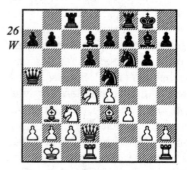

26
W

13 &d5! &xd2?! (13...&d8 saved the pawn, but now White's attack will almost certainly see him through) **14 &xe7+ &h8 15 &xd2.** The e7-pawn is gone and the d6-pawn will fall shortly, leaving White with an easily winning endgame.

(B) Something that I know novices often worry about when playing the Dragon, is that White might play &(d4)xc6, and hence they unnecessarily prepare ...&c6 with ...&d7. When pushed for a foundation for this fear, they struggle, eventually pin-pointing the now isolated a-pawn as a weakness.

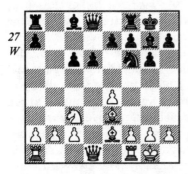

27
W

While this pawn is undeniably isolated, Black in fact has no more pawn islands than before the exchange took place. What he does have though, is a terrific half open b-file for a rook to exert (in conjunction with the latent Dragon bishop power) some devilish pressure on b2. In addition, Black now has a firm grip on the d5-square, which is useful for both keeping out a white knight, and perhaps helping to prepare a later ...d5. Therefore ♘xc6 is a move that Black should usually hope for, rather than fear, and when given the choice, should more often prefer to recapture with the b7-pawn rather than with a piece. The exception to this is if White can follow up the trade on c6 with a quick and successful e5. Such a position is arrived at below after 6 ♗c4 ♘c6?!

28
W

7 ♘xc6! bxc6 8 e5 dxe5? 9 ♗xf7+ and Black can resign.

(C) Although Black plays ...d6, usually as early as move 2, it is generally accepted that if he can later achieve the pawn break ...d6-d5 without repercussion, then he has at least equalized. A brief explanation for this is that the inevitable opening up of the centre following a timely ...d5, results in White's centrally posted pieces becoming targets for the black rooks. At present, this may sound somewhat vague but all will become clear as you read on.

(D) Always keep an eye out for the possibility of playing ...♘g4, attempting to exchange off White's dark-squared bishop (although preferred, the light-squared bishop is no mean catch either). White should usually guard against this mainly post-development threat, as the e3-bishop has difficulty moving away due to its important centre-defending role. However do NOT fall for ♗b5+, one of the oldest tricks in the book (well, this book anyway!). For example in the following position after 6...♘g4??

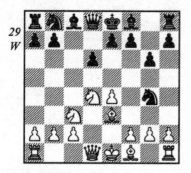

29
W

7 ♗b5+! ♗d7 8 ♕xg4+-.

(E) Finally in the same vein as ...♘g4, another move to look out for is ...♕b6. This may surprise the reader as although here the queen may attack the (often poisoned) pawn on b2, on b6 it can be in the firing line of a potential ♘(d4)-f5, unleashing the bishop on e3. Indeed I am far from saying that ...♕b6 is always a good move, rather indicating and I agree vaguely, that particularly when the opening has drifted off of the well-known tracks, the move ...♕b6 can occasionally pose awkward problems for White.

3 Early Deviations

After the normal sequence of moves 1 e4 c5 2 ♘f3 d6 3 d4 cxd4 4 ♘xd4 ♘f6 5 ♘c3 g6 the most commonly played moves are:

6 ♗e3 which is dealt with in chapters 4-7
6 ♗e2 which is dealt with in chapter 8
6 ♗c4 which is dealt with in chapter 9
6 h3 which is also dealt with in chapter 9
6 g3 which is dealt with in chapter 10
6 f4 which is dealt with in chapter 11

In this chapter I would like to discuss the following less common, but often problematic continuations:

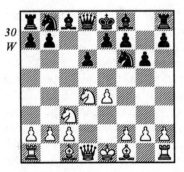

30
W

A: 6 ♗g5

B: 6 ♘d5?!
C: 6 ♗b5+
D: 6 ♘de2
E: 6 ♖g1?!

However, first I would like to deal with some even earlier divergences and methods of coping, and hopefully, refuting them. A common complaint about openings books, particularly from weaker players who are memorizing variations 'parrot fashion', is "But what if I am not playing a Grandmaster?" or "What if my opponent has not read this book?". In short, "What if I am confronted by an unmentioned move?".

The obvious answer is to stay calm and not to panic. To begin with, this unknown move that your opponent has just unleashed could well transpose into another variation. e.g. after 6 ♘b3, although Black may have other alternatives, at the very least he can aim to transpose into lines detailed in chapter 8. Secondly, it is extremely unlikely, in an opening with as much published theory as the Dragon, that White has come up with a move of such subtle brilliance that it refutes your favourite opening out of hand! Indeed, the Dragon *is* renowned for new moves being discovered that change the evaluation of a whole line, but these are usually around move 22 or 23, not move 6!

Ruling out the above two possibilities, leads one to the conclusion that any early new move not detailed in opening theory (or perhaps more relevantly to the reader, any early White move not mentioned in this book), is almost certainly not good and is probably quite bad!

Clearly the next question might be: "So okay, I suspect that this new move that my opponent has just played is bad, but what do I do now?".

Black's plans are obviously transferable between variations and the answer is that if you can see no obvious refutation, then you should draw both from the knowledge gained in the previous chapter, and from the ideas against more usual White continuations. From these deliberations you will be able to determine at least one relevant plan and hence a specific response, although remember there is possibly more than one satisfactory reply.

Take here for example the move 6 ♗d3?!. As a junior this move was played against me on several occasions, and yet I was unable to find this move in any Openings book. On d3 the bishop performs neither of the functions that it would do on the more usual c4 or e2 squares.

Although 6 ♗d3?! develops the bishop and prepares 0-0, bishops are not intended just to defend pawns (in this case the adequately-protected e4 pawn). Clearly the light-squared bishop has no future along this diagonal and its current placing has the detrimental effect of interfering with the white queen's protection of the d4 knight.

The game **Kinlay-Ward**, Langley Park U-18 ch 1982, continued: **6...♗g7 7 0-0 0-0 8 ♗e3 ♘c6** Satisfactory although 8...♘g4! securing White's dark-squared bishop is even better. **9 ♘xc6?! bxc6 10 ♖e1?! ♘g4 11 ♕d2 ♘xe3 12 ♖xe3?** Clearly losing, but after 12 ♕xe3 both 12...♖b8 Δ 13...♖xb2 (even after 13 ♖ab1) or 12...♕a5 leave Black with a lovely position. Note 12...♕b6 13 ♕xb6 axb6 is also a very favourable endgame for Black due in main to his two bishops v bishop and knight advantage. **12...♗h6-+.**

Before returning to the main 6th move divergencies, I would like to take the reader back to as early as move two. After 1 e4 c5, if 2 ♘c3, how should Black continue so as to fit in with the Dragon set-up, bearing in mind White may still opt for an Open Sicilian? The obvious choice is **2...♘c6** and then after **3 ♘f3**, the correct move is **3...g6**. An early h4 is not something Black should fear, and after **4 h4 h5!?**

technically we return to the confines of this book with **5 d4 cxd4 6 ♘xd4** as in the game **Wessels-Ward**, Guernsey 1991, which continued: **6...♗g7 7 ♘xc6?! bxc6 8 ♗e2 d6 9 f4 ♘f6 10 ♕d3 ♕b6** *(31)*

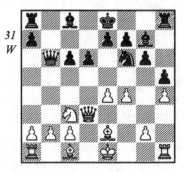

11 ♗e3 ♕xb2 12 ♖b1 ♕a3 13 f5 ♗a6! 14 ♕xa6 ♕xc3+ 15 ♗d2 ♕g3+ 16 ♔d1 0-0 17 ♗f3 d5 18 ♕xc6 ♖ac8 19 ♕a4 dxe4 0-1.

Clearly h4 does not have to be met by ...h5. After the usual move order, the game **Velimirović-Watson**, Bor 1986, continued **6 h4?! ♘c6 7 h5** (7 ♗e3?! ♘g4!) **7...♘xh5 8 g4 ♘xd4! 9 gxh5 ♘c6 10 hxg6 fxg6 11 ♗h6?** (11 ♕d5!? though it is unlikely that after either 11...e6, 11...♗g4 or 11...♕a5 White has sufficient compensation for the pawn. Note not 11...♗g7? in view of 12 ♖xh7!) **11...♗xh6 12 ♖xh6 ♕b6∓**.

One advantage of the Dragon over many other Sicilian variations is the simplicity with which the first few moves can usually be made. In, for example, the Sicilian Najdorf where correct move-orders have become a science, after the relatively innocuous 2 ♘c3, Black cannot simply reply 2...♘c6. This is because in an Open Sicilian, a Najdorf player would rather develop the b8 knight to d7. After delaying its deployment with 2...d6, he then faces the dilemma of what to do after 3 ♘ge2. White might still play 4 d4 and yet if Black plays 3...♘f6 hoping ultimately to reach the position shown below *(32)*, White could play 4 g3. In such a 'Closed' Sicilian position, Black might have preferred to have his g8 knight go to e7 instead.

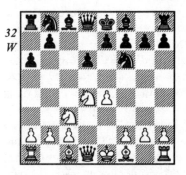

In the Sicilian Dragon, 'tricky' move orders are not really a problem. Nonetheless, on occasion Black must apply a little common sense. One important point to note is that after 1 e4 c5 2 ♘f3, Black must play 2...d6 rather than 2...♘c6. Obviously the latter is not a bad move, but if followed by a kingside fianchetto, this becomes the 'Accelerated Dragon'. Although these two separate defences may transpose (particularly in the Classical variations), there are two main differences which are highlighted briefly below:

a) 2...♘c6 3 d4 cxd4 4 ♘xd4 ♘f6 5 ♘c3 g6 6 ♘xc6 bxc6 7 e5 ♘g8 when Black has the half open b-file and an extra centre pawn but is somewhat lacking in development.

b) 2...♘c6 3 d4 cxd4 4 ♘xd4 g6 5 c4! when White has a bind on the d5 square (known as the 'Maroczy Bind').

Now the purpose of 2...d6 becomes clear. It guards the f6 knight against an early e5 as occurs in the former case (often referred to as the 'Hyper-Accelerated Dragon'). This then allows an early 'guarded' ...♘f6, forcing ♘c3, preventing the c4 intermezzo played in (b). Another useful tip is that if after 2...d6 3 d4 cxd4 4 ♘xd4 ♘f6, White defends his e4 pawn with 5 f3?!, then it would seem likely that he is trying to get in c4 before playing ♘c3. If Black so chooses he can now abandon the kingside fianchetto and immediately seize the initiative with 5...e5!? Δ...d5.

We have already established that after 1 e4 c5, 2 ♘c3 is easily met by 2...♘c6 (2...d6 is also possible) but what after 2 ♘f3 d6 3 ♘c3 (33)?

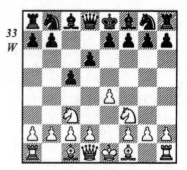

Although **3...♘f6** is playable, Black may regret not being able to develop the knight to e7, should White opt for a Closed Sicilian set-up with 4 g3.

As I once discovered to my cost **3...g6?** is bad in view of **4 d4 cxd4 5 ♕xd4!**. I can recall disliking 5...♘f6 because of 6 e5 ♘c6?! 7 ♗b5± though the rather ugly 5...f6± that I played is hardly better.

Therefore I would suggest **3...♘c6** when after **4 d4 cxd4 5 ♘xd4** Black must play **5...g6** in order to obtain a Dragon formation. I stress this point because I have seen too many juniors who supposedly play the Dragon, come up with 5...♘f6 here. Let me be clear on this, 5...♘f6 is not a bad move, but it is the 'Classical' Sicilian and two of White's main moves here prevent Black from obtaining a successful kingside fianchetto, i.e. 6 ♗g5 g6?! 7 ♗xf6! and 6 ♗c4 g6?! 7 ♘xc6! bxc6 8 e5 when although 8...dxe5?? 9 ♗xf7+! wins immediately, the alternatives:

a) 8...d5 9 exf6 dxc4 10 ♕xd8+ ♔xd8 11 ♗g5;

b) 8...♘d7 9 exd6 exd6 10 0-0 ♘e5 11 ♗b3; and

c) 8...♘g4 9 ♗f4 ♕b6 10 ♕f3! all lead to a clear White advantage.

Therefore after 5...g6, things are likely to transpose into a main line after, say, 6 ♗e3 or 6 ♗e2. However a move which sticks in my mind, yet I do not recall ever having seen documented is **6 ♘d5** *(34)*.

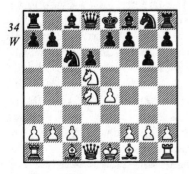

This occurred while I was watching the 1982 British Championship game, **Bellin-Miles** in Torquay. It took me a while to notice that White's threat was simply to forget his other pieces, concentrating on the knights with the rather cheeky 7 ♘b5 Δ ♘(b or d)c7+. Once I excluded the obvious pawn-weakness-invoking moves 6...♘f6? and 6...e6?! I began to fear for the safety of my (and Miles'!) beloved Dragon as 6...a6 7 ♗e3 Δ 8 ♘xc6 bxc6 9

♗b6+- also looked grim. I was eager to know and therefore awaited Miles' move with anticipation. Finally the move came: **6...♗g7!**, White did continue with 7 ♘b5 to which Black replied **7...♖b8**. After **8 ♘bc7+ ♔f8** it soon become apparent that White will suffer more for the six consecutive knight moves than Black will for the inability to castle. The rest of the game shows Miles gradually increasing his space advantage, eventually strangling his opponent like a boa-constrictor. **9 ♘b5 a6 10 ♘bc3 e6 11 ♘f4 b5 12 a3 ♗b7 13 ♗d3 ♘f6 14 0-0 ♔e7 15 ♘h3 ♖e8 16 f4 ♔f8 17 ♕e1 ♔g8 18 ♔h1 ♘g4 19 ♗d2 f5 20 exf5 exf5 21 ♕g3 d5 22 ♖ae1 ♕d7 23 ♘g5 ♘f6 24 ♕h3 d4 25 ♘d1 ♖bd8 26 a4 h6 27 axb5 axb5 28 ♘f3 ♕d5 29 ♔g1 ♘e4 30 ♖e2 ♖e6 31 ♖fe1 ♖de8 32 ♗c1 h5 33 ♘f2 ♗f6 34 ♘xe4 fxe4 35 ♘d2 e3 36 ♘f3 ♗g7 37 f5 ♖f6 38 fxg6 ♖ef8 39 ♖f1 ♘e5 40 ♖ee1 ♘xf3+ 0-1.**

After 41 ♖xf3 ♖xf3 42 gxf3 ♖xf3 43 ♕g2 (forced in view of 43...♖g3+) 43...♖g3! 44 ♕xg3 ♕h1 mate. Let us now return to White's five more commonly played and hence usually documented alternatives to the main lines. Before I start though I would like to say now that I am slightly loathe to include the latter three as I consider them barely worthy of attention.

A) **Ghinda-Sax**
Malta OL 1980

6 ♗g5   ♗g7
7 ♗b5+

7 ♕d2 perhaps intending some sort of Yugoslav Attack set-up without f3 is adequately met by 7...h6!? when in Nacino-Garcia, Haifa 1976, White continued 8 ♗h4 (8 ♗e3?! ♘g4 9 0-0-0 ♘xe3∓) 8...♘bd7 9 f4 (Black also fared well in Murey-Taimanov, Moscow 1966, after 9 0-0-0 a6 10 ♗c4 0-0 11 f3 e5!? 12 ♘de2 ♘xe4! 13 ♗xd8 ♘xd2 14 ♖xd2 ♖xd8 15 ♖xd6 b5 16 ♗d5 ♖a7 17 ♖d1 ♖f8!) 9...a6 10 f5?! g5 11 ♗g3 b5 12 a3 ♗b7 13 ♗d3 ♖c8 14 ♘f3 0-0 (△ 15...♖xc3∓) 15 e5 dxe5 16 ♘xe5 ♘xe5 17 ♗xe5 ♖c5 18 ♗xf6 ♗xf6∓. You won't often see two better black bishops!

7 ...   ♗d7
8 ♕e2   ♘c6! *(35)*

While 8...0-0 can hardly be bad, I would like to highlight the glut of Black possibilities, with three good alternatives:

a) 8...h6 (a move which seriously questions White's winning chances) 9 ♗h4 ♘c6 10 0-0-0 ♘h5 11 ♗xc6 bxc6 12 ♘f5 gxf5 13 ♕xh5 ♗xc3 14 bxc3 ♕a5 15 exf5 ♕xc3 16 ♖he1 ♕a3+ 17 ♔d2 ♕a5+ 18 ♔c1 ♕a3+ 19 ♔d2 ♕a5+ 20 ♔c1 ♕a3+ ½-½ Kwiatkowski-Ward, London Lloyds Bank 1992.

b) 8...♗xb5!? 9 ♘dxb5 a6 10 ♘d4 ♘c6 11 0-0-0 ♘d7 12 ♗e3 ♖c8, when Black, angling for the c4-square can look forward to the usual play along the c-file.

c) 8...a6!? 9 ♗xd7+ ♘bxd7 10 0-0-0 ♖c8 11 ♘b3 (11 ♘d5 h6 12 ♗h4 ♕a5 13 ♔b1 ♘xd5 14 exd5 ♘f6 15 ♘b3 ♕c7∓ was Ulybin-Ivanchuk, USSR 1985) 11...0-0 12 f4 ♖xc3!? 13 bxc3 ♕c7 14 ♖he1 h6 15 ♗h4 ♖c8 16 e5 ♘h5 17 e6 fxe6 18 ♕xe6+ ♔h7 19 f5 ♘f4! 20 fxg6+ ♔h8 21 ♕e4 ♕xc3 22 ♖d2 ♘dc5 23 ♕xf4 ♘d3+ 0-1 Gobleja-Tiviakov, USSR schools 1986.

9 0-0-0   ♖c8!?

Played instead of 9...0-0. Now not only is White weak on d4, but he must also guard against a later possible exchange sacrifice on c3. Therefore he must now make a decision on c6.

10 ♗xc6	**bxc6**
11 f4	**0-0**
12 e5	**dxe5**
13 fxe5	**♘d5**
14 ♘xd5	**cxd5**
15 e6?	

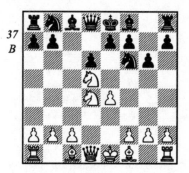

37
B

Although it is tempting for White to eliminate his isolated e-pawn, attacking Black's pawn structure in the process, he would have been better off with either 15 ♖hf1, 15 ♖he1 or 15 ♔b1. Nevertheless with moves like ...♗e6, ...♖e8, and ...♕b6 at his disposal, Black has little to fear. The text move seems to activate all of Black's pieces at once, culminating in a devastating Black attack.

15 ...	fxe6
16 ♘xe6	**♕b6!**
17 ♘xg7	**♖f2!** *(36)*

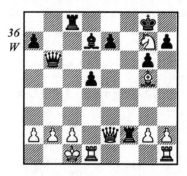

36
W

18 ♕d3	♔xg7
19 ♖d2	♗f5
20 ♗e3	♗xd3
21 ♗xf2	**♕f6**
0-1	

B) **A.Smith-Ward**
Ramsgate 1989

6 ♘d5?! *(37)*

If your opponent plays a move like this, you should begin to smell a rat. In Estrin-Govbinder, USSR 1943, Black didn't and fell into the trap with 6...♘xe4? 7 ♗b5+ ♗d7 8 ♕e2 f5 (dare I say it, not 8...♘f6?? 9 ♘xf6#) 9 f3 ♘c6 10 ♘b3 ♘c5 11 ♘xc5 dxc5 12 ♗f4 ♖c8 13 0-0-0 ♔f7 14 ♗c4 e6 15 ♘c7±.

6 ...	♗g7
7 ♘xf6+	

7 ♗b5+ ♗d7 8 0-0 ♘c6! (△ 9...♘xd4-+) 9 ♘b3 0-0 10 ♖e1 a6 11 ♗f1 ♖c8 12 ♗e3 (12 ♘xf6+ ♗xf6 13 c3 ♘e5 14 ♘d4 ♘c4∓) 12...♘xd5 13 exd5 ♘e5 14 ♗d4 ♗f5 15 c3 g5!∓ Estrin-Averbakh, Moscow 1939.

7 ...	♗xf6
8 ♗h6	

This, in conjunction with White's last move, is logical in that it prevents Black from castling. The problem is that it leaves the knight on d4 and White's queenside far too weak.

8 ...	**♕b6!?**
9 ♗b5+	♗d7

10 ♗xd7+	♘xd7
11 c3	♕xb2
12 0-0	♕xc3
13 ♘b5	♕c4∓
14 a4	♗xa1
15 ♕xa1	♘e5
16 f4	♕c5+
17 ♔h1	♘g4
18 h3 *(38)*	

A nice 'Smothered Mate' occurs after 18 ♕xh8+ ♔d7 19 ♕xa8 ♘f2+ 19 ♔g1 ♘h3+ 20 ♘h3+ 21 ♔h1 ♕g1+ 22 ♖xg1 ♘f2 mate.

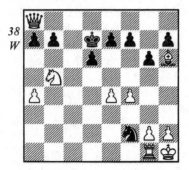

38
W

18 ...	♘f6
19 e5	dxe5
20 fxe5	♘d5
21 e6	f6
22 ♖d1	♖d8
23 ♕a2	g5
24 ♕d2	♖g8
25 h4	a6
26 ♘d4	♘c3
27 ♕c2	♖xd4
28 ♖xd4	♕xd4
29 ♕xh7	♕xh4+
30 ♔g1	♕e1+
31 ♔h2	♕xe6

0-1

C) 6 ♗b5+

Whereas 6 ♘d5?! is at least good for 'cheapo' value, I simply cannot condone this move, which offers White nothing. If anything, the advantage White has in Open Sicilians is that of space, and this move only serves to remove this without compromising the Black position at all. In variation (A), I suppose 7 ♗b5+ fits in with a quick development system, but by playing it on its own, White merely succeeds in swapping off what is generally Black's least active minor piece. This trade will weaken White's grip on the c4 square and enable a black rook faster access to the c-file.

6 ...	♗d7
7 ♗xd7+	

7 ♕e2?! ♘c6 8 ♗e3 ♗g7 9 0-0-0 ♘g4!? 10 ♘xc6 bxc6 11 ♗xc6 ♗xc6 12 ♕xg4 ♗xc3 13 bxc3 ♕a5∓.

7 ...	♕xd7 *(39)*

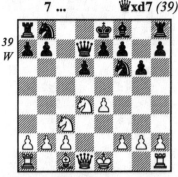

39
W

With c4 such a key square and a target particularly for a black knight, White will have difficulty finding a good square for his dark-squared bishop.

D)   **6 ♘de2**   **♗g7**
     7 ♘f4 *(40)*

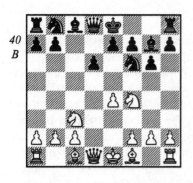

The text is harmless, but the only real alternative, 7 g3, at best only transposes to chapter 10. By my own admission, d5 is a very good square for a white knight, perhaps explaining why White's queen's knight is generally more valuable in the Dragon than his king's knight. However, this manoeuvre, played now in favour of other developing moves, is too time-consuming and it is for this reason that contrary to advice in the previous chapter, Black doesn't have to think twice about exchanging it off immediately.

     7 ...   **♘c6**
     8 ♗e2   **b6!?**

Although clearly 8...0-0 would also be satisfactory.

     9 ♘fd5   **♘xd5**
     10 exd5   **♘d4**
     11 ♗e3   **♘xe2**

And with the bishop pair, unsurprisingly, Black is fine.

E)   **6 ♖g1!?**

When I had this move played against me (and no, not because of the touch and move rule!), I had to prevent myself from laughing before simply developing my pieces. While I consider it only fair to keep my opponent anonymous, it appears that some other texts warrant this move a place in theory. Although (partly to be thorough and partly for fun), I will give some moves here; suffice it to say that I can only hope that should there ever be a second edition of this book, it doesn't include a variation (F) 6 ♖b1!?.

     6 ...   **♘c6**
     7 ♗e3   **♗g7**
     8 ♗b5?!   **♗d7**
     9 ♗e2   **♖c8**
     10 g4   **h5!**
     11 gxh5   **♘xh5**
     12 ♗xh5   **♗xd4!**
     13 ♗xd4   **♘xd4**
     14 ♕xd4   **♖xh5**
     15 0-0-0   **♕a5**
     16 f4   **♗e6∓** *(41)*

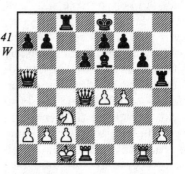

This is Papp-Sapi, Budapest 1981.

4 Yugoslav Attack – Introduction

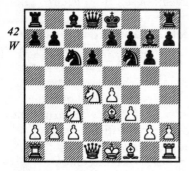

42
W

The 'Yugoslav Attack', sometimes referred to by the Russians as the 'Rauzer Attack', is without a doubt the most aggressive set-up that White can adopt against the Sicilian Dragon. White places his dark-squared bishop on e3 where it helps support the centre and then plays f3 (note that should White combine f3 with the less attentive ♗g5, then even after the usual developing moves, Black is likely to have a ...♘xe4 trick at his disposal). The latter pawn move bolsters e4 whilst guarding his important e3-bishop against an awkward ...♘g4. In addition after moving his queen (usually to d2) intending 0-0-0 White may have a later g4 in mind. Indeed to the first-time Dragon player this may look pretty fearsome but the good news is that White's plan is fairly

transparent with, generally speaking, little room for subtlety.

White's basic idea is ultimately to checkmate Black by infiltration down the h-file. His queen can enter the fray via a trade of bishops on h6 whilst the h1-rook offers support after h4-h5 (and hxg6, with or without g4). Once this queen and rook alignment has been achieved, all that remains is to remove the one key defender: the black knight on f6. This can be done either by g5 (as long as White can deal with ...♘h5), the simple ♘d5, or even both, as in the following hypothetical, though not untypical game highlighting the danger to Black:

1 e4 c5 2 ♘f3 d6 3 d4 cxd4 4 ♘xd4 ♘f6 5 ♘c3 g6 6 ♗e3 ♗g7 7 f3 ♘c6 8 ♕d2 0-0 9 ♗c4 ♗d7 10 0-0-0 a6? 11 h4 b5 12 ♗b3 ♘e5 13 h5 ♘xh5?!. Played here, this move merely succeeds in accelerating White's attack. However White will eventually come down the h-file, particularly if Black has to meet hxg6 with ...hxg6 due to the pin from White's b3-bishop. **14 g4 ♘f6 15 ♗h6 ♗xh6** Delaying this exchange achieves nothing as White can always play ♗xg7 ♔xg7 ♕h6+ anyway, although perhaps 15...♗h8 here would be a

better practical try. **16 ♕xh6 ♖c8**
Too little too late! However 16...e6
preventing 17 ♘d5, would appear
to lose to the rather annoying but
thematic sacrifice 17 ♘f5! exf5
(17...gxf5 18 g5+-) 18 ♘d5 ♖e8 19
g5!+-. **17 ♘d5 ♖e8 18 ♘xf6 exf6
19 ♕xh7** mate was the threat! **18
g5 ♘h5 19 ♖xh5! gxh5 20 ♘f6+
exf6 21 gxf6 1-0** *(43).*

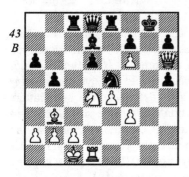

43
B

Impressed or depressed? Do not
worry, but for the moment note that
as Black, you are going to have to
play a bit more accurately than that
if you want to last more than 21
moves or, better still, win! In fact
it pains me to see (as I do only too
often) this sort of game take place,
a not uncommon conclusion being
a Black declaration of "I don't
think that this opening is for me!".
There is a common misconception
going around that the Dragon is all
about learning reams and reams of
theory and if theory in one given
week implies that it is refuted, well
then that's just tough luck! Although I could hardly argue that

'knowing games' is not a good
thing, through experience I have
learnt that however good the two
players concerned are, it is always
dangerous to accept their moves
(and even their annotations) as gos-
pel. Rather one should view games
with an open mind, accumulating a
wealth of ideas/principles and in
practice engaging the brain! Home
analysis is of course extremely
valuable with regards to critical
variations.

So starting from the beginning,
where did Black go wrong in the
previous game? He made no apparent positional errors and so does
this mean that the Dragon is all
about tactics?

The answer to the latter question
is 'No', but they do come into it a
lot, and particularly in the next
three chapters of this book. Besides, isn't it the rumours of 'do or
die' excitement that attracted you
to this opening in the first place?
Whether or not the answer to this
is "Yes!", to avoid more than your
fair share of dying, read on!

The first and most critical mistake that Black made was 10...a6?
after which he is objectively lost.
The Yugoslav Attack invariably
involves attacks on both wings. If
both sides settle for pawn storms
then it will be Black's fortress that
falls first. The simple reason for
this is that it is Black who has
weakened his defensive structure
with ...g6 whilst White's a-, b- and

c-pawns remain at home. Black has no target this way and hence it will take him far longer to 'get at' the white king. When time is of the essence, Black should attack with pieces and not pawns. Certainly I have never been checkmated by the white pawns but it is the rooks behind them that pose the threat. Black has a half-open file readily available for his rooks and he should not delay in using it.

Indeed a good example of such use is demonstrated in the first of three distinct memories that I have of the Yugoslav Attack when learning how to play the Dragon as a young junior:

A) I am afraid that I couldn't tell you who were the original players in the following game but I once saw it in an old book and then had the same game several years back. I have also lost count of the amount of times that I have had the position after 17...♕xc3. As far as I am concerned the game is a classic example of how piece attacks are quicker than pawn attacks and, even though I cannot take the credit, I feel privileged to have played the game.

1 e4	c5
2 ♘f3	d6
3 d4	cxd4
4 ♘xd4	♘f6
5 ♘c3	g6
6 ♗e3	♗g7
7 f3	♘c6
8 ♕d2	0-0
9 ♗c4	♗d7
10 0-0-0	♕a5
11 h4	♖fc8
12 ♗b3	

12 h5? ♘xd4 13 ♕xd4 ♘g4-+.

12 ...	♘e5
13 h5	♘xh5
14 g4	♘f6
15 ♗h6	♗xh6
16 ♕xh6	♖xc3!

The first real example of the thematic exchange sacrifice described in chapter 2. It prevents ♘d5, which would remove the remaining key defender on f6, and shatters White's defensive structure all in one go. Also the relevance of the apparently greedy 13...♘xh5 is highlighted. Black will not even be any material down!

| 17 bxc3 | ♕xc3 (44) |

44
W

| 18 ♔b1 |

Played to prevent ...♕a1+ and ...♕xd4+. It would be putting it mildly to say that Black arrives at an extremely favourable ending after 18 ♘e2 ♕a1+ 19 ♔d2 ♘xf3+ 20 ♔e3 ♕xd1 21 ♖xd1 ♘xg4+ 22 ♔xf3 ♘xh6.

18 ...	♖c8
19 g5	♘h5
20 ♖xh5	

This in conjunction with White's last move was the only way to break down Black's defence.

20 ...	gxh5
21 ♕xh5	♘c4
22 ♗xc4	♖xc4
23 ♖d3	

Unfortunately for White, he is unable to bring anything else into the attack. 23 ♖h1 allows 23...♕xd4, when the queen's excellent defensive qualities are demonstrated, covering both h8 and g7. Now the race is effectively over, as White is forced on the defensive with nothing to show for his attacking efforts but an offside queen!

23 ...	♕e1+
24 ♔b2	♕f2!
25 g6	

Desperation, but there is no other way to defend both d4 and c2.

25 ...	hxg6
26 ♕d5	♗e6
27 ♘xe6	♕xc2+
28 ♔a3	♖a4 mate

B) The next game is one which many will recall as being the original 'Dragon slayer'. Considered a brilliancy at the time, this World Championship Candidates' Final encounter won White the *Informa-tor* series best game competition with 89 out of a possible 90 votes! Funnily enough, today's Dragon protagonists of both colours place little importance on this game. 16...♖e8 for quite a while has been considered fine for Black and hence White has been dabbling in alternatives to 16 ♘de2 in the search for an ultimate refutation of the Dragon (well, in the 10...♖c8 line anyway!).

Karpov-Korchnoi
Moscow Ct (2) 1974

1 e4	c5
2 ♘f3	d6
3 d4	cxd4
4 ♘xd4	♘f6
5 ♘c3	g6
6 ♗e3	♗g7
7 f3	♘c6
8 ♕d2	0-0
9 ♗c4	♗d7
10 h4	♖c8
11 ♗b3	♘e5
12 0-0-0	♘c4
13 ♗xc4	

With reference to chapter 2, the reader should note that it is rarely advisable for White to concede his dark-squared, rather than his light-squared bishop. If he did, then he would have trouble neutralizing the powerful 'Dragon bishop', thus hardening both his attacking and defending duties. Hence if 13 ♕d3?!, then 13...♘xe3 (admittedly the black knight is very well placed on c4, but Black is often happy to exchange a rook for White's dark-squared bishop) 14 ♕xe3 ♕b6! *(45)*

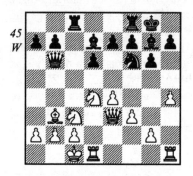

Now an excellent diagonal for the black queen, the immediate threat being 15...e5-+) 15 ♕d2 ♕c5 when Black, knowing his king is much safer in the absence of the e3-bishop, can roll his a- and b-pawns in search of the b3-bishop. For example:

a) 16 h5 ♘xh5 17 ♘d5 ♖fe8 18 ♘f5 ♗xf5 19 exf5 ♘g3 20 fxg6 hxg6 21 ♕g5 (after 21 ♖h3 ♘f5∓, White's only hope of trebling on the h-file is far too slow in view of simplification threats that will arise after ...♘d4) 21...♘xh1 22 ♖xh1 (both 22 ♘xe7+ ♔f8! and 22 ♕xg6 fxg6 23 ♘f6+ ♔h8 24 ♖xh1+ ♗h6+ are winning for Black) 22...♕d4 23 c3 ♕e5 when White is lost, as long as Black avoids 25 ♕xg6 fxg6?? (25...e6!) 26 ♘f6+ ♔f8 27 ♘d7(or h7) mate!

b) 16 g4 b5 17 g5 (17 h5 is still too slow, and is met well by 17...b4 when 18 hxg6 bxc3!, 18 ♘a4 ♕a5,

18 ♘d5 ♘xd5 19 ♗xd5 ♗xd4, and 18 ♘ce2(or b1) a5 intending ...a4, are all very good for Black) 17...♘h5 18 ♘d5 ♖fe8 19 ♘e2 b4! (intending ...a5-a4 but discouraging both 20 a3 and 20 c3) 20 ♘ef4 (Black's b-pawn is out of bounds with 20 ♕xb4 losing to the rather amusing bishop hunt 20...♕xb4 21 ♘xb4 a5 22 ♘d3 a4 23 ♗d5 e6 24 ♗b7 ♖b8 25 ♗a6 ♖b6 26 ♗c4 d5 27 exd5 exd5 and 20 ♘xb4 a5 21 ♘d3 ♕b6 leaving Black with good compensation) 20...♘xf4 21 ♘xf4 ♗b5 (Δ 22...♕e5) 22 ♔b1 a5 23 ♕d5 e6 24 ♕xd6 a4 winning a piece (Kengis-Lanka, Latvia 1973).

13 ...	♖xc4
14 h5	♘xh5
15 g4	♘f6
16 ♘de2	

This move, guarding against a possible exchange sacrifice on c3, was originally annotated with an '!', but as mentioned before, is currently out of fashion!

16 ...   ♕a5?!

This move unfavourably mixes the two systems recommended for Black in chapter 5. Indeed, there you will find more on 16...♖e8! which prevents the forthcoming trade of bishops.

17 ♗h6   ♗xh6

When all's said and done, probably Black's best chance now lies in 17...♗h8!? 18 ♗xf8 ♔xf8, when he will have at least some compensation (and a pawn!) for the exchange. For example, 19 ♔b1 (19 ♗e3 intending to meet 19...b5 with 20 e5 perhaps looks better, but even then some complications still arise after 20...♘xg4, and 19...b5 is far from forced) 19...♖b4 (19...♗e6 20 ♘f4 21 ♘xe6 fxe6 22 ♘e2 ♕e5 23 c3 ♗g7 24 ♘c1 h6 *(46)* reached below in Chudinovsky-Jakmimainen, Krasnodar 1977, left Black with the better prospects, particularly on the attacking front. With the kingside nicely blockaded, he can launch a queenside pawn storm and hop his f6-knight round to somewhere more exciting.)

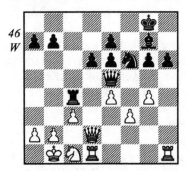

46
W

20 g5 (20 ♘c1 ♗e6 21 ♘b3 ♕b6 Δ...a5-a4; if 22 a3 then both 22...♖xb3 and 22...♖c4 23 ♘d4 ♘xe4 {or 23...♖xd4 24 ♕xd4 ♘xe4} look at least playable, if not good for Black) 20...♘h5 21 ♘c1 ♗e6 22 ♘b3 ♕e5 23 ♖xh5! ♗xb3! (23...gxh5?! 24 f4 ♕g7 25 f5 ♗xb3 26 f6!±) 24 ♖xh7 ♗xa2+ 25 ♔c1 (25 ♔xa2?! ♕a5+ 26 ♔b1 ♖xb2+ 27 ♔xb2 ♕b4+ 28 ♔c1 {28 ♔a2

loses to 28...♗xc3 29 ♕c1 ♕a4+ 30 ♕a3 ♕xc2+} 28...♗xc3 29 ♖xf7+ ♔e8 30 ♕xc3 ♕xc3 31 ♖h7 ♕xf3 leaves Black with a winning queen vs two rooks endgame. White's rooks are uncoordinated and his few remaining pawns weak) 25...♗g7 26 ♖dh1 (26 f4? ♕xc3! 27 ♕xc3 ♗xc3 28 bxc3 ♖xe4 and Black has a lovely endgame) 26...♗c4 27 ♕h2 ♕xh2 with an approximately equal endgame; Almroth-Hernod, Sweden 1974.

18 ♕xh6   ♖fc8
19 ♖d3! *(47)*

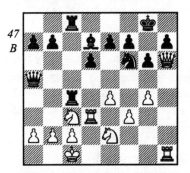

47
B

A fine move offering further support to the c3-knight. Clearly 19 g5 ♘h5 20 ♘g3 or 20 ♘f4 (20 ♖xh5 gxh5 21 ♘d5 ♖xc2+ 22 ♔b1 ♔h8! is inconclusive) allows 20...♖xc3, when Black will have at least enough play for a draw. However, now 20 g5 is threatened.

19 ...   ♖4c5?
It is worth noting here that one defensive idea that Black may occasionally choose to consider is

...♕d8-f8. Here 19...♕d8 is foiled by 20 ♘d5! when Shamkovich's analysis runs 20...♖xc2+ 21 ♔b1 e6 22 ♘5c3 ♖xe2+ 23 ♘xe2 ♗b5 24 ♖d2 ♗xe2 25 ♖xe2±. In fact, Black's position has probably gone already, as his only other real try, 19...♗e6, appears to lose to 20 g5 ♘h5 21 ♘g3 ♕e5 22 ♘xh5 gxh5 23 ♕xh5 ♕g7 24 f4 b5 25 f5 b4 26 ♖dh3!! with a decisive attack, e.g. 26...bxc3 27 ♕xh7+ ♕xh7 28 ♖xh7 cxb2+ 29 ♔b1+- or 26...f6 27 g6! bxc3 28 ♕xh7+ ♕xh7 29 ♖xh7 cxb2+ 30 ♔b1 ♔f8 31 g7+ which is also curtains for Black.

> **20 g5!**   **♖xg5**
> **21 ♖d5!**   **♖xd5**
> **22 ♘xd5**   **♖e8**
> **23 ♘ef4!**

Consistently accurate. White does not want the black king to escape, as it would do after 23 ♘xf6+ exf6 24 ♕xh7+ ♔f8 with e7 being the flight square.

> **23 ...**   **♗c6**

It is necessary for Black to prevent White from posting his other knight on d5 after 24 ♘xf6+. 23...♗e6 simply loses to 24 ♘xe6 fxe6 25 ♘xf6+ exf6 26 ♕xh7+ ♔f8 27 ♕d7.

> **24 e5!**

Another excellent move, effectively ending the game. White has the idea of playing ♘xf6+ exf6 followed by ♘h5, but wants to cut out the possibility of ...♕g5+.

> **24 ...**   **♗xd5**
> **25 exf6**   **exf6**

> **26 ♕xh7+**   **♔f8**
> **27 ♕h8+**   **1-0**

C) In my youth, seeing this game was not very encouraging, but perhaps what hurt most were the comments of ex-World Champion Bobby Fischer, that playing against the Dragon was a simple case of prying open the king's rook's file and then sac, sac, ... mate! Anyway, after a nice but very much overrated win against Bent Larsen's Dragon in 1958, Fischer remarked "Will Black succeed in reinforcing the variation? Time will tell."

Well, it has. It is now 1994 and the Dragon is going as strong as ever. As for the other point, experience has taught me that it is generally Black who does most of the piece (or exchange) sacrificing, although it occasionally helps for him to hedge his bets by stocking up on pawns!

Returning to the nitty-gritty, after **6 ♗e3 ♗g7 7 f3, 7...♘c6** is sensible (7...0-0 intending 8...♘c6 retains marginally less options but is of course also good) after which 8 ♕d2 is usual. However on several occasions I have seen **8 ♗c4** which offers Black an alternative to the obvious 8...0-0 in the risky but interesting **8...♕b6**. Now 9 ♗b3?! occurred in **Tayeb-Ernst, Manila OL 1992**, after which Black won a pawn with **9...♘xe4!**

10 fxe4 ♗xd4 11 ♗xd4 ♕xd4 12 ♕xd4 ♘xd4. Better options are 9 ♗b5, 9 ♘cb5, and 9 ♘f5!? ♕xb2 10 ♘xg7+ ♔f8 when complications set in, that in light of results, lead one to the conclusion that Black might as well avoid them.

Hence back to the obvious **8...0-0** when 9 ♕d2 will transpose into chapter 5 and anything silly (such as 9 h4?!) could well be asking for 9...♕b6. In fact White's only justification for the 8 ♗c4 move-order lies in the obscure **9 ♕e2** *(48)*.

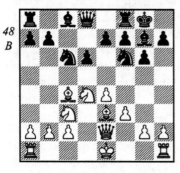

48
B

This strange move, which keeps an extra eye on the c4-square but temporarily at least removes the ♗e3-h6 possibility, has, quite frankly, never impressed me. Whilst I am not convinced that 'normal' Dragon moves are not okay, I go along with old texts that say that Black does well with **9...♘a5!?** hoping to exploit the lack of retreat squares for the d4-knight (note that 9...♘xe4? falls for White's trap i.e. 10 ♘xc6 ♘xc3 11 ♘xd8 ♘xe2 12 ♘xf7 d5 13 ♘h6+!+-). After 9...♘a5!? **10 ♗d3**

(10 ♗b3?! e5! 11 ♘db5 a6 12 ♘a3 ♘xb3 13 axb3 d5 and Black is already on top) **10...e5 11 ♘b3 ♗e6** White is in no position to exploit Black's currently backward d6-pawn. **Tal-Gufeld**, Sukhumi 1972, continued **12 0-0 ♖c8 13 ♖fd1** (the greedy 13 ♗xa7?! only attracts unbearable pressure on b2 and c3 after 13...♘c4) **13...♘c4 14 ♗xc4 ♗xc4 15 ♕f2 b6 16 ♖d2 ♕c7 17 ♖ad1 ♘e8! 18 ♕h4 f5 19 exf5 gxf5∓**.

The reader will note that any lines that I have given so far in this chapter involve White developing his bishop to c4. However, I am often asked why White should bother with such a move, followed by ♗b3, when it only ends up giving itself up for the black knight that soon materializes on c4. In other words why doesn't White save two valuable tempi by leaving it at home on f1?

To answer this, let us take a look at the crucial Yugoslav Attack position from which the main diversions take place *(49)*.

49
W

Black has completed all of his obvious developing moves and it is now White to play. In order to determine White's sensible options, it helps to look at what Black might do now with an extra move. Of course Black may choose 9...♗d7 preparing to bring a rook to the c-file though I would be the first to admit that the bishop doesn't actually do an awful lot on this square. In fact in the absence of a white bishop on c4, Black would do better to seek a more active post for his light-squared bishop along the a2-g8 diagonal. Thus after 9...♘xd4!? 10 ♗xd4 ♗e6 the bishop is ready to help in an attack on the white king when 0-0-0 is played. Of even more importance is that from the diagram position Black is threatening to open things up with 9...d5. This pawn break, described in chapter 2, challenges White's pawn centre and has the ultimate aim of exposing White's centrally posted pieces to the black rooks. The move ...d5 also paves the way for a later thrust of Black's e7-pawn, when of course he will not have to worry about a backward d-pawn! However it is important that the timing is right. For example, were Black to play 8...d5?! (instead of 8...♘c6) then White could secure a pawn on e5 with 9 e5 ♘e8 10 f4 f6 11 0-0-0 fxe5 12 fxe5 ♘c6 (12...♗xe5?! 13 ♘f3±) 13 ♘f3 e6 14 ♗h6±. However, should White have to ex-

change knights on c6 before playing e5, then the d5-pawn is a strength rather than a weakness for Black, who can also obtain counterplay down the newly opened b-file (a result of ...bxc6).

White's most popular (and best) ninth move alternatives are:

9 ♗c4 covered in chapter 5
9 g4 covered in chapter 6
9 0-0-0 covered in chapter 7

As well as being sensible, these moves are all designed to prevent 9...d5, although it is probable that this is Black's best reply to 9 0-0-0 anyway. Certainly in my view both 9 h4?! and 9 ♗e2?! are best met by 9...d5!. Then any variations that arise can be compared favourably to the ones discussed in chapter 7, as 9 0-0-0 must be a more useful move.

Finally the only other move that I have ever seen is the premature and uninspiring **9 ♘b3** *(50)*.

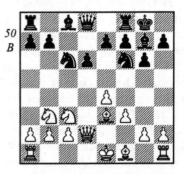

50
B

As the e6-square is no longer under White's control, Black now does well to post his bishop there (but as you will discover this is often okay even when ♘xe6 is a possibility) and after **9...♗e6** White's two documented practical tries to date are:

a) **10 0-0-0 ♖c8 11 g4 ♘b4** (with ...♖xc3 in mind) **12 ♔b1 ♘d7 13 ♗d4 ♘e5 14 ♗e2 a5** with a more than comfortable game and good attacking chances for Black in **Shuchinsky-Veresov**, Moscow 1940.

b) **10 ♘d5 ♗xd5 11 exd5 ♘e5** and now:

b1) **12 0-0-0 ♕c7 13 ♔b1 ♖fc8 14 c3 a5 15 ♘d4 ♘c4 16 ♗xc4 ♕xc4** and not only is White's d5-pawn in line for more pressure than Black's e7-pawn, but with c3 pro-

voked, a queenside pawn storm with good prospects was the order of the day in **Barcza-Filip**, Bucharest 1953.

b2) **12 ♗e2** unambitiously combines Yugoslav and Classical lines (see chapter 9) and leaves White rather planless, for example **12...♕c7 13 0-0 ♘c4 14 ♗xc4 ♕xc4 15 ♖ad1 ♖fc8 16 ♖f2 ♘d7 17 ♗g5 ♗xb2 18 ♗xe7 ♘b6 19 ♗xd6 ♖d8∓ Bronstein-Winter**, USSR v Great Britain (radio match) 1946.

b3) **12 c4 ♖c8 13 ♖c1 b5!? 14 cxb5 ♖xc1+ 15 ♕xc1** when both **15...♘xd5** and **15...♕a8!** Δ **16...♘xd5** leave Black better as White has lost his centre and is lacking in development.

5 Yugoslav Attack 9 ♗c4

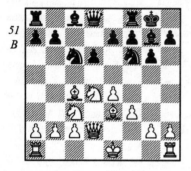

51
B

Despite my advice on why you should read this book from the beginning to the end, no doubt lots of readers (and I hope there are lots of readers!) will have jumped straight to this chapter. Indeed it is quite possible that you are even flicking through this at a bookstall, wondering whether you should add this to your already quite large Dragon collection (or desperately trying to prepare for your next round game!). Whatever the case may be, it is quite likely that you are about to see some fresh material on an old idea.

Yes, this author believes that the best form of defence *is* 'attack' and in system 1, the focus is concentrated on the ...♕a5 variation. Many people have told me that this is supposed to be bad, yet nobody has ever really convinced me of why. In system 2, some instructive

and some recent games are illustrated in the more common ...♖c8 line. The assessments in ...♖c8 Dragon theory are subject to particularly rapid changes, but the reader should note that there is no mention of the most topical ...h5 variations (often referred to as the 'main line'). For a long time to come, I am sure that Black will have the resources at least to hold his own there, but nonetheless, in this book at least, it is not what I am advocating.

System 1: ...♕a5

I would like to be able to give an exact move number for ...♕a5, but as you will see, even this is a talking point. Dragon expert William Watson once told me that he leaves his queen on d8 to protect the e7-pawn. In system 2 you will see why this can be important, but with nothing quite like over-achieving, the queen zooms into the attack with bigger fish to fry! In addition, the queen makes way for the f8-rook to go to c8. This is not only important so that the a8-rook can (if required) attack down the b-file, but as will become apparent, the black king has at its disposal the f8-square.

As a general overview, games 1 and 2 will look at a quick h4-h5. Games 3 and 4 will cover h4 in conjunction with g4, whilst the quiet but popular idea of an early ♔b1 is the subject of games 5-7.

Game 1
Morris-Ward
Lloyds Bank U-16 1983

1	e4	c5
2	♘f3	d6
3	d4	cxd4
4	♘xd4	♘f6
5	♘c3	g6
6	♗e3	♗g7
7	f3	0-0
8	♕d2	♘c6
9	♗c4	♗d7

Black clears the c-file for a rook and having selected the 9 ♗c4 option, it is once again decision time for White.

10 ♗b3

White is counting on having to play this move anyway and so gets it out of the way now. This and the other two main tenth move alternatives (as well as 10 g4), are likely to transpose, although 10 ♗b3 does allow Black the possibility of 10...♘xd4 11 ♗xd4 b5 (intending to hassle the bishop with a quick ...a5-a4). Evidently in this game Black passes up this chance, preferring the more usual continuation.

10 0-0-0 is of course sensible, though often it seems that many players like to go it alone with their h-pawn first. For the moment, let us assume that in pure caveman style, White decides that he will only need one rook (the one on h1) to give mate. He can then batter his way down the h-file and infiltrate with his queen via ♗h6. The only obstacle that will then keep White from glory is the f6-knight (defending h7) and White has just the move to cure that, ♘d5. However, although by this stage Black will not have had the chance to play the thematic ...♖xc3 (with this very much on his mind), the c3-knight is of course pinned to the white king. Note ...♕a5 will have been played, but 0-0-0 won't! On 10 h4, I have come to the conclusion that 10...♘e5 is probably the correct move order. 10...♕a5 is alright, but it allows the annoying 11 ♘b3. I say this despite achieving a little bit of fame for the following game: 11...♕c7 (11...♕b4!? 12 ♗d3 ♘a5 is an interesting alternative) 12 h5 ♘e5 13 ♗e2 ♘c4 14 ♗xc4 ♕xc4 15 ♗h6 ♗h8?! 16 ♗xf8 ♖xf8 17 hxg6 fxg6 18 0-0-0 ♗e6 19 ♘d5 ♘xd5 20 exd5 ♗f5 21 g4 ♗d7 22 ♖de1? ♗e5 23 ♖xe5 dxe5 24 ♕h2 ♕f4+ 25 ♘d2 ♕xh2 26 ♖xh2 e4! 27 fxe4 ♗xg4 28 c4 h5 29 ♔c2 ♔g7 30 c5 g5 31 ♔d3 h4 32 d6 exd6 33 cxd6 h3 34 e5 ♗e6 35 ♘e4 g4 36 ♘g5 ♗f5+ 37 ♔d4 g3 38 ♖xh3 ♗xh3 39 ♘xh3 g2 40 d7 ♔f7

41 ♔d5 ♔e7 42 e6 ♖f3 43 ♘g1 ♖f1 44 ♘e2 g1♕ 0-1 Nunn-Ward, British Quickplay 1988.

In fact, the above did little but make me very happy and my opponent as sick as a parrot! It shows how resourceful the bishops can be in the Dragon, but it is very doubtful that before White blundered on move 22, Black had sufficient compensation for the exchange.

Returning to 10 h4 ♘e5, after 11 ♗b3 ♕a5, the only outstanding way that White might be able to exploit this move order is with 12 ♗h6 (as 12...♗h8 is not really on and there is no rook available to chop on c3). Then 12...♗xh6 13 ♕xh6 lures the white queen away, with 13...♖fc8 threatening 14...♖xc3. Then 14 ♘de2 ♗e6!? (or 14...♗b5) is fine for Black and on 14 0-0-0, of course 14...♖xc3! anyway, e.g. 15 bxc3 ♕a3+!? (or 15...♕xc3 16 ♘e2? ♘d3+!∓) 16 ♔b1 a5 17 h5 a4 18 ♗d5 ♘xd5 (18...♖a6!? may even be better) 19 exd5 ♘c4 20 ♕c1 ♕xc3 (threatening 20...♘a3+) 21 ♖d3 ♕b4+ 22 ♔a1 ♘e5 23 ♖dd1 ♕c3+ 24 ♕b2 ♕xb2 25 ♔xb2 ♖a5 and Black holds the endgame advantage.

Finally 10 ♘xc6? bxc6 merely gives Black control over the d5-square and a half-open b-file which should be used to its full advantage; and what can one say about 10 0-0 ?!. Probably all Dragon players will come up against this at some time or other and it really is illogical. To make progress on the kingside now White would probably have to play f4 anyhow. Meanwhile Black can carry on with the traditional Sicilian queenside play as in the following game: 10...♘e5 11 ♗b3 ♖c8 12 ♘de2 b6 13 ♗h6 ♘c4 14 ♗xc4 ♗xh6 15 ♕xh6 (and not 15 ♗xf7+?? ♔g7-+) 15...♖xc4 16 ♖ad1 b5 17 ♖d2 b4 18 ♘d1 ♕b6+ 19 ♔h1 ♖c5 20 ♘g3 ♘h5 21 ♘xh5 ♖xh5 22 ♕f4 ♗e6 23 ♖e1 ♖a5∓ Mordue-Ward, British Ch (Eastbourne) 1990.

10 ...	♕a5
11 h4	♖fc8 *(52)*

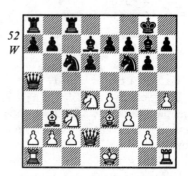

52
W

A frequently occurring position, although 11 h4 may be replaced by 11 0-0-0.

12 h5

The lovely thing about the ...♕a5 variation is that whether or not White knows the limited theory, there is always plenty of room for dubious innovation on his part. One of my favourites is 12 ♔f2?! (played now or at some other juncture). Fearing a queenside attack,

White mistakenly believes that his king will be safer on f2. However after 12...♘e5, 13 ♖ag1 ♘eg4+! 14 ♔e1 (if 14 fxg4 then 14...♖xc3! with ...♘xe4+ in mind, is horrendous for White) 14...♘xe3 15 ♕xe3 ♕c5 (threatening 16...e5) 16 ♕d3 ♘xe4 17 ♘xe4 ♕xd4, Black was soon victorious in Fournier-Ward, Le Touquet 1992.

Again, we will see a lot more of 12 0-0-0 ♘e5, and 12 g4 is covered in game 3.

12 ...   ♘xh5

An ability that is quite handy for Black is knowing when to and when not to accept an offered h-pawn. One might suggest that is good to do so provided ...♘c4 has not yet been played. Indeed it is true that ...♘xh5 is less likely to be safe after the knight has been swapped for the b3-bishop. However the best thing to do is look at the reason why Black should voluntarily accelerate White's attack. Of course, if it were a race solely for checkmate then such a decision would be pure madness. Rather Black is stocking up on pawns and encouraging White to weaken his kingside pawns further, in anticipation of an endgame. In the Sicilian Dragon, Black must not be afraid to sacrifice the exchange. Often this will involve ...♖xc3 (a white knight) crippling the white queenside and perhaps winning the new c3-pawn. As you will soon discover, this structure-wrecking

may be sufficient compensation on its own, but with that extra pawn (on h5) bagged, there should be no worries!

13 0-0-0   ♘e5
14 ♘de2 (53)

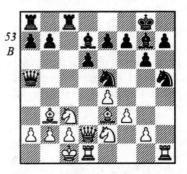

53
B

Very Karpovian! A surprisingly common try, but although White guards against an exchange sacrifice on c3, there is a flaw. The difference between it being played here and in system 2 is the presence of both the b3-bishop and the e5-knight. Fortunately for Black it is his trusty steed that wins the day. As it eyes up f3, White's attack (namely the g2-g4 thrust) is put on ice whilst Black temporarily refrains from playing the obvious 14...♘c4.

14 ...   ♗e6!

Although this game was played some time ago, even today I am particularly proud of this move. The point is that if White trades bishops, although Black's kingside is slightly weakened, White no longer has d5 for his knight. Most of all though, he will have lost his grip on c4, a square on which a knight is bound to materialize. Meanwhile White must do something about 15...♗xb3 as 16 cxb3 allows 16...♕xa2 and 16 axb3 ♕a1+ 17 ♘b1 ♘xf3! is the end.

15 ♔b1   ♘c4
16 ♗xc4   ♖xc4
17 g4   ♘g3!

17...♘f6 was okay, but this move destroys the White position. It is a sacrifice that cannot be declined.

18 ♘xg3   ♖xc3

Aesthetically pleasing, although 18...♗xc3 also wielded the axe. Then if 19 bxc3? Black has 19...♖b4+! 20 cxb4 ♕xa2+ 21 ♔c1 ♕a1 mate.

19 b3

19 a3 is not much better as Black has a few good continuations including 19...♖xa3 20 bxa3 ♗c3!.

19 ...   ♖ac8
20 ♖c1 *(54)*

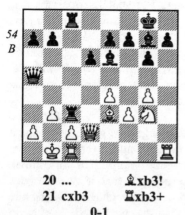

20 ...   ♗xb3!
21 cxb3   ♖xb3+
0-1

On 22 axb3 ♕a1 is mate.

Game 2
Holmes-Ward
London Lloyds Bank 1991

1	e4	c5
2	♘f3	d6
3	d4	cxd4
4	♘xd4	♘f6
5	♘c3	g6
6	♗e3	♗g7
7	f3	0-0
8	♕d2	♘c6
9	♗c4	♗d7
10	h4	♕a5

Once more I would like to add that possibly 10...♘e5 (which would transpose to this game) is more accurate.

| 11 | h5 | ♘e5 |
| 12 | ♗b3 | ♘xh5 |
| 13 | 0-0-0 | ♖fc8 | *(55)*

14 g4

The most natural though not the best continuation, after which Black should be quietly (or loudly!) confident. Three alternatives spring to mind:

a) 14 ♘d5 (Often given as "!?" though "interesting" is not exactly how I would describe the positions

reached) 14...♕xd2+ 15 ♖xd2 ♔f8
(The only adequate way to defend
e7) 16 g4 ♘f6 when we arrive at
another crossroads:

a1) 17 ♗h6?! (remarkably, suggested by many textbooks as the
best way for White to try for an
advantage) 17...♗xh6 18 ♖xh6
♘xd5 19 ♗xd5 ♔g7! 20 ♖dh2
♖h8 21 ♗xb7 ♖b8 22 ♗d5 (22
♗a6 will receive the same treatment) 22...♖b4 23 c3 ♖xd4! 24
cxd4 ♘xf3 25 ♖h1 ♗xg4. Black
has a monstrous kingside, and with
the d4-pawn weak and his rooks in
a tangle White is in big trouble.

a2) 17 ♘xf6 ♗xf6 18 ♖xh7 (18
♖dh2 ♘c4 will reach a similar position) 18...♘c4 19 ♗xc4 ♖xc4 20
g5 ♗g7 21 ♖dh2 ♖ac8! (guarding
against 22 ♖h8+ and not falling for
21...♖xd4?? or 21...♗xd4?? when
Black will either lose his unprotected a8-rook or worse still have
the two white rooks catch his king
in a mating net) 22 f4! (after 22
♘b3 ♗e5 23 f4 ♗g7 leaves the
e4-pawn an easy target and 23 ♖g2
♔g8 is also better for Black)
22...♗g4 (once more the d4-knight
is immune) 23 c3 ♔g8 24 ♖7h4
♗h5. The position is about level,
although Dragon optimists might
claim that the two bishops give him
an edge.

a3) 17 ♖dh2 ♘xd5 18 ♗xd5 ♖c7
19 ♗h6 ♗xh6+ 20 ♖xh6 e6 21
♗b3 ♖ac8=. If Black wants, he
might be able to mix things up
more with 18...♘c6!?.

b) 14 ♗h6. Karpov's move
which quite frankly doesn't impress me. 14...♗xh6 (drawing the
queen away. 14...♘d3+ is an interesting alternative) 15 ♕xh6 ♖xc3!
(Black is forced to make this good
move anyway, as White threatened
16 g4 ♘f6 17 ♘d5+-) 16 bxc3
(Note that the desperate 16 ♖xh5
will not get White a draw after
16...gxh5 17 ♕g5+ ♔h8 18 ♕xe7
♖xb3! 19 ♘xb3 ♕d8-+) 16...♘f6!
(16...♖c8 and 16...♕xc3 are more
obvious but I like this move as it
removes any chance of ♖xh5. Now
17 g4 would transpose to the detailed memory (A) in chapter 4) 17
♔b1 (White is hoping for
17...♕xc3? when 18 ♘e2, intending 19 ♘f4-d5, will give him the
chance to try to remove the key
defensive f6-knight. On 17 ♘e2
♗b5 18 ♘f4 ♗c4! Black has the
upper hand) 17...♖c8 18 ♘e2 ♗e6!
19 ♗xe6 (Again 19 ♘f4 should be
met by 19...♗c4 when 20 ♘d5
♗xd5 21 ♖xd5 ♕xc3 leaves Black
in control and 20 ♗xc4 ♘xc4 21
♘d5 ♕b5+ is fatal) 19...fxe6 20
♕h3 (White cannot allow
20...♘c4) 20...♖c6! 21 ♕xe6+
♔f8. Black currently has no pawns
for the exchange. However with a
knight itching to get to c4, his attack is likely to prove deadly.

c) 14 ♔b1 ♖xc3 15 ♕xc3 (Leading to a foretaste of the main text
ending. It may be argued that
White is slightly better off by having refrained from g2-g4. However

whilst Black keeps up his queen-side play, he is also able to stamp his authority on the kingside. 15 bxc3 ♖c8 16 ♗h6 ♕xc3 is certainly not an improvement for White) 15...♕xc3 16 bxc3 ♖c8 17 ♔b2 (or 17 ♘e2?! a5 18 a3 a4 19 ♗a2 ♗b5∓) 17...a5 18 a3 ♘f6 19 ♗f4 ♘e8 20 ♗g5 a4 21 ♗a2 ♘c6 22 ♖d3 ♘f6 23 ♘xc6 ♗xc6 24 ♖d4 h5 25 ♔c1 ♔f8 26 ♔d2 ♖a8 27 ♖b4 ♖a5 28 ♗e3 e6 29 c4 ♘d7. A draw was the eventual outcome in Spassky-Stein, USSR 1967, but the lack of open files and weaknesses in Black's camp necessitate an assessment of "∓".

14 ...   ♘f6
15 ♗h6 *(56)*

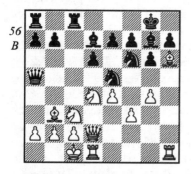

There is no beating about the bush for White now, but it is already too late for subtlety. After the cautious 15 ♔b1, I would firstly like to demonstrate some more ideas for Black in the endgame that might arise after 15...♖xc3 16 ♕xc3 ♕xc3 17 bxc3 ♖c8 18 ♔b2 a5 19 a3 (19 a4? ♘c4+

20 ♗xc4 ♖xc4 leaves the a4-pawn easy pickings) 19...a4 20 ♗a2 ♗e8!? (Note it is a common theme in these positions for Black to hold back with ...♘c4. White's light-squared bishop doesn't do a lot and Black, wanting to have a knight on c4 as a permanent fixture, prepares ...♘f6-d7-b6-c4) 21 ♖h3 ♘fd7 22 ♘e2 ♖c6 23 ♗d5 ♖a6 24 ♗xb7 ♘c4+ 25 ♔c1 ♖a5 26 ♗d4 ♘xa3 and the newly obtained passed a-pawn eventually won Black the day in Ezmakov-Keene, Corr. 1967/70.

Secondly though, 15...♘c4!? also looks good. It is interesting that in the following game White, being an International Master, was the big favourite. However, not known in recent times as a 1 e4 player, this is how he chose to respond when first confronting the Dragon: 16 ♗xc4 ♖xc4 17 ♘b3 ♕d8 18 ♕h2 ♖xc3!? 19 bxc3 ♕c7 20 e5 dxe5 21 ♗d4 ♗e6 22 ♗xe5 ♕c6 23 ♖d3 ♗c4 24 ♖d4 h6 25 ♕g3 a5 26 g5 hxg5 27 ♕xg5 a4 28 ♘d2 ♗d5! 29 ♗xf6 ♗xf6 30 ♕xd5 ♕xc3 *(57)*.

Even with an extra rook, White is unable to cope with the Dragon bishop. 31 ♖hh4 ♖c8! 32 ♕xb7 ♕xc2+ 33 ♔a1 and 0-1 Berg-Meyling, Copenhagen 1993. 33...♕d1+ 34 ♕b1 ♖c1 is hopeless and 34 ♔b2 ♕c1 is mate.

The other direct route to the black king is with 15 ♕h2. This intends to meet 15...♖xc3 with 16 ♗d2! and so best is 15...e6!?. This move is not often good, but here it more than adequately fulfils its task (namely preventing 16 ♘d5). A rare practical outing saw 16 ♔b1 b5 17 ♗g5 ♖xc3 18 ♗xf6 ♗xf6 19 bxc3 ♕xc3 20 ♕xh7+ ♔f8 (Burger-Barnes, US Open Ch 1971). Having conceded his dark-squared bishop, White can make no progress and deserves everything that is coming to him (which is a loss!).

15 ...   ♗xh6!

15...♖xc3!? 16 bxc3 ♘xf3!? has apparently been analysed out to a draw and so isn't applicable here!

16 ♖xh6

What I particularly like about 15...♗xh6! instead of 15...♖xc3!? is that in ignorance, White is more likely to respond with 16 ♕xh6?!. Then as shown in memory (A) at the start of chapter 4, 16...♖xc3! tears his position apart. The text move introduces a new plan for White. 17 ♖dh1 followed by 18 ♕h2 seems obvious, but in actual fact 17 ♖dh1 may threaten 18 ♖xh7 in view of 18...♘xh7 19 ♕h6.

16 ...   ♖xc3!

Remember that from the moment Black captured White's h-pawn (or indeed from the moment Black played the Dragon), this is the move that he must be prepared to play.

17 ♕xc3

The last major divide is reached, and it has to be said that 17 bxc3 may offer White more chance of a draw. The lowdown on 17 bxc3 is as follows:

17...♖c8 18 ♔b2 ♕b6 19 ♔a1(or c1) ♕c5 20 ♔b2 a5 21 ♖dh1 (intending 21...a4? 22 ♖xh7) 21...e6!. Black has given his king an escape square and having reached this position on a few occasions with a maximum score, I can attest to its credibility as "∓". One good plan after 22 a3 a4 23 ♗a2 is 23...♗b5!? intending to secure the knight on c4 with 24...♗c4.

All very well so far, but White should replace 19 ♔a1 with 19 ♕h2! and if now 19...♕c5 then 20 ♖xh7 ♕xc3+ 21 ♔b1 ♘xh7 22 ♖h1 e6 23 ♕xh7+ ♔f8 24 ♕h6+ ♔e7 25 ♕g5+ f6 26 ♖h7+ ♘f7 27 ♕xg6 ♕e1+ 28 ♔b2 ♕c3+ with a perpetual check. Therefore if Black wishes to obtain the full point then he should search the latter for an improvement (and I have a sneaky suspicion that there is one) or else dabble in 18...♘c4+ 19 ♗xc4 ♖xc4 20 ♘b3 (if 20 ♖dh1 then ♖a4! threatens to get the mate in first) 20...♕e5 when the game is in the balance though still very much alive.

17 ...   ♕xc3

18 bxc3 *(58)*

This is the starting position of a typical endgame arising from a Dragon exchange sacrifice.

18 ...   ♖c8

Black must avoid the temptation of 18...♘h5? because of 19 gxh5! ♔g7 20 hxg6 ♔xh6 21 gxf7 ♖f8 22 ♖g1!±. I have reached the above position on several occasions during my illustrious career(?!) and although 18...b5 is not stupid, the other move that I have favoured is 18...♔g7. White must now make a relatively insignificant decision about where his rook should go (although judging from the amount of time usually spent on this retreat, White doesn't see it that way). White selected 19 ♖6h1 in Kett-Ward, London Barbican Open 1986, when play continued along similar lines to the main text with 19...g5 20 ♖hf1 ♖c8 21 ♔b2 a5 22 a3 a4 23 ♗a2 ♖c5 24 ♘f5+ ♗xf5 25 exf5 h6 26 ♖d4 b5 27 ♖e1 ♖c7 28 ♖e3 h5 29 gxh5 ♘xh5 30 ♖b4 ♖c5 31 c4 (My opinion is that White's very slim hopes lie on the queenside, i.e. with a possible rook

penetration and ultimate creation of a passed pawn. With currently five isolated pawns, 31 c4 represents White's only alternative to a slow painful death) 31...bxc4 32 ♖xa4 ♘f4 33 ♖a7 ♘d5 (White has got his passed pawn but, while this never gets going, the black knights dominate the centre of the board) 34 ♖e4 ♔f6 35 ♖a4 ♖b5+ 36 ♔c1 ♘c3 (a fork!) 37 ♗xc4 ♖b1+ 38 ♔d2 ♘xa4 39 ♗a2 ♖b2 40 ♗b3 ♘c5 41 ♔c1 ♘xe4 42 ♔xb2 ♘xf3 0-1.

19 ♔d2

There is not much to choose between this and 19 ♔b2. White hopes here that his king will be of more use when centralized.

19 ...   ♔g7

20 ♖h4

Encouraging Black to play a move that he was going to play anyway. As a result White loses a tempo, but there is nothing more frustrating than having time on your hands with nothing to do (and believe me, there really is little for White to do).

20 ...   g5

The point behind this move is to fix the white kingside pawns. The f3-pawn is a real weakness (along with the c3-pawn) and the pressure on g4 renders f3-f4 practically impossible. Eventually Black intends to get his majority rolling after which his knights will find some terrific outposts.

21 ♖h2   ♖c5

A solid move. This is often a good square for a black rook in the

Dragon. Easily transferable from the queenside to the kingside and vice versa, here it can aspire to things other than the already useful c-file operations.

22 ♖e1   e6

Although Black retains the possibility of a ...d5 break, the main reasons for this move are to blunt the white light-squared bishop and to take away the f5-square from the white knight. White's rooks continue to wonder aimlessly and are never likely to be in a position to attack the d6-pawn. This of course should always be a consideration when contemplating ...e6.

23 ♖e3   a5

This inevitable move has taken surprisingly long to surface. White's reply is forced. After 24 a4? Black could win the a4-pawn with 24...♘c4+ 25 ♗xc4 ♖xc4 or 24...♗xa4!? 25 ♗xa4 ♘c4+ 26 ♔e2 ♘xe3 27 ♔xe3 ♖xc3+ with 28...♖c4 regaining the piece.

24 a3   a4
25 ♗a2   ♗b5!? *(59)*

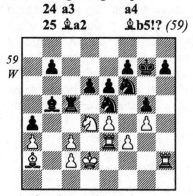

A plan that we have already seen. With 26...♗c4, Black intends to

get a knight to c4. White cannot allow Black to achieve this aim as his a-pawn will certainly fall (if not the exchange). He would then be fighting a hopeless cause and so he must take steps to intercept the black bishop's journey.

26 ♘xb5   ♖xb5
27 ♖h1   ♖b2

In these type of endgames where Black has sacrificed the exchange, it will nearly always favour him to keep the other rook on. This way, not only are there twice as many white rooks available to be caught in forks and pins, but there is less danger should White be able to create an outside passed pawn (knights for example are notoriously bad at stopping passed rook pawns). However this does certainly not mean that the black rook's role is of that of a defender. Far from it, and here we see that despite being outnumbered, it is indeed the black rook that has found its way to a key file. The black rook will often be particularly useful for attacking isolated pawns. The next few moves see it forcing a white rook to defend the 'lame duck' bishop on a2.

28 ♖a1   h5!

Having tied White up on the queenside, Black makes a break on the kingside where he believes he has some comparatively redundant pieces waiting to get in on the action.

29 gxh5   ♘xh5
30 c4

As if it were possible, White further reduces the scope of his light-squared bishop. Nevertheless he must do something to try to banish the troublesome black rook.

30 ...	♘f4
31 ♔c3	♖b6
32 ♖b1	♖xb1
33 ♗xb1	

His bishop just seems to go from bad to worse, but at least White has a glimmer of hope. An ingenious manoeuvre of his rook or king to mop up the black a- and b-pawns, followed by a quick a-pawn promotion should do the trick! Unfortunately that is never really going to be on the cards and, besides, his position is about to take another turn for the worse.

| 33 ... | ♘g2! |

The black kingside majority was always going to appear. Well, now it is quicker than expected as the f3-pawn is doomed.

| 34 ♖e2 | ♘h4 |
| 35 f4 | |

If 35...♘exf3 were allowed, then the black g-pawn would motor home.

| 35 ... | gxf4 (60) |

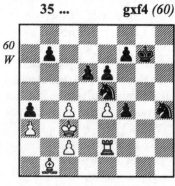

60
W

| 36 ♖h2 | ♘hf3 |
| 37 ♖f2 | ♔h6 |

Now for the icing on the cake! White is powerless to prevent a king penetration.

38 ♗a2	♔h5
39 c5	dxc5
40 ♗c4	♔h4
41 ♗f1	♘g5
42 ♖h2+	

After 42 ♖xf4+ ♔g3, the rook is trapped.

42 ...	♔g4
43 ♖g2+	♔h5
44 ♖h2+	♔g6
45 ♗d3	f3
46 ♖h4	f2
47 ♗f1	♘ef3

0-1

With his e-pawn going and a knight destined for g3 or d2, White throws in the towel.

As I have previously mentioned, it took me a little while to realize that it is okay to give up the exchange, even when it doesn't lead to mate. As you have just seen (and will continue to do so), there are certain structural and positional compensations to be had. I hope that this game has gone some way toward removing any doubts about ...♖xc3 that the reader may have had.

Game 3
Cullip-Ward
Guildford Masters 1991

| 1 e4 | c5 |
| 2 ♘f3 | d6 |

3 d4	cxd4
4 ♘xd4	♘f6
5 ♘c3	g6
6 ♗e3	♗g7
7 f3	0-0
8 ♗c4	♘c6
9 ♕d2	♗d7
10 0-0-0	

Assuming that White is going for the h4 and g4 set-up, then he may choose to omit 10 0-0-0. However this has little to gain and a lot to lose, e.g. 10 h4 ♘e5 11 ♗b3 ♕a5 12 g4 ♖fc8 13 h5?! ♖c4! (not only possible, but good here as the b2-pawn is undefended. The big threat is 14...♖xd4 and 15...♘xf3+) 14 ♗xc4 ♘xc4 15 ♕c1 d5 (ignoring the e3-bishop for the moment in favour of blasting open the centre. If 16...dxe4 is allowed then the White position will fall apart) 16 ♘b3 ♕c7 17 exd5 ♘xd5! 18 ♘xd5 (or 18 ♗f2 ♘f4 threatening 19...♘xb2 amongst others, leaves Black with excellent compensation) 18...♕g3+ 19 ♔e2 (If 19 ♗f2 then 19...♕xf3 when White might be a rook up, but has his king all over the shop and his pieces either *en prise* or completely un-coordinated) 19...♗b5!. The white king won't last the distance.

10 ...	♕a5
11 h4	

After 11 g4 ♘e5 12 ♗b3 ♖fc8, 13 h4 will transpose, 13 ♔b1 is found in game 5 and that leaves one other try; 13 g5?! prevents White from trading dark-squared bishops

(thus hindering his own attack) and Black has a good alternative to 13...♘h5 (which would be met by 14 ♘de2 △ ♘g3) in 13...♘e8!? (playable as there is no longer a dire need either to protect, or prevent White getting at h7) 14 h4 b5 15 h5 (15 ♘d5 ♕xd2+ 16 ♖xd2 ♔f8 will leave Black holding all the trumps in the endgame, i.e. with the usual queenside play) 15...♘c4 16 ♗xc4 bxc4 17 hxg6 hxg6 18 ♖h4 ♖ab8 19 ♖dh1 e6 20 ♕h2 ♔f8 (A purpose has been found for the e8-knight; it defends both the g7-bishop and the f6-square. White's attack will soon grind to a halt, whereas Black's is just beginning) 21 ♖h7 (threatening 22 ♖xg7 and 23 ♕h8+) 21...♔e7 22 f4 *(61)*

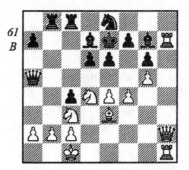

61
B

22...♖xb2!! 23 ♔d2 (After 23 ♔xb2 ♖b8+ 24 ♔c1 ♕xc3∓, threats include 25...♕xe3+, 25...♗xd4, and 25...♖b2xa2-a1) 23...♖b3!! 24 axb3 cxb3 25 ♖xg7 ♖xc3! 26 ♖a1 ♖xc2++ 0-1 Razuvaev-Kornakin, Moscow 1967.

11 ...   **♘e5**
12 ♗b3   **♖fc8**
13 g4 *(62)*

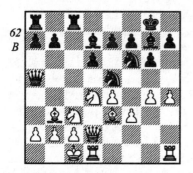

62
B

13 ♔b1 is found in games 5 and 6. 13 h5 has just been discussed in detail and 13 ♗h6?! ♗xh6 14 ♕xh6 ♖xc3! has also already turned up.

13 ...   **♘c4**

A natural progression, Black wishing to double his rooks on the c-file. 13...♖c4, which is dubious in an interesting sort of way, is a blatant attempt to trade a rook for the white dark-squared bishop. To bring in some additional (to the text) ideas, game 4 illustrates the other alternative, 13...b5!?.

14 ♗xc4

14 ♕d3, opting to preserve the light-squared bishop instead, has never made much sense to me. After 14...♘xe3 15 ♕xe3, White's attack is already down to warp factor 1 and Black has satisfactory continuations in 15...♖c5 (intending 16...♖ac8) and 15...♕c5 with a queenside pawn storm in mind, and perhaps even a timely ...e5.

14 ...   **♖xc4**
15 ♘b3

A reflex reaction. White considers his queenside to be a little bare and so offers some cover. The drawback is that the long a1-h8 diagonal is now less blocked. As you will see, in this game White takes the precaution of playing 16 ♔b1. I would like to look at how things might turn out if White forgets this move, starting with if Black has his heart set on an early exchange sacrifice. On 15 h5, *ECO* gives 15...♖xc3 (for 15...♖ac8 see notes to White's 16th move) 16 ♕xc3 ♕xa2 17 hxg6 hxg6 18 ♕b3 ♕a6 19 ♗h6 ♕a1+ 20 ♔d2 ♕a5+ 21 ♔e2 (21 ♕c3? ♗xh6+ 22 ♖xh6 ♕g5+ 23 ♕e3 ♕xe3+ 24 ♔xe3 ♗xg4!∓) 21...♗xh6 22 ♖xh6 as 'unclear'.

Similarly after the text 15 ♘b3 ♕a6 and then 16 h5 Black again has 16...♖xc3!? if he wants. Then after 17 bxc3 (17 ♕xc3 allows the useful discovered attack ...♘xe4, either before or after ...♕xa2) 17...♕xa2 18 hxg6 ♗e6!, Black is generally considered to have some good compensation, e.g. 19 gxh7+ ♔h8 20 g5 ♘d7 (and with his king position fairly safe, Black plans a now not unfamiliar knight trek around to the c4-square).

It is I suppose worth mentioning that 15 ♘de2 still doesn't find its place here. White reinforces his knight on c3, but while at some point a double exchange sacrifice might not be out of the question, Black should not be averse to simple chess. It is sometimes overlooked that the purpose of doubling the rooks on the c-file is not just to threaten ...♖xc3 (making ♕xc3 impossible), but to pile the pressure on the c2-pawn. Consequently both 15...♖ac8 and 15...b5 (intending ...b4) leave Black very much in the driving seat.

15 ...   ♕a6
16 ♔b1

White defends that which the black queen continues to eye up. The reader may have noted that the interpolation of both White's, and Black's, 15th moves supply White with another idea; whilst the black bishop remains on d7, the e4-e5 pawn thrust may force the black knight away, as ...dxe5 can be met by g5. This is always a move that Black (and indeed White) should consider, although here Black has little to fear from 16 e5?!. The h-file is not yet open and so 16...♘e8 (or 16...♘xg4 17 fxg4 ♗xg4 18 ♖de1?! dxe5 19 ♗h6 ♗f6∓ was Beliavsky-Velimirović, Szirak IZ 1987) 17 h5 (17 ♘d5 ♕xa2 leaves White in more danger) 17...♖xc3!? 18 bxc3 ♗xe5 is better for Black.

16 h5 is a critical alternative (16 ♔b1 transposes to the game) and having already analysed 16...♖xc3!?, some new ideas crop up after 16...♖ac8 17 hxg6 *(63)*.

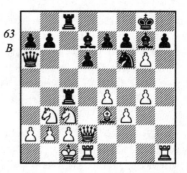

A dilemma often facing Black is whether he should recapture on g6 with his h-pawn or his f-pawn (this being a fine example). Generally speaking, ...hxg6 will leave his pawn structure better, but leave him more susceptible to a mate down the h-file. On the other hand ...fxg6 may buy the black king more time, though possibly leave him open to problems along the b3-g8 diagonal. Often it is suggested that with a white bishop on d4, ...hxg6 is the correct response as his dark-squared defender is not so easy to trade off (♗d4-e3-h6 takes time). Meanwhile ...fxg6 appears more universally playable and this is what I would like to look at here. Note 17...hxg6?! holds several hidden resources for Black (in case of inaccurate White play) but seems to go down the tubes to 18 e5! dxe5! (18...♘e8 19 ♕h2! and 18...♘xg4 19 fxg4 ♗xg4 20 ♕h2! both seriously question Black's survival) 19 ♗h6! (even better than the materialistic 19 g5) 19...♗h8 20 ♗g5!, when with 21 ♖xh8+ just one of the threats, Black at least appears to be heading for a defeat.

So, 17...fxg6 18 e5 (making use of this move while he still can. After 18 ♗d4 ♗e6 19 ♔b1 b5 20 ♘d5, Black was fine and opted for some reasonable compensation with 20...♘xd5!? 21 exd5 ♖xd4!? 22 ♘xd4 ♗xd5 in Coleman-Ward, British Ch 1988) 18...♘e8 19 ♕h2 h5!?. Now 20 gxh5 ♗xe5 21 ♕g2 ♗f5! and with such a strong attacking force, things should soon start to happen around a2, c3, and c2. 20 exd6?! ♗xc3 21 bxc3 ♖xc3∓ is even worse for White, who should try the solidifying 20 ♗d4!. After 20...♖xd4!?, two of my own games have continued:

a) 21 ♘xd4 ♗xe5 22 ♕d2 ♖c4 23 ♘de2 hxg4 24 ♕g5 gxf3 25 ♕xg6+ ♘g7 26 ♕h7+ ♔f7 27 ♖df1 ♗f5 28 ♖xf3 ♗f4+ 29 ♖xf4 ♖xf4 30 ♕h6 ♖g4∓ Morrison-Ward, Kent Schools 1983.

b) 21 ♖xd4!? ♖xc3!? 22 bxc3 ♗xe5 23 ♕d2 ♗e6 24 gxh5 ♕xa2 25 ♖g1 ♘f6 26 ♖xg6+ ♔f7 27 f4 ♗xd4 28 ♕xd4 ♕a3+ 29 ♔d2 ♗xb3 30 cxb3 ♕b2+ 31 ♔d3 ♕xb3 32 ♖g5 ♘xh5!∓ Baumann-Ward, London Barbican Open 1991. Admittedly these lines can be very hairy and although I won both games, I particularly can't advise (b) to anyone with a heart condition!

16 ...   ♖ac8
17 ♗d4? *(64)*

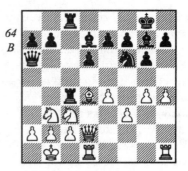

At first glance this looks like a very solid move. From d4 the bishop keeps in on all of the action. However it is just about to be knocked off its perch and then White is in for a shock. 17 e5?! ♘e8 again leads nowhere for White in view of 18 ♘d5 ♖xc2! and 17 ♗h6 can be given the usual treatment of 17...♗xh6 (17...♗h8 is actually playable here) 18 ♕xh6 ♖xc3!. This only really leaves 17 h5 when Black has the choice between the reliable 17...♗e6 and the more adventurous 17...♗xg4!? as in the following instructive game:

18 e5! (White must decline this sacrifice, e.g. 18 fxg4?! ♖xc3! 19 bxc3 ♘xe4-+ or 19 hxg6 ♖xc2 20 gxf7+ ♔f8 21 ♕xc2 ♖xc2 22 ♔xc2 ♕c4+ 23 ♔d2 ♘xe4+ 24 ♔e1 ♗e5 0-1 was McCurdy-Keene, Örebrö 1966) 18...♗xf3 19 exf6 ♗xf6 20 hxg6 hxg6 21 ♗g5 (21 ♘d5 ♖xc2 22 ♘xf6+ exf6 23 ♕d4 ♖2c4! seems fine for Black as 24 ♕xf6? loses to 24...♕xa2+!! 25 ♔xa2 ♖a4+ 26 ♔b1 ♗e4+ and 24 ♖h8+! ♔xh8 25 ♕xf6+ ♔g8 26

♕xf3 ♕c6 leads to a satisfactory ending) 21...♗xc3! 22 bxc3 ♖xc3? 23 ♗f6!! ♗xh1 24 ♕h6 1-0 Wahls-Ward, London Lloyds Bank 1987.

Clearly everything went horribly wrong! However things might have turned out different had Black played 22...♗xh1! 23 ♖xh1 ♖xc3. This way Black could have met 24 ♗f6 with 24...♖h3! and responded to 24 ♕h2 with the stunning 24...♕xa2+!! 25 ♔xa2 ♖xc2+ 26 ♕xc2 ♖xc2+ arriving at the position below *(65)*.

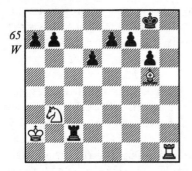

65
W

With six pawns for two pieces in the endgame, it is Black with all the practical chances.

17 ...   e5!

It is rare to see this move cause so much damage to anyone other than Black himself. The g7-bishop blocks itself out, but it intends to see the light of day again soon. Incidentally this and my next move were not entirely of my own creation. I had read about this idea when learning the Dragon as a junior. Being rather a decisive combi-

nation, it is all the more puzzling as to why I had previously played 17...♗e6. Still, after 18 h5 b5 19 e5 b4!? 20 exf6 bxc3 21 bxc3 exf6 22 hxg6 fxg6 23 ♖de1 ♗f7 24 g5 ♖a4 25 c4 ♖axc4 26 ♖ec1 ♖xd4!? 27 ♕xd4 fxg5 28 ♕g4 ♖c4 29 ♕xg5 h5 30 ♕d8+ ♔h7 31 ♕e7 ♕a3 32 c3 ♖a4 33 ♖h2 ♗xb3 34 axb3 ♕a1+ 35 ♔c2 ♕xc3+ 36 ♔d1 ♖d4+ 37 ♔e2 ♕c1 0-1 Sampson-Ward, British Ch 1987, I suppose that I shouldn't complain! Clearly in view of the main text, 17...♗e6 has no precise theoretical interest, but the ideas (particularly of sacrificing a rook for the dark-squared bishop, and then attacking with the – also defensive – two bishops) are worth bearing in mind.

18 ♗e3   ♗xg4! *(66)*

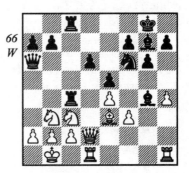

66
W

19 ♖hf1

After 19 fxg4 ♖xc3! 20 bxc3 ♘xe4 21 ♕d3 ♘xc3+ 22 ♔c1 ♕a3+ 23 ♔d2 e4, even if the white king escapes all of the turmoil, he will be material down as his pawns are dropping like flies. The text is no real improvement.

19 ... Ξxc3!
20 bxc3 $\&$xf3!

This bishop was offered before, so why not again? Its purpose of facilitating ...$\&$xe4 is just the same as before.

21 $\&$xd6

Stubborn to the end. 21 Ξxf3 $\&$xe4 22 $\&$e1 $\&$xc3+ 23 $\&$c1 $\&$e2+ 0-1 was Arbakov-Bykhovsky, Vilnius 1967. White has assumed that Black will see 24 $\&$d2 (if 24 $\&$b1 then 24...$\&$a3) 24...e4 25 Ξf2 Ξxc2+! 26 $\&$xc2 $\&$xa2 mate.

21 ... $\&$xd1
22 $\&$xa6   bxa6
23 Ξxd1 $\&$xe4
24 Ξd7 $\&$xc3+

0-1

White is not hopeful of halting Black's kingside majority!

Game 4
Martín Gonzalez-Ravi Sekhar
Thessaloniki OL 1984

1 e4	c5
2 $\&$f3	d6
3 d4	cxd4
4 $\&$xd4	$\&$f6
5 $\&$c3	g6
6 $\&$e3	$\&$g7
7 f3	$\&$c6
8 $\&$d2	0-0
9 $\&$c4	$\&$d7
10 0-0-0	$\&$a5
11 h4	Ξfc8

12 $\&$b3 $\&$e5
13 g4   b5!? (67)

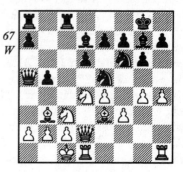

Black is holding back on ...$\&$c4 so that he can meet $\&$xc4 with ...bxc4 and then attack down the b-file.

14 h5 $\&$c4
15 $\&$xc4

15 $\&$d3?! as usual doesn't impress me. Black could simply play 15...$\&$xe3 and say "Thanks very much", but Hakki-Ravi Sekhar saw 15...$\&$e5 16 $\&$d2 (if 16 $\&$e2 then 16...Ξxc3!?) 16...$\&$c4 (a repetition to show who's boss!) 17 $\&$d3 b4!? 18 $\&$xc4 bxc3 19 hxg6 hxg6 20 g5 Ξxc4!? 21 $\&$xc4 Ξc8 22 $\&$b3 $\&$e8 23 $\&$b1 cxb2 24 $\&$d5 $\&$a6 25 Ξd3 $\&$c7 26 $\&$b3 $\&$a4 27 $\&$xb2 $\&$b5. All of Black's pieces are descending on the white king and its solitary defender, the queen.

15 ...   bxc4
16 $\&$h6

16 hxg6?! is too committal. Now Black has some air for his king which consequently removes the $\&$d5xe7 mate threat that White has

in the text. Indeed an impressive Black continuation was 16...fxg6 17 ♕h2 ♖ab8! 18 ♘d5 c3! 19 ♘xf6+ exf6 20 ♕xh7+ ♔f7 21 ♘f5 gxf5 22 ♖xd6 cxb2+ 23 ♔b1 ♕a4 24 ♖d2 ♖h8 0-1 Aijala-Ljubojević, Dresden 1969.

There is no doubt that b2 is an awkward pawn for White to defend, and the following manoeuvre is an unambitious yet common way for White to solve this problem: 16 ♔b1 ♖ab8 17 ♔a1 ♕b4 18 ♖b1 ♖c5 19 hxg6 fxg6 20 g5 (rarely a good idea, but White evidently has no others) 20...♘h5 21 ♖hg1 ♖a5 *(68)*

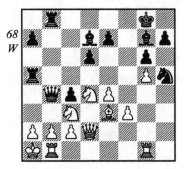

The c3-knight cannot move in view of ...♖xa2+ and ...♕a4 mate. Based on this concept, one of Black's plans is ...♖b6-a6 and ...♖xa2+) 22 a3 ♖a6 23 ♖gd1 ♕b7 24 ♕e2 ♗e6 25 f4 (25 ♘xe6 loses to 25...♗xc3 26 ♔a2 ♕xb2+ 27 ♖xb2 ♖xb2+ 28 ♔a1 ♖xa3 mate) 25...♗f7 26 ♖g1?! ♘xf4! 27 ♕d2 ♘h5 28 ♖gf1 ♕b4 29 ♖f2 ♘g3 (intending 30...♘xe4 31 ♘xe4 ♖xa3+ 31 bxa3 ♕xa3 mate) 30

♖xf7 ♔xf7 31 ♕f2+ ♔g8 32 ♔a2 ♘xe4! 0-1 Sziva-Matveeva, European Girls 1986.

16 ...   ♗h8

As there is no exchange sacrifice to be performed on c3, Black has no good reason to pull the white queen towards his king with 16...♗xh6?. Instead Black prefers to keep the enemy queen obstructing the king, and opts to withdraw the bishop to the corner, from where it is still very much in the game.

17 ♔b1

The downside of 16...♗h8 is that it leaves the black king very short of squares. As mentioned earlier, the threat is 18 ♘d5. 17 ♘f5!? was the old recommendation, but after 17...♖e8!? (intending to carry on as usual with 18...♖b8), I'm not sure I believe in the suggested 18 hxg6 fxg6 19 ♗g7(!).

17 ...   ♖c5!

Protecting the queen and thus parrying the threat admirably; 18 ♘d5? can now be met by 18...♘xd5.

18 ♘f5?!

As Black is not going to play 18...gxf5?? 19 ♕g5+ mating, this move appears to be detrimental. The chance to challenge the pawns around the black king is not worth the problems that White now faces along the a1-h8 diagonal. Now must be the time to try something down the h-file (before Black completes his task on the b-file). However after 18 hxg6 fxg6 19 ♕h2 (19 ♔a1 is the same old story) 19...♖b8 20 ♘de2 ♗e6, Black's attack remains by far the more impressive.

18 ...	♗xf5	
19 gxf5	♖b8	

Now 20...♘xe4 is a very real threat.

20 hxg6	fxg6	
21 e5		

White is desperately trying to neutralize the Dragon bishop, but he also has a few major pieces to deal with.

21 ...	♕b4	
22 ♘a4	♕xa4	
23 exf6	♖xb2+!	
24 ♔c1		

If 24 ♔xb2 then 24...c3+ 25 ♕xc3 ♗xf6! is the most efficient way of terminating the proceedings.

24 ...	c3	
25 f7+	♔xf7	
26 fxg6+	♔e8 (69)	

0-1

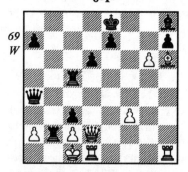

69
W

And what a horrible way to go! ...♖b1+ will force mate (if required!) in the very near future.

Game 5
Prasad-Ward
London 'Chess for Peace' 1987

1 e4	c5	
2 ♘f3	d6	
3 d4	cxd4	
4 ♘xd4	♘f6	
5 ♘c3	g6	
6 ♗e3	♗g7	
7 f3	0-0	
8 ♕d2	♘c6	
9 ♗c4	♗d7	
10 h4	♘e5	
11 ♗b3	♕a5	
12 0-0-0	♖fc8	
13 ♔b1 (70)		

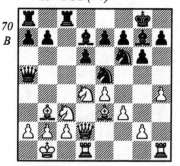

70
B

A waiting move. Game 7 sees ♔b1 played in conjunction with the positional ♗g5, but ♔b1 with h4 is a very popular partnership. As a change from the diagrammed position above, White may have opted to replace h4 with g4. Then in contrast to the text, 13...b5!? would not even be a pawn sacrifice as 14 ♘cxb5?! ♕xd2 15 ♗xd2 16 ♗xb5 17 ♘xb5 allows 17...♘xf3 when White has by far the weaker pawns. Alternatively 14 h4 enables Black to carry on with his plan of 14...♘c4 15 ♗xc4 bxc4 (intending ...♖ab8 and ...♕b4) and 14 g5 ♘h5 only succeeds in blocking things up. Then even the suggested plan of 15 ♘ce2 (Δ ♘g3) fails to impress as White can achieve little down the h-file.

13 ...   b5!?

So far we have seen how Black plays ...♘c4 immediately, to facilitate the doubling of his rooks on the c-file, and how he plays it after ...b5, in order to follow up ...bxc4 with an attack along the b-file. It is the second of these plans which here is once more called into action. Nonetheless after 13...♘c4 14 ♗xc4 ♖xc4 15 ♘b3 there are plenty of channels for Black to investigate (especially if for some reason he is unhappy with the text suggestion). Of the queen moves available, possibly the least documented is 15...♕e5!?.

Probably White does best to meet this with 16 ♗d4! ♕e6 when in practice two follow-ups are:

a) 17 h5 a5 18 h6 ♗h8 19 ♘d5 a4 20 ♗xf6 ♗xf6 21 ♘xf6+ ♕xf6 22 ♘d4 ♖ac8 23 ♖he1 a3 24 bxa3 ♗a4 with reciprocal chances; Hebden-Jönsson, London 1988.

b) 17 g4 ♖ac8 (17...a5!?) 18 ♖he1 ♗c6 19 ♘d5 ♗a4 20 c3 b5?! (20...♘xd5!?) 21 ♕h2 and with no clear way forward for Black, White definitely has the upper hand; Koch-Nen.Ristić, Dortmund 1989.

However, I had my appetite whetted when in a simultaneous, I

once followed some old analysis of Dueball's: 16 g4 ♖ac8 17 f4?! *(71)*

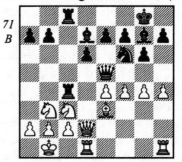

17...♕xc3!! 18 bxc3 ♘xe4 19 ♕d3 ♘xc3+ 20 ♔c1 ♘xa2+ 21 ♔d2 ♘b4 22 ♕f1 ♖xc2+ 23 ♔e1 ♖8c3 24 ♗d4 ♖xb3 25 ♗xg7 ♖e3+ 0-1 Wellby-Ward, Leicester 1991.

14 ♘cxb5

Experience has taught me that a lot of Yugoslav Attack players are 'all mouth and no trousers'. Indeed it no longer surprises me that when the chance comes along to win a pawn and exchange queens, many go for it like a shot!

a) 14 ♗g5?! ♘c4 15 ♗xc4 bxc4 16 ♗xf6 exf6!? 17 ♘d5 ♖c5 18 ♕xa5 ♖xa5 19 ♖he1 f5 20 ♘e3 fxe4 21 fxe4 ♖b8 22 ♘d5 (22 ♘xc4 ♖a4-+) 22...♗e5∓ Ansell-Ward, London 1989.

b) 14 ♘d5 ♕xd2 15 ♖xd2 ♘xd5 16 ♗xd5 ♖ab8 17 ♘e2 ♖c7 18 a3 ♘c4 19 ♗xc4 bxc4 20 c3 f5 21 exf5 gxf5 22 h5 ♔f7 23 h6 ♗f6 24 ♔c1 ♖cb7 25 f4 ♗c6 26 ♖g1 ♗e4 27 ♗d4 e5 28 ♗f2 exf4 29 ♘d4 ♖g8 30 b4 cxb3 31 ♔b2 ♖g6 32 ♘e2 ♗g5 33 ♖d4 ♗xh6 34 ♘c1 f3 35 g3 ♗g7 36 ♖a4 ♗xc3+ 37 ♔xc3 b2 38 ♘d3 ♗xd3 39 ♔xd3 b1♕+ 40 ♖xb1

♖xb1 41 ♗xa7 ♔e6 0-1 Markzon-Ward, Canaries 1993.

c) A more theoretically important game is Tolnai-Jovičić, Leibnitz 1990: 14 h5 ♘c4 15 ♗xc4 bxc4 16 ♗h6 ♗xh6 17 ♕xh6 ♖ab8 18 ♘d5 ♘xd5 19 exd5 ♕a3 20 ♘b3 cxb3 21 bxa3 bxc2+ 22 ♔a1 cxd1♕+ 23 ♖xd1 ♗f5 24 g4 ♗c2 25 ♖c1 when after 25...♖c7 the position would be equal (or perhaps 'drawish' is more accurate!).

Some may be satisfied with this, but I feel that a closer inspection of this game's early stages is called for; firstly after 14 h5(?!), there seems nothing wrong with 14...♘xh5 15 g4 ♘f6 when ...♖xc3 should be next on the agenda.

Also interesting is 16...♖ab8!? (instead of 16...♗xh6). This keeps the white queen on d2 so that 17 ♘d5 can be met by 17...c3! and 17 ♗xg7 ♔xg7 18 hxg6 by 18...♕b4!. This motif of leaving a white pawn on g6 to do something else more vital than recapturing, is often worth considering.

Therefore if White is hoping to follow the above game, then he is more likely to transpose with 14 ♗h6, as after 14...♘c4 15 ♗xc4, 15...bxc4 is very doubtful in view of 16 ♘d5!. Nevertheless, with this move order, Black does have another alternative in the traditional 14...♗xh6 15 ♕xh6 ♖xc3. This can't be as good as when we have seen this in previous lines, yet *ECO* now gives 16 bxc3 ♕xc3 17 ♘e2

♕c5 18 ♘f4 a5! 19 h5 a4 20 ♘xg6 ♘xg6 21 ♖d5 ♕a3 22 hxg6 fxg6 23 ♖g5+ as "=" (Matulović-Jovčić, Yugoslavia 1970). Not even convinced of the final assessment, I believe that this game warrants the 'fine comb' treatment.

14 ...   ♕xd2

Levy suggests that with 14...♕d8(!?), Black should be able to obtain enough counterplay on the queenside files to compensate for the sacrificed pawn. My own feelings on this move are mixed as my one and only outing with it didn't leave me entirely convinced (though this was some time ago). This game is the first of three practical demonstrations, which may help readers to reach their own conclusions:

a) 15 ♘c3 ♖ab8 16 g4 ♘c4 17 ♗xc4 ♖xc4 18 h5 ♕c7 19 ♘d5 ♘xd5 20 exd5 g5 21 ♘b3 h6 22 ♗d4 ♗xd4 23 ♘xd4 ♕b7 24 ♘b3 ♖f4 25 ♖he1 ♖xf3 26 ♖xe7 ♕c8 27 ♖de1 ♗xg4 28 ♘d4 ♖f4 29 ♘c6 ♖a8 30 ♕c3 ♕f8 31 ♕a3 ♖f6 32 ♖xa7 ♖e8 33 ♖g1 ♗xh5 34 b4 ♗g6 35 ♖g2 ♖f1+ 36 ♔b2 ♕g7+ *(72)*

37 ♕c3 (37 c3 ♖b1 mate; 37 ♔b3 ♖f3+ -+) 37...♖b1+ 38 ♔xb1 ♕xc3 39 ♘e7+ ♔h7 40 a3 ♕e1+ 0-1 Kuznecov-Ward, Oakham 1986.

b) 15 a4?! a6 16 ♘c3 ♖ab8 17 ♖he1 ♘c4 18 ♕d3 ♘xe3 19 ♕xe3 ♖c5 20 g4 ♕a5 21 ♘de2 ♗e6 22 g5 ♘d7 23 ♘d5 ♗xd5 24 exd5 ♘e5 25 ♘d4 ♖b7 26 ♘c6 ♘xc6 27 dxc6 ♖xc6 28 ♕f4 e6 29 h5 ♕c5 (threatening 30...♖xb3) 30 ♖e2 ♖b4 31 ♕h2 ♕xg5 32 ♖xd6 ♖xd6 33 ♕xd6 ♕f6 34 c3 ♖xb3 35 hxg6 hxg6 0-1 N.Littlewood-J.Ward, Sheffield 1984.

c) 15 ♕e2!? a6 16 ♘a3 ♕c7?! (16...a5!?) Santo Roman-Leriche, French Team Ch 1992.

15 ♖xd2

For 15 ♗xd2 see game 6.

15 ...   ♖ab8

16 a4

Other possibilities:

a) 16 ♘xa7? is bad because after 16...♖c7, Black can guarantee winning the two pieces for a rook. White may also have two pawns as well, but his queenside is incredibly difficult to push with so many black minor pieces around.

b) 16 ♘a3 a5 17 c3 a4 18 ♗d1 ♖xc3 is winning for Black.

c) after 16 ♘c3 an endgame may be reached in which the Dragon bishop demonstrates its superiority over a knight: 16...a5! 17 a4 (White cannot allow Black to play this move as a black knight would ultimately wreak havoc on c4) 17...♘c4 18 ♗xc4 ♖xc4 19 ♖d3

♖cb4!? 20 ♘db5 ♗xb5 21 axb5 ♘d7 22 b3 ♘e5 23 ♖d4 ♘g4! 24 ♖d3 (24 ♖xb4 ♘xe3-+) 24...♘xe3 25 ♖xe3 ♔f8 26 ♖d1 ♖c8 27 ♘a4 ♖xb5 28 ♖d5 ♖cb8 29 ♖ed3 ♗e5 30 ♖xb5 ♖xb5 31 ♖d5 ♖xd5 32 exd5 ♗g3 33 h5 gxh5 34 c4 ♔g7 35 ♔c2 ♔f6 36 ♔d3 ♗e1 37 ♘b6 ♗b4 38 ♘d7+ ♔g5 39 ♔e4 ♗d2 40 c5 dxc5 41 ♘xc5 ♔h4 42 ♔f5 ♔g3! 0-1 M.Schlosser-Ward, Oakham 1990. After the intended 43 ♘e4+ ♔xg2 44 ♘xd2, Black has 44...h4 45 ♘e4 h3 46 ♔f4 (46 ♔g4 f5+ is a nice touch!) 46...h2 47 ♘g3 h5 and White is in zugzwang.

16 ...   a6

17 ♘a3   ♗e8! *(73)*

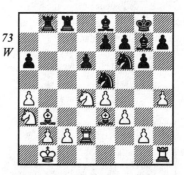

The cards are on the table. Black intends to manoeuvre his f6-knight to either c5 or c4. As we soon see, White can find no antidote to this plan.

18 ♔a2   ♘fd7

19 ♘e2   ♘b6

20 a5   ♘bc4

White is in a complete mess and the knight on c4 is devastating. As if the e3 and d2 fork isn't enough, the build-up on b2 is immense. There is no point to 21 ♘xc4 as after 21...♘xc4, 22 ♗xc4 allows 22...♖xb2+. Therefore White chooses to offload the exchange, but his troubles are far from over.

21 ♗f4	♘xd2
22 ♗xd2	♗b5
23 ♘xb5	axb5
24 h5	♘c4

A case of history repeating itself! White doesn't fancy 25 ♗c1 ♖a8 and so opts to go down fighting. Unfortunately for him, his fire-power is somewhat limited.

25 hxg6	♘xd2
26 ♗xf7+	♔f8
27 ♘f4	

Black had correctly negotiated the first 50-50, but White keeps up with the one-movers!

27 ...	hxg6
28 ♗xg6	♖a8
29 ♘e6+	♔g8 (74)

0-1

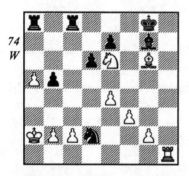

White is a rook down. His checks will soon vanish and even 30 b4 is terminated by 30...♖xc2+ 31 ♔a3 ♘c4+ 32 ♔b3 ♖b2 mate.

Game 6
Ansell-Ward
Hastings Challengers 1991

1 e4	c5
2 ♘f3	d6
3 d4	cxd4
4 ♘xd4	♘f6
5 ♘c3	g6
6 ♗e3	♗g7
7 f3	♘c6
8 ♕d2	0-0
9 ♗c4	♗d7
10 0-0-0	♕a5
11 h4	♖fc8
12 ♗b3	♘e5
13 ♔b1	b5!?
14 ♘cxb5	♕xd2
15 ♗xd2	♘c4 (75)

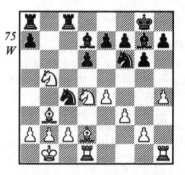

As usual one of Black's aims is to win White's dark-squared bishop, but here a very big threat is 16...e5, winning a piece. After 15...♖ab8, Black also has some compensation for the pawn.

16 ♘c3

The move that theory recommends. It is natural for White to

want to keep the cover around his king, and in a rare Dragon annotation, Karpov gives 16 ♗xc4 ♖xc4 17 b3 ♖c5 18 ♘c3 ♘g4! 19 fxg4 ♗xd4 as leaving Black with active play.

16 ...   ♘xd2+!?

Black has a tactic which temporarily regains him his pawn, but 16...♘xe4?! 17 ♘xe4 ♗xd4 18 ♗g5! ♗e5 19 ♗xe7 ♘xb2 20 ♖xd6! ♗e8 21 ♖d5 left White clearly better in Kuzmin-Garcia, Hastings 1973.

17 ♖xd2   h5!?

Phase 2 of the master plan. Black knows that he will have good dark-square compensation and this move fixes the h4-pawn. There will never be any back-rank worries, and not only will he always have ....♗h6 available (i.e. as g4-g5 is now out of the question), but the control of g4 dissuades White from playing f4.

18 ♖d3

Meanwhile White, who appears to be under no great pressure, has the problem of how to make progress. There is no doubt that White's very cagey play here doesn't really hit the mark. However, although White is a pawn up, the application of the basic liquidation rule wasn't successful either after 18 ♖e1 ♖c5 19 ♘d5 ♘xd5 20 ♗xd5 ♖b8 21 ♗b3 a5 22 a4 ♗xa4!? (another idea worth remembering) 23 ♗xa4 ♖c4 24 ♗b5 ♖xd4 25 ♖xd4 ♗xd4 26 c4 ♗f2∓ in Fogaraši-Ward, Oakham 1988.

18 ...   ♖ab8
19 ♘de2   ♔f8

Defending the e7-pawn and removing any ♘f4xg6 tricks.

20 ♖hd1   ♗e8!

Preventing 21 e5 and heralding the start of a plan that by now the reader should be accustomed to.

21 g3

White just can't seem to think of anything to do, but to be fair, no constructive plans stand out. The key to his troubles is his inability to challenge along the a1-h8 diagonal.

21 ...   a5

It should be noted that this move must always be well timed. Pawns cannot move backwards and often it is this a-pawn alone that prevents what would otherwise appear to be an endless supply of white knights taking up refuge on b5 (i.e. after ...a5, a4).

22 a4   ♘d7

Here we go again.

23 ♘d4   ♘c5
24 ♖e3   ♖b4 *(76)*

76
W

All of a sudden the heat really is on, but there is no way out of the kitchen! Note how with White in such a muddle, Black is eager to avoid straight swaps. In particular, it doesn't look as though he would trade his bishops for the Crown Jewels!

25 ♘cb5

White must guard both d4 and b3. This task proves too much though, as the text relinquishes the a4-pawn (and another bishop to boot).

    25 ...   **♘xa4**
    26 ♗xa4

Sadly necessary as next in line for the chop would be the white knights or the b2-pawn.

    26 ...   **♖xa4**
    27 ♖a3   **♖b4**

Of course there is no point in exchanging as 28 ♖xa5 loses to both 28...♖b8 and 28...♗xb5 29 ♘xb5 ♖xb2+.

28 c3

A bit grim, but there is nothing doing. 28 ♖b3 ♖xb3 29 cxb3 drops a piece to 29...e5 30 ♘xd6 ♖d8.

    28 ...   **♖xb5**
    29 ♘xb5   **♗xb5**
    30 ♖d5

Of course White's position is resignable now. Even if he were able to win a pawn (which he is not), he would still be lost.

    30 ...   **♖b8**
    31 ♔c1

31 ♖xa5 ♗c4 and 32...♗xc3.

    31 ...   **a4**
    32 f4   **♔e8**
         0-1

Enough is enough.

I hope that these last two games have shown the reader just how successful a queenside assault can be, even when the queens are off. I do not pretend to claim that after 14...♕xd2, Black is winning the resulting endgame/middlegame (whatever). Indeed I really do not know. What is abundantly clear though, is that Black has very good practical chances and thus after 14 ♘cxb5, we can conclude that he has reasonable compensation for the pawn.

Game 7
Sievers-Ward
Guildford Masters 1991

1 e4	c5
2 ♘f3	d6
3 d4	cxd4
4 ♘xd4	♘f6
5 ♘c3	g6
6 ♗e3	♗g7
7 f3	♘c6
8 ♕d2	0-0
9 ♗c4	♗d7
10 0-0-0	♕a5
11 ♗b3	♖fc8
12 ♖he1?! *(77)*	

When my opponent played this, I simply couldn't believe my eyes. I mean, there are many books on the Yugoslav Attack, but I have yet to see one on the Yugoslav Defence! In actual fact it is not so bad, as it soon transposes into a more streamline variation. After 12 ♔b1 ♘e5, to recap and fill in the gaps, we have seen enough of 13 h4 and 13 g4, but a few other possibilities deserve a mention:

a) 13 ♘d5?!. Not much of a mention for this though! It appears that White is going for a draw, but in my opinion even if he gets it, he will have to suffer first. Black should exchange off the queens and the d5-knight. Then he can either secure the bishop-for-knight edge with ...♘c4, or hunt down White's light-squared bishop with ...b5 and ...a5. The c-file should be used to pressurize the c2-pawn, which if pushed to c3, can be hassled with a timely ...b4.

b) 13 ♗h6?! ♗xh6 14 ♕xc3 ♖xc3! (as if you didn't know this by now!) 15 bxc3 ♕xc3. Not having weakened his kingside pawn structure, White questions whether Black has enough for the exchange. However Black's own king is in no danger and so he can harass the b3-bishop at will. He already has one pawn in the bag and to increase the discomfort of the white light-squared bishop (and so that he can continue to attack), Black will choose to keep the queens on. Sedov-Yudovich, Lvov 1968, continued with 16 ♕d2 ♕c5 17 ♕e2 b5 18 f4 ♘c4 19 ♗xc4 bxc4 20 ♕e3 ♘g4 21 ♕g3 e5 22 fxe5 dxe5 23 ♘e2 ♘f2 24 ♘c3 (24 ♖xd7 ♕b5+ -+) 24...♘xh1 25 ♖xh1 ♗c6 and Black was a pawn up with positional pluses as well.

c) 13 ♗g5. White abandons any attacking notions he may have had in favour of some positional play. He hopes that after ♗xf6 ♗xf6 ♘d5, he will be able to weaken Black's pawns with ♘xf6+ exf6?. However this is never likely to be successful as Black will always have ...♔g7 (instead of ...exf6). Play might continue with 13...♖c5! (exploiting the bishop's departure from e3 and defending the queen. It is useful to have a rook along the fourth rank and Black can now double if he wants) 14 f4 (Again 14 ♗xf6 ♗xf6 15 ♘d5 ♕xd2 16 ♘xf6+ ♔g7 17 ♘h5+ ♔h6!? 18 ♖xd2 ♔xh5 is weird but fine for Black, and 14 ♖he1 transposes to the main text) and now Black has two interesting and good alternatives:

c1) 14...♘c6!? (threatening 15...♘xe4) 15 e5!? dxe5 16 ♗xf7+ ♔xf7 17 ♘b3 ♘e4! with complications not unfavourable to Black.

c2) 14...♘c4!? 15 ♗xc4 ♖xc4 16 ♘b3 ♕xc3!! *(78)*.

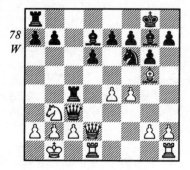

This is the second time that we have seen this idea. Here the rooks aren't even doubled yet, but after 17 bxc3 ♘xe4, Black has the likes of ...♖ac8 and ...♗f5 to follow up the immediate pawn grabbing, giving him excellent chances.

d) 13 ♕e2. White covers c4, forgets an attack and switches to centralization mode. With time on his hands, Black can play for a slow build-up with 13...a6, having ...b5 and ...♘c4 in mind as a follow-up. Alternatively he can reproduce a familiar pawn sacrifice with 13...b5!?. Then after 14 ♘cxb5 ♖ab8 15 ♘a3 (15 c4 a6 16 ♘a3 ♗e8!? 17 ♕d2 ♕c7 18 ♖c1 ♘fd7 19 ♗a4 ♘c5 20 ♗xe8 ♖xe8 21 ♖c3 ♖b7 22 ♘b3 ♘a4 23 ♖c2 and White had the worse of it in Gipslis-Stein, Moscow 1967) 15...d5 16 exd5 ♘xd5, Black probably has enough compensation.

12 ...	♘e5
13 ♗g5	♖c5
14 ♔b1	b5!

White chooses not to attack. Black doesn't follow suit. If White does nothing now, then after 15...♘c4, if the b-file is opened up for a black rook, it will all be one-way traffic.

15 f4

15 ♗xf6 ♗xf6 16 ♘d5 ♕xd2 17 ♖xd2 (17 ♘xf6+ ♔g7!) 17...♔g7 18 ♘xf6 ♔xf6 19 ♗d5 ♘c4 20 ♖f2 ♖ac8 21 f4 e6 22 e5+ dxe5 23 fxe5+ ♔e7 24 ♗xc4 ♖xc4 25 ♘f3 h6 left Black with an endgame advantage in Perenyi-Radosavljević, Hungary 1983.

15 ...	♘c4
16 ♗xc4	

As he no longer has a bishop on e3, it may appear more logical to move the queen. However after (say) 16 ♕d3, White is threatening nothing whilst Black can continue to build up the pressure on b2 and c3.

16 ...	bxc4
17 e5	♖b8! *(79)*

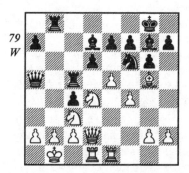

17...dxe5 was also not bad, but the text is more appealing. Black temporarily sacrifices a piece and in doing so forces the opposing dark-squared bishop offside.

18	exf6	exf6
19	♗h4	♕b4
20	♕c1	♕xc3
21	♘b3 *(80)*	

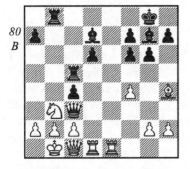

80
B

21 ... cxb3!!

The point behind the original sacrifice.

22	bxc3	bxa2+
23	♔xa2	

White can for the time being at least remain a queen for a piece up with 23 ♔a1. However after 23...f5! threatening 24...♗xc3+ 25 ♔xa2 ♖a5+ 26 ♕a3 ♖b2+ 27 ♔a1 ♖xa3 mate, the cards really are stacked against him.

23	...	♖a5+
24	♕a3	♗e6+
25	♖xe6	♖xa3+
26	♔xa3	fxe6

Black is now a clear pawn up (27 ♖xd6?? ♗f8-+) and just for good measure his kingside pawns have been ironed out. The rest takes a little time, but he gets there in the end.

27	c4	♔f7
28	c5	♗f8
29	♗f2	d5
30	c4	dxc4
31	♖c1	e5
32	fxe5	fxe5
33	♖xc4	♔e6
34	♔a4	♔d5
35	♖c2	♔c6
36	♖e2	♗xc5
37	♗xc5	♔xc5
38	♖xe5+	♔d6
39	♖e2	♖b7
40	♔a5	♖e7
41	♖d2+	♔e5
42	♔a6	♔f4
43	♖d4+	♔e3
44	♖g4	♔f2
45	♖g5	♖f7
46	h4	♖f4
47	g4	♔g3
48	h5	♖xg4

0-1

System 2; ...♖c8

In system 1, we saw the f-rook coming to c8, after the black queen had ventured to the aggressive a5-square. In these lines, the queen stays put for the time being, whilst the a-rook quickly enters the game via the c-file. The coverage of this popular variation is not as complete as system 1, and is intended more as food for thought. I have focused my attention on some more recent games in order to add new ideas to old theory.

Game 8
Gelemerov-Nesis
Corr. 1991

1 e4	c5
2 ♘f3	d6
3 d4	cxd4
4 ♘xd4	♘f6
5 ♘c3	g6
6 ♗e3	♗g7
7 ♗c4	♘c6
8 f3	0-0
9 ♕d2	♗d7
10 0-0-0	♖c8
11 ♗b3	

A necessary retreat. e.g. 11 h4??
♘xd4 12 ♕xd4 ♘g4 winning a
piece.

11 ...   ♘e5 *(81)*

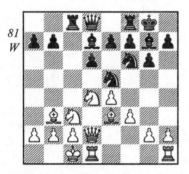

81
W

12 ♗h6?!

A weaker player's instinctive
move to exchange off the Dragon
bishop. 12 h4 and 12 g4 are the
subject matter of games 9 to 11,
which leaves a couple of untested
alternatives:

a) 12 ♗g5 ♘c4 13 ♗xc4 ♖xc4
14 e5 (as the reader will soon discover, a common theme devised to
cause the d7-bishop some grief)
14...dxe5 15 ♘de2 ♖c7 (the threat
was 16 ♗xf6 and 17 ♕xd7) 16
♘b5 (16 ♗xf6 exf6 17 ♘b5 is no
improvement, as 17...♗f5! is still
playable) 16...♗f5! 17 ♘xc7 ♕xc7
18 ♘c3 ♖c8 19 ♖he1 b5 (another
interesting try is 19...♘e8!? with
...♘d6-c4 in mind) 20 ♔b1?! (20
g4!? ♗e6! 21 ♘xb5 ♕b6 22 ♘c3
e4! 23 fxe4 ♘xg4 and Black's
pieces are all trained on the white
king) 20...b4 21 ♘e4 ♘xe4! 22
fxe4 ♗e6 23 ♕xb4 (Wahls-Alter-
man, Manila OL 1992). Black has
adequate compensation and although he won in 66 moves with
23...h6?!, better would have been
23...♕xc2+! 24 ♔a1 ♕xg2.

b) 12 ♔b1 ♘c4 13 ♗xc4 ♖xc4
14 ♘b3 (if 14 g4 or 14 h4 then
14...b5!? is the most active response) 14...♗e6 15 ♖he1 ♕b8!?
16 ♗d4 b5 and Black had no problems in Yudasin-Romero Holmes,
Lyon 1992.

12 ...   ♗xh6!
Drawing the queen away from its
defensive tasks on the queenside.

13 ♕xh6   ♖xc3!
The usual!

14 bxc3   a5!?
Hunting the white bishop,
though 14...♕a5 is also good.

15 a3
15 a4? is too weakening and after
15...♕c7 16 ♕e3 ♕c5, White's a-
pawn is doomed.

15 ...   a4

16 &a2	♕a5
17 ♕e3	♖c8
18 ♔d2? *(82)*	

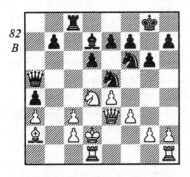

82
B

White doesn't like 18 ♔b2 as he is hoping to utilize the b-file for his rooks later. Nevertheless that would be eminently preferable to the text.

18 ...   ♘eg4!

This is not the first time that we have seen the one-two killer blow with the black knights.

19 ♕e1

If 19 fxg4 then 19...♖xc3 is to say the least, bleak!

19 ...	♕xc3+
20 ♔e2	♕xa3
21 ♖a1	♕e3+

0-1

White is not only short of pawns, soon he will be short of pieces.

Game 9
Nunn-Ljubojević
Amsterdam OHRA 1988

1 e4	c5
2 ♘f3	d6

3 d4	cxd4
4 ♘xd4	♘f6
5 ♘c3	g6
6 &e3	&g7
7 f3	0-0
8 ♕d2	♘c6
9 &c4	&d7
10 h4	♖c8
11 &b3	♘e5
12 0-0-0	

Black brilliantly punished move-order inaccuracies after 12 h5?!, with 12...♘xh5 13 g4 ♖xc3! 14 bxc3 ♘f6 15 &h6 ♕a5 16 0-0-0? ♘xf3!! (note the similarity with system 1, but with a rook on f8, preventing any &xf7+ saviour) 17 ♘xf3 ♕a3+ 18 ♔b1 ♘xe4 0-1 Samplieri-Bertolucci, Corr. 1985-87.

12 ...   ♘c4

As briefly mentioned before, 12...h5 is perhaps considered to be the Dragon main line, but that's not to say it's necessarily any better.

13 &xc4	♖xc4
14 h5	

The fastest and most popular method of progression is to sacrifice the h-pawn. However 14 g4 is a slower alternative, when Black can choose to return to the realms of system 1 with 14...♕a5 or play the more consistent 14...b5!?, a favourable practical example being: 15 h5 b4 16 ♘d5 e6 (16...♘xd5!?) 17 ♘xf6+ (17 ♘xb4 ♕a5 18 a3 ♖b8 with reasonable play for the pawn) 17...♕xf6 18 hxg6 hxg6 19 ♕h2 ♖fc8 20 ♖d2 e5 21 g5 ♕d8

22 ♘b3 (22 ♘f5!?) 22...♕c7 23
♔b1 a5 24 ♕f2 ♖c6 25 f4?! a4 26
♘d4 b3! 27 f5 exd4 28 ♕h4 bxc2+
29 ♔c1 ♕b6! 30 ♕h7+ ♔f8 31
♖dh2 gxf5 32 exf5 ♕xb2+! 33
♔xb2 dxe3+ 0-1 Prokopp-Deuel,
Corr. 1986.

14 ...   ♘xh5

Black takes this now so that he
has more to give back later.

15 g4

The prophylactic 15 ♘de2 is
tricky, but certainly no better.
Black should not continue with
15...♖e8? 16 ♗h6 ♗h8? 17 ♖xh5!
gxh5 18 ♕g5+, but with 15...♕a5!.
Then 16 g4 can be met with
16...♘g3!, and 16 ♗h6 with
16...♗xc3! 17 ♘xc3 ♖fc8, when
White's queenside is under severe
pressure.

15 ...   ♘f6 (83)

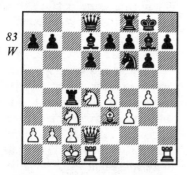

83
W

The advantage of the ...♖c8 lines
is that whilst the black queen remains at home, a black rook arrives
quickly on the c4-square. This obviously means that doubling and
even trebling is possible, but there
is another point to it. The d4-
knight, as well as the c3-knight,
should now feel less secure. Above
is the standard position from which
there are several diversions.

16 ♗h6

The most direct move, which
may appear simple, but in fact in-
vites many complications. 16 ♘b3
and 16 ♔b1 are covered in game
10, whilst 16 e5, 16 ♘d5 and 16 b3
are all discussed in game 11. After
re-iterating how in the Dragon particularly, lines are very much dic-
tated by trends, I would have to say
that generally in recent years, the
text move and Karpov's old favourite 16 ♘de2, have gone out of
fashion.

On 16 ♘de2, 16...♖e8!? prevents White trading off the Dragon
bishop. White then has:

a) 17 ♗h6 ♗h8 and now:

a1) 18 ♕g5 ♕c7 19 ♕h4 b5!?
(19...♖ec8!?, 19...♗e6) 20 e5!? (or
20 ♗g5 b4!) 20...dxe5 21 ♗g5
h5!? 22 ♕h2 ♘xg4! 23 fxg4 ♗xg4
(Zganec-Piriši, Zalaegerszeg
1986). Black has two excellent
bishops and more than enough
pawns for the piece. In fact this
variation brings back fond memories. At the 1984 British Under-16
Championship, a once deadly rival
of mine had just lost to me for the
second time in a fortnight with this
'suggestion'. Fed up, he consequently went to the *'Any Questions?'* evening to ask Raymond

Keene about his recommendation. The reply was met with great laughter. Mr Keene said that he had recommended it, but he hadn't said that it was any good!

a2) 18 e5 ♘xg4 (as the reader will soon discover, this theme of obtaining three very good pawns for a piece, is always cropping up) 19 fxg4 ♗xe5! 20 ♗f4 ♕a5 21 ♗xe5 ♕xe5 22 g5 (Both 22 ♕h6 ♕g7 and 22 ♘d5 ♖xg4 leave Black with the better practical chances) 22...b5! 23 ♘d4 b4 24 ♘ce2 ♖ec8 25 ♖h4 ♗a4! 26 b3 ♖xc2+! 27 ♕xc2 ♕xg5+ 28 ♖f4 ♖xc2 29 ♔xc2 e5 30 ♖ff1 ♗d7! 31 ♘f3 ♗f5+ 32 ♔b2 ♕g2 33 ♖de1 ♗d3 34 ♘h4 ♕e4 0-1 (Eisen-Nesis, Corr. 1982).

b) 17 e5 ♘xg4 18 fxg4. More of the same, although this time 18...♗xg4! is better as Black has no problems on his back rank.

16 ...   ♘xe4!

Black must be careful as White is not far from delivering mate down the h-file. The differences between this and system 1 must be observed. Now 16...♗xh6? 17 ♕xh6 ♖xc3 is inadequate because of 18 g5! ♘h5 19 ♖xh5 gxh5 20 ♖h1. The text, unleashing a discovered attack on White's d4-knight, sees the beginning of a forced sequence, from which either side deviates at their own peril.

17 ♕e3! *(84)*

Briefly, the alternatives are good for Black:

a) 17 ♘xe4? ♖xd4 18 ♕h2 ♗e5 19 ♕h4 ♖xd1+ 20 ♔xd1 f5.

b) 17 fxe4? ♖xd4 18 ♕h2 ♖xd1+ 19 ♘xd1 ♗e5!.

c) 17 ♕h2?! ♗e5! 18 f4 ♗xd4! 19 ♖xd4 ♖xd4 20 ♗g7! ♖d1+!! 21 ♘xd1 ♔xg7 22 ♕xh7+ ♔f6 and the black king will escape.

In all of the above lines, of course with pawns to boot, Black is never worried about losing the f8-rook for White's dark-squared bishop.

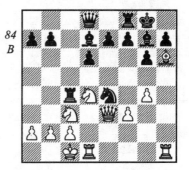

17 ...   ♖xc3!

Necessary to prevent this knight from later hopping into d5.

18 bxc3

And not 18 ♕xe4? ♗xh6+ 19 ♖xh6 e5! (with ...♕g5+ in mind).

18 ...   ♘f6

Returning to the vital role of protecting the h7-pawn.

19 ♗xg7   ♔xg7

20 ♖h2

Preparing to treble the major pieces. 20 ♕h6+ ♔h8! and 20 ♘e2 ♕a5! are both worthy of consideration.

20 ...   ♖g8
Bringing the rook to where it will be able to defend.

Counterattacking with 20...♕c7!? is also not out of the question.

21 ♘e2
The knight did little on d4, so White starts to re-route it.

21 ...   ♗c6
22 ♘g3   ♔f8
Played so that 23 g5 can be met safely by 23...♘d5.

23 c4   ♖g7
The storm has died down and we are beginning to see the position for what it really is. Black may have an awkwardly placed rook, but his structure is faultless. He has two pawns for the exchange and White has plenty of pawn weaknesses.

24 ♖e2	**a6**
25 g5	**♘d7**
26 f4	**f5!**
27 gxf6	**♘xf6**
28 c5	**d5**
29 ♕d4	**♕a5**
30 c3	**♘d7** *(85)*

85
W

The black king is safe, but the white pawns are in trouble.

31 c4	**♕a3+**
32 ♔b1	**♕b4+**
33 ♖b2	**♕xc4**
34 ♘e2	**♘xc5**
35 ♖c2	**♕xd4**
36 ♘xd4	**♗a4**
37 ♖xc5	**♗xd1**
38 ♘e6+	**♔f7**
39 ♘xg7	**♔xg7**
40 ♖xd5	**♗f3**

0-1

Black has three pawns for the exchange, and as the piece is a bishop, White doesn't bother testing Black's technique.

The following is an amazing game, demonstrating perfectly the concept that Dragon expert Thomas Ernst has aptly named 'Pawn Power'!

Game 10
Westerinen-Ernst
Gausdal 1991

1 e4	**c5**
2 ♘f3	**d6**
3 d4	**cxd4**
4 ♘xd4	**♘f6**
5 ♘c3	**g6**
6 ♗e3	**♗g7**
7 f3	**0-0**
8 ♕d2	**♘c6**
9 ♗c4	**♗d7**
10 0-0-0	**♖c8**
11 ♗b3	**♘e5**
12 h4	**♘c4**

13 ♗xc4   ♖xc4
14 h5   ♘xh5
15 g4   ♘f6
16 ♘b3

A fairly innocuous looking, yet currently popular continuation. White withdraws his knight from the firing line and prevents ...♕a5, whilst creating his own threats down the d-file. Of a similarly cagey nature is 16 ♔b1, which was played in an earlier encounter between these two Grandmasters: 16...♖e8! 17 ♘d5 e6 (17...♘xd5!?) 18 ♘xf6+ ♕xf6 19 c3 (19 ♕h2!? h6 20 ♕xd6 ♖d8 gives chances for both sides) 19...♖xd4! 20 ♗xd4 e5 21 g5 (after 21 ♗xa7 ♕xf3 22 ♕xd6 ♕xe4+ 23 ♕d3 ♕xd3+ 24 ♖xd3 ♗xg4, the black bishops work superbly well with the passed pawns) 21...♕xf3 22 ♕e3! ♗xg4 23 ♖df1 exd4 24 ♕xf3 ♗xf3 25 ♖xf3 ♖xe4 and Black went on to win the endgame; Westerinen-Ernst, Gausdal 1990.

16 ...   ♖e8

16...♕c7 is the best of the alternatives.

17 e5 *(86)*

Serra-Martín, Spanish Ch 1991 saw 17 ♗h6 ♗h8 18 ♗g5 b5!? 19 e5 ♘xg4 20 fxg4 ♗xe5 21 ♘d5 ♗xg4 22 ♖df1 ♗e6 23 ♖h6 ♕d7 24 ♘e3 ♖a4 25 ♔b1 f6 26 ♖fh1 fxg5 27 ♖xh7 ♖h4 28 ♖7xh4 gxh4 29 ♖xh4, which not surprisingly, Black went on to win.

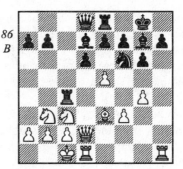
86
B

17 ...   ♘xg4!
18 fxg4   ♗xg4
19 ♖dg1   ♗xe5!?

19...h5 20 e6! and 19...dxe5 20 ♕xd8 ♖xd8 21 ♘d2 are both worse than the text.

20 ♗d4

White, who has plenty of open lines for his rooks, knows that if he can remove the Dragon bishop, his checkmating task will be much easier.

20 ...   ♖xd4!

Black chooses to preserve it!

21 ♘xd4   h5 *(87)*

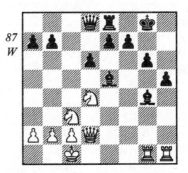
87
W

In exchange for White's additional rook, Black might be opti-

mistic and say that he has four extra
potential queens! Certainly these
pawns are a barrier between his
king and the enemy rooks, and he
retains two raking bishops.

22 ♘d5!

White sets about bringing his
knights in on the act. No doubt he
will be happy to trade them for
bishops, but at the same time he
will not want the black pawns to
wind up connected too near his
back rank.

22 ...	e6
23 ♘e3	♛b6
24 c3	♗xd4
25 ♛xd4?!	

White bravely accepts the challenge of an endgame, but it must be
more logical to keep the queens on
(and hence Black's king on its toes)
with 25 cxd4.

25 ...	♛xd4
26 cxd4	f5
27 ♔d2	

It appears that there are plenty of
rook versus pawns endgames to be
had. If 27 ♘xg4 hxg4, then Black
has just his rook to help along his
pawns (but there remain a lot of
them).

27 ...	♔g7
28 ♖c1	♗f3
29 ♖h3	♗c6
30 ♘c4	♔f6
31 ♘a5	♗g2
32 ♖h2	♗d5
33 ♖c7	♖e7
34 ♖xe7	♔xe7 *(88)*

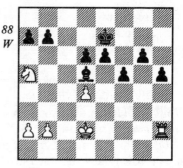

Incredible. Now Black only has
a bishop to compliment his pawns.
Nobody is saying that he is winning these endgames, but he must
certainly be having the most fun.
Irrespective of 'correct' play,
Black's practical chances are excellent as his plan of pushing the
pawns is the easier. The danger is
that these pawns might get
blocked, when he has no more
pieces!

35 ♔d3	b5
36 ♘b3	♔f6
37 ♘c1	f4
38 ♔d2	♔f5
39 ♘d3	♔g4
40 ♖e2	g5
41 ♘b4	♔f3
42 ♘xd5	exd5

Well that's it, now there's no
turning back.

43 ♔e1	h4
44 ♖f2+	♔g3
45 ♔f1	h3
46 ♔g1	g4

White has managed to get his
king over, but the pawns still look

very menacing. Ideally, White wants to get a passed pawn of his own and so he sets about doing so.

47 ♖c2	♔h4
48 ♖c7	g3
49 ♖xa7	♔g4
50 ♖g7+	♔f3
51 a3	

Slow, but necessary in order to be able to create a passed pawn.

51 ...	♔e2
52 ♖e7+	♔d3
53 ♖f7?	

The vital mistake. 53 b3! is best, when 53...f3 54 a4 bxa4 55 bxa4 h2+ 56 ♔h1 f2 57 ♖f7 ♔e2 58 ♖e7+ ♔d2 59 ♖f7 will lead to a draw by repetition.

53 ...	♔e3
54 ♖e7+	♔xd4
55 ♖f7	♔e3
56 ♖e7+	♔f3
57 ♖e6	h2+
58 ♔h1	♔f2 (89)

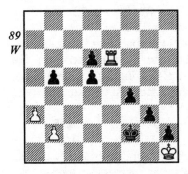

89
W

0-1

Touchdown!

Before this chapter's final game, I would just like to say a few words about correspondence games. With plenty of time for each move, it is clear that postal encounters make important contributions to the state of theory (especially here in the Dragon). In particular, a lot of imaginative ideas have come from the games of Gennadi Nesis. Therefore you can imagine my shock when a Latvian Grandmaster informed me that in fact this innovative character is actually quite weak at over-the-board chess. However he followed up this startling revelation by saying that nevertheless he is Khalifman's trainer, and hence they do a lot of studying together. Need I say more?

Game 11
Wibe-Nesis
Corr. 1989-91

1 e4	c5
2 ♘f3	d6
3 d4	cxd4
4 ♘xd4	♘f6
5 ♘c3	g6
6 ♗e3	♗g7
7 f3	♘c6
8 ♕d2	0-0
9 ♗c4	♗d7
10 0-0-0	♖c8
11 ♗b3	♘e5
12 h4	♘c4
13 ♗xc4	♖xc4
14 h5	♘xh5
15 g4	♘f6

16 e5 *(90)*

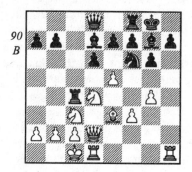

Completing the 16th move divergences, we have:

a) 16 ♘d5 (not with a great reputation) 16...e6 17 ♘xf6+ ♕xf6 18 ♕h2 ♖fc8 19 ♕xh7+ ♔f8 20 ♔b1 d5 21 exd5 e5 22 ♗h6! with mutual chances; Gudiev-Nesis, Corr. 1993.

b) 16 b3 (creating a hole, but putting the question to the black rook) 16...♖c5 17 ♗h6 ♗h8! 18 ♘f5!? ♖e8 19 ♗e3 ♖c8 20 ♘d5 ♗xf5 21 ♕h2 e6! and Black had the better of the complications; Bericat-Copié, Corr. 1986.

16 ...   dxe5!?

The reader should now be familiar with the idea behind the alternative 16...♘xg4!?. One practical example of this is: 17 fxg4 ♗xg4 18 ♖dg1 dxe5 19 ♖xg4 ♖xd4!? 20 ♗xd4 exd4 21 ♘e4 ♕d5 22 ♖gh4 ♕xa2 23 ♕b4 h5 24 ♔d2 ♖c8 25 ♖d1 ♕e6 26 ♔c1 f5 27 ♘d2 ♕d5 28 ♔b1 e5 29 ♖h2 d3 30 c4 ♕d7 31 ♖g2 ♖c6 32 ♘f3 e4 Hellers-Ernst, Sweden 1987 *(91)*.

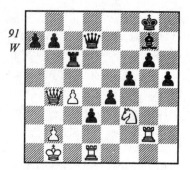

And I'm sure that White, who resigned shortly, would agree that he was overwhelmed by 'Pawn Power'!

17 ♘b3   ♖c6

Preparing to solve the d-file problems with 18...♖d6.

18 ♗c5   h6!?

A subtle *intermezzo*. If 18...b6? immediately, then 19 g5! is very strong for White.

19 ♖xh6   b6
20 ♖h4?!

After 20 ♗f2 ♖d6 21 ♕g5 ♖xd1+ 22 ♘xd1, 22...♗xh6 is good for Black. Hence White should probably try 20 ♗a3!?, as with the d1-rook still on the board, playing 20...♗xh6? is not unlikely to lead to mate down the h-file.

20 ...   bxc5
21 ♕h2   ♖e8

Black begins to safeguard his king in an ingenious manner.

22 ♖h1   ♔f8
23 ♖h8+   ♘g8
24 ♖h7   g5!

Allowing the c6-rook to help out in the defence.

25 ♘xc5   ♗c8

Not 25...♖xc5?, falling for the deadly 26 ♖xg7! ♔xg7 27 ♕h8+ ♔f8 28 ♖h7.

26 ♖xg7   ♔xg7
27 ♕xe5+   ♔f8
28 ♖h7   ♖g6
29 ♘3e4   f6
30 ♘e6+

The flash 30 ♕e6 is easily parried by 30...♖g7.

30 ...   ♗xe6
31 ♕xe6   ♖g7
32 ♘xg5 *(92)*

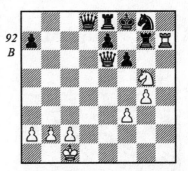

The last sneaky try. If now 32...♖xh7??, then disaster strikes in the form of 33 ♕f7+!! ♖xf7 34 ♘e6 mate.

32 ...   fxg5
0-1

6   Yugoslav Attack 9 g4

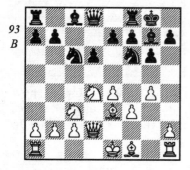

93
B

9 g4 is very much a multi-purpose move. The first point to note is that White retains g4-g5 as an option, thus preventing Black's thematic ...d6-d5 break. It also looks like a fairly aggressive move, but:

a) White is kidding himself if he believes that he can launch a successful onslaught without putting his own king in safety first.

b) Even if he does castle queenside, his king can hardly be classified as safe, and in fact practice shows that nearly all attacking lines are favourable to Black.

Therefore instead, 9 g4 can be seen perhaps more as a restraining, or space-gaining move. However, as White is often well advised to 'bale out' into an endgame, it is not clear whether an expansion of kingside pawns

should be seen as a strength, or as a weakness. I am advocating two systems for Black, though both starting with 9...♗e6. The first involves an early exchange of knights on d4, followed by a quick and simple development of the major pieces; a tried and tested system with a solid reputation. The second, in contrast, is more complicated in that it tends to involve more manoeuvring of the minor pieces, and while very interesting, is still relatively untested.

System 1: 9...♗e6 with ...♘xd4

Game 12
Miles-Keene
London 1982

1	e4	c5
2	♘f3	d6
3	♘c3	♘c6
4	d4	cxd4
5	♘xd4	g6
6	♗e3	♘f6
7	f3	♗g7
8	♕d2	0-0
9	g4	♗e6 (94)

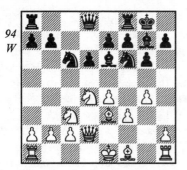

94
W

As 10 ♘xe6?! is laid to rest in system 2, the question of whether Black should exchange on d4 first is slightly irrelevant. The problem with 9...♘xd4 10 ♗xd4 ♗e6 used to be 11 ♘d5!?, which keeps the black queen out of a5 after 11...♗xd5 (11...♘xd5?! 12 ♗xg7 ♔xg7 13 h4 is clearly better for White as Black is lacking in counterplay) 12 exd5 ♖c8 13 h4 ♕c7 14 ♖h2 (not 14 0-0-0? ♘xd5 or 14...♘e4, both ∓). However more recently in Varga-Komljenović, Andorra 1991, Black apparently improved on 14...e5 15 dxe6 fxe6 16 h5 ♕c6 17 0-0-0 ♕xf3 18 hxg6 hxg6 19 ♗g2! ♘e4 (19...♕g3 20 ♗xb7±; 19...♕xg4 20 ♗h3 ♕e4 21 ♖e1±) 20 ♗xf3 ♘xd2 21 ♗xb7± Karpov-Mestel, London 1982, with 14...h5!? when White's over-optimism left him struggling after 15 0-0-0?! (15 g5 △ ♗h3!?) 15...hxg4 16 ♗d3 g3 17 ♖h3 ♘h5 18 ♗xg7 ♔xg7 19 ♗f5 ♕c4! 20 ♗xc8 ♖xc8 21 ♕d4+ ♔h7 22 ♕xc4 ♖xc4 23 ♖hh1 ♘f4. Clearly

though after 9...♗e6, 10 ♘d5? is not playable.

10 0-0-0

10 ♗e2?! looks like a wasted move after 10...♘xd4 11 ♗xd4 ♕a5, but see game 18 for an even better response! 10 h4 can be met by 10...♘xd4 11 ♗xd4 ♕a5 12 h5 ♖fc8!?, but reacting in the centre with 10...d5! is the logical reply to White's premature wing play. For example, 11 h5 ♘xd4 12 ♗xd4 dxe4 13 h6 ♗h8 14 g5 e3! 15 ♗xe3 ♘d5∓ Van der Wiel-Miles, Utrecht 1986, and 11 g5 ♘h5 12 0-0-0 ♘xd4 13 ♗xd4 dxe4 14 ♗xg7 ♔xg7 15 ♕xd8 ♖axd8 16 ♖xd8 ♖xd8 17 fxe4 h6∓ Rastes-Petursson, Dubai OL 1986.

Finally the short but instructive game Trapl-Barczay, Dečin 1978, saw 10 g5?! ♘h5 11 ♗e2?! ♘xd4 12 ♗xd4 ♗xd4 13 ♕xd4 ♕a5 14 ♕d2 ♕e5 (incidentally, if secure, this is a great square for the queen as it is allowed both to attack and defend) 15 0-0-0 ♖ac8 16 ♔b1 ♖c5! 17 h4 ♘f4 18 ♗d3 ♖fc8 (all of Black's pieces are doing things, and White's days are numbered) 19 h5 ♖xc3! (the usual treatment!) 20 bxc3 ♖xc3 21 hxg6 fxg6 22 ♕h2 h5 23 gxh5 ♔h7 24 ♕h4 g5 25 ♕e1 ♘xd3 26 ♖xd3 (26 cxd3 ♕b5+ 27 ♔a1 ♖c2+-) 26...♕b5+ 27 ♔c1 ♕xd3 1-0.

10 ...	**♘xd4**
11 ♗xd4	**♕a5**

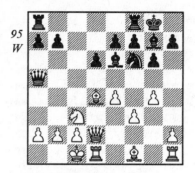

95
W

12 a3

The first critical decision has been made and it should be noted that this pawn really was *en prise*. For example, if 12 h4?! ♗xa2 13 h5 (13 b3?? traps the bishop, but unfortunately allows 13...♕a3 mate!) 13...♗e6 14 hxg6 hxg6 15 ♔b1 (15 ♕h2 ♖fc8 16 ♘d5 ♗xd5 17 exd5 ♕a1+ 18 ♔d2 ♕a4 19 c3 ♕b3 20 ♔c1 a5∓) 15...♖fc8 16 ♕h2 ♖c6 17 ♗e2 ♖ac8 when White has no way through with a double exchange sacrifice on c3 looming.

The main alternative is 12 ♔b1, but after the simple 12...♖fc8, Black has a threat which must be parried:

a) 13 h4? was met by 13...♖ab8 in J.Polgar-Zsu.Polgar, Vejstrup 1989, which continued 14 ♘d5 ♕xd2 15 ♖xd2 ♘xd5 16 exd5 ♗xd4 17 ♖xd4 ½-½. A warning should go out to all readers not to believe everything that they read (with the possible exception of this book!) as the validity of this game must be questioned. I mean, is it likely that two such distinguished players would miss 13...♖xc3! 14 ♕xc3 ♕xa2+ 15 ♔c1 ♗xg4! 16 fxg4 ♕a1+ 17 ♔d2 ♘xe4+ 18 ♔e1 ♘xc3 19 ♖xa1 ♗xd4 when Black has three soon-to-be massive pawns for the exchange?

b) 13 ♘d5?! leaves Black with a comfortable endgame after 13...♕xd2 14 ♘xf6+ ♗xf6 15 ♖xd2 ♗xd4 16 ♖xd4 ♖c5 17 h4 ♖ac8.

c) 13 ♗xf6? is a misguided attempt at equality after 13...♗xf6 14 ♘d5 ♕xd2 15 ♘xf6+ ♔g7!. However, not only do I prefer Black's position, but besides he can refute White's unambitious play with 13...♖xc3! 14 ♕xc3 ♕xa2+ 15 ♔c1 ♗xf6 16 ♕e3 (the only move in view of 16...♗g5+) 16...♕xb2+ with an absolutely juicy position with which I will leave the reader to find the forced win (or if all else fails, promote the a-pawn!).

d) 13 a3. Therefore not really avoided and met well by 13...♗c4!? (13...♖ab8 △...b5 is also playable), intending to exchange on f1, and prepare doubling with ...♖c4 (which will also threaten ...♘xe4).

12 ...   ♖fc8

It might be argued that 12...♖ab8!? as detailed in game 13 is more accurate and, as the reader will learn, these two moves can be interchanged.

13 h4

For 13 g5 see game 14.

13 ...   ♖ab8

14 ♘d5

The somewhat less tedious 14 h5 is covered in games 16 and 17.

14 ...   ♛xd2+
15 ♖xd2   ♝xd5

In this variation, there are three types of ending (with rooks) that Black may arrive at: knight versus bishop, bishop versus bishop, and pawns versus bishop. As the former, for which I personally am more likely to opt, may not be everybody's cup of tea; the latter two which may be reached after 15...♘xd5, are discussed in game 15.

16 exd5 *(96)*

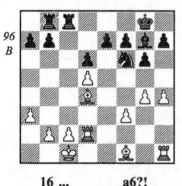

96
B

16 ...   a6?!

The reader may be slightly confused as to why I have included this game when, as detailed in the next game, a significant improvement has been found in 16...b5!. I must confess that I played the text move for a while as a junior with great success and considered the position as an inevitable case of good knight versus bad bishop. Although I would not go as far saying that there is no such thing as a 'bad'

bishop, I have since learnt never to underestimate them when other pieces are on the board. Indeed after 16...a6?! (16...a5?! is no better) White's greater board space (converted often into wins by top players) prompted English Grandmaster John Nunn to recommend this as a weapon in his extremely popular book *Beating the Sicilian*. Here, good technique is shown which should help remind the reader that these type of positions can be lost.

17 ♝h3!

White is very careful to contain the black knight. If he played 17 g5?! hoping for 17...♘d7?! 18 ♝h3, Black could respond with 17...♘h5!. Then after the dark-squared bishops are exchanged, the knight could wreak havoc and with at least one black rook entering the game along the c-file, White's d-, f- and h-pawns would soon become targets. Miles' move is in fact an improvement on 17 ♝e2, which was nevertheless assessed as a slight advantage to White, the game Karpov-Miles, London (Phillips & Drew) 1982, continuing 17...♘d7 18 f4 ♘c5 19 ♖h3 ♖c7?! (19...♝xd4 20 ♖xd4 e5 21 fxe5! dxe5 22 ♖d1±) 20 ♖e3 b5 21 ♝xg7 ♔xg7 22 ♖d4 a5 23 b4! ♘a4 24 bxa5±.

17 ...   ♘d7

The reader will no doubt be surprised with the ease in which the resulting double rook ending is won, and in light of this, perhaps Black should opt for 17...♖c7!?, retaining the possibility of ...♘h5.

18 g5   ♖c7
19 ♗xd7!

Although the notes to White's 17th imply that he can retain a small plus by keeping the minor pieces on, Miles is not convinced, believing his best is to remove the knight while he can. His decision certainly appears justified.

19 ...   ♖xd7
20 h5   ♗xd4
21 ♖xd4 *(97)*

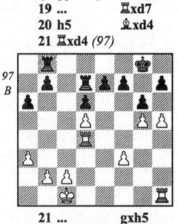

21 ...   gxh5

A horrible move to have to play but with a white pawn on g5 and ♖dh4 coming, there is a real chance that Black will be mated down the h-file.

22 ♖xh5   ♖c8
23 c3

White clearly has a superior position, but he must play carefully not to let his advantage slip. For example, Black can generate some activity after 23 ♖dh4?! ♖c5! 24 c4 ♖dc7.

23 ...   ♖c5
24 ♔d2   ♖dc7

25 ♔e3   ♖c4
26 ♖d2   ♖7c5
27 f4   ♖a4

A minority attack is too slow as after, say, 27...b5 (Δ...a5 and ...b4), White has 28 ♔f3. This cuts out ...♖g4, enabling him to follow up with f5-f6 and ♖dh2 creating a mating net.

28 ♖dh2   ♖xd5
29 ♖xh7   ♖f5
30 ♖h8+   ♔g7
31 ♖2h7+   ♔g6
32 ♖h4!   ♔g7

33 ♖g8 mate was threatened and 32...f6 encouraged a monstrous g-pawn.

33 ♖8h7+   ♔f8
Or 33...♔g8 34 g6±.

34 b3!   ♖xa3
35 ♖h8+   ♔g7
36 ♔e4   e6 *(98)*

If 36...♖c5 then 37 f5 spells doom for the black king.

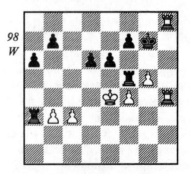

37 ♖b8!   d5+

White was threatening 38 ♖hh8 Δ ♖bg8 mate. Probably best was 37...♖c5! 38 ♖hh8 f5+ 39 ♔d4 ♖d5+! 40 ♔c4 (40 ♔e3 ♖xb3)

40...b5+ 41 ♔b4 ♖a2 42 ♖bg8+
♔f7 43 ♖a8 a5+ when things are
not so clear.

38	♔d3	♖xf4
39	♖xf4	♖xb3
	1-0	

Bearing in mind my aforementioned lack of objectivity regarding
the knight vs bishop endgames that
arise from this variation, the next
game was to be a great challenge to
me, as I owe a great deal of success
as a junior to the Dragon. Was the
expert Sicilian basher to give me a
lesson that I would never forget?
The answer is "No" and in fact I
had to wait a few years later to
discover that it is far from all one-
way traffic. The occasion I remember vividly was a game in the
Lloyds Bank Masters in which I
was somewhat unfortunately
paired against my girlfriend (or at
least she had been until the previous night! I will leave her un-
named in case she is too embar-
rassed—to have been playing 9 g4,
that is!). Although my score-sheet
mysteriously disappeared, I can recall:

a) For the first time considering
White's pawn on d5 as a strength
rather than a weakness.

b) Suffering an awkward amount
of pressure on my e7-pawn from
the white rooks which was easily
transferable to the h-file.

c) Having both of my rooks and
my knight apparently tied up sin-
gle-handedly by the supposedly
bad white bishop.

d) Having been extremely re-
lieved to hear and extremely quick
to accept a rather sympathetic draw
offer!

Of course I put that display down
to a lack of concentration (that's
my excuse and I'm sticking to it!),
which is evidently required, but ab-
sent at one vital stage in the following game.

Game 13
Nunn-Ward
Simul, Sevenoaks 1983

1	e4	c5
2	♘f3	d6
3	d4	cxd4
4	♘xd4	♘f6
5	♘c3	g6
6	♗e3	♗g7
7	f3	0-0
8	♕d2	♘c6
9	g4	♗e6
10	0-0-0	♘xd4
11	♗xd4	♕a5
12	a3	♖ab8!?
13	h4	b5

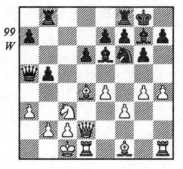

99
W

The point. Whilst ...♖fc8 is a very useful move, Black has temporarily foregone it in favour of a more direct route to the white king, down the b-file. This move order effectively removes the specific relevance of games 16 and 17 (although the ideas there are interesting), as after 14 h5?!, Black can improve on 14...♖fc8 with 14...b4! 15 ♘b1 (15 axb4? ♕a1+ 16 ♘b1 ♗a2-+) 15...♖fc8 when Black has a dangerous initiative. This was used well in Kondali-Martinovski, Yugoslavia 1954, after 16 hxg6 hxg6 17 ♗d3 ♗a2 18 ♖h3 ♕a4 19 axb4 ♖xb4 20 ♘c3 ♖xb2!! 21 ♔xb2 ♕xd4-+. The two drawbacks of this move order are as follows:

a) White is now virtually forced into entering an endgame with 14 ♘d5 which removes a lot of the excitement. After 13...♖fc8, 14 h5 is more tempting as White's own attacking prospects are at least present, in contrast to the line given above.

b) After playing through game 15 you will notice that the pawns vs bishop endgame is unreachable, as the black rook is still on f8. However it will be seen that Black cannot force such an ending anyway, making the situation unique. Black can prevent White from playing a possible favourite variation, but then White can if he so chooses, return the favour! Confused? Read on ...

14 ♘d5   ♕xd2+

15 ♖xd2   ♗xd5
16 exd5   a5

A very reasonable move. Also good is 16...♖fc8!?, arriving at a position that could have come from 13...♖fc8 (or 12...♖fc8 and 13...♖ab8) and 16...b5! (instead of 16...a6?! – see game 12).

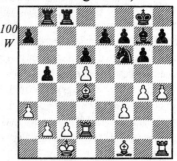

From the illustrated position, the following have been tried in practice:

a) 17 g5 (17 ♗xa7?! ♖a8 18 ♗d4 b4 and in view of the mate threat on a1, Black will not only regain his pawn, but will have easy access for his rooks and dark-square domination after ...♘d7) 17...♘h5 18 ♗xa7?! ♖a8 19 ♗d4 b4 20 ♗xg7 ♔xg7 21 ♗b5 bxa3 22 b3 (pawns would drop like flies after 22 bxa3?! and while they don't last too long this way, at least White retains a potentially dangerous b-pawn) 22...♖c3 23 ♖d3 ♖xd3 24 ♗xd3 ♘f4 25 ♗c4 ♘g2! 26 ♗b5 ♘xh4∓ Klinger-Ward, Oakham 1986.

b) 17 ♗h3 ♖c7 18 g5 ♘h5 19 ♖e1 b4 20 axb4 ♖xb4 21 ♗xg7 ♔xg7 when Black's penetration of

White's fourth rank outweighs the pressure on his e7-pawn, giving him the upper hand; Stein-Hodgson, Copenhagen 1985.

c) 17 ♔b1 ♖c7 (17...a5!? Δ 18 h5 b4 or 18 ♗h3 ♖c4! 19 b3?! ♘e4∓ due to the usual superiority of dark-over light-squared bishop) 18 h5 ♗h6 19 ♖d1 ♗f4 20 hxg6 fxg6 21 ♗d3 with an unclear position, though probably preferable for White due to his two bishops vs bishop and knight advantage.

17 h5?? (101)

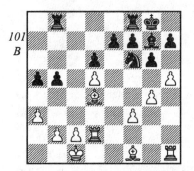

101
B

I had just won the club championship in this year and I was rather unlucky in that local reporters present for this special occasion chose this moment to take my photograph, along with the trophy. All of a sudden John appeared expecting a move, and foolishly not wanting to 'pass', I confidently bashed out the natural 17...♘d7 and returned to my photo shoot! John immediately found the whole situation most amusing and accompanied very audible laughter with the comment that 17...♗h6! might have forced his resignation. My face turned a beetroot red colour, but I soon dismissed this as the price of fame and got on with the game. As it turned out the last laugh was with me.

17 ...   ♘d7?!
18 ♗xg7   ♔xg7
19 ♖dh2

In view of Black's next move, perhaps White should exchange on g6 first, but I still prefer Black.

19 ...   g5!?
20 h6+

Practically forced. If Black is allowed to play ...h6 then not only will his knight have a choice of delightful dark squares, but his king will be a threat too. Now it is not so much the possibility of f4 which prevents 20...♔f6 but rather the problem of defending the h7-pawn after 21 ♗d3.

20 ...   ♔h8

Obviously if the white rooks could find a way to the seventh or eighth rank, then the position of the black king would be exposed. However this is not possible as the black knight is a real monster.

21 ♗d3   ♘e5
22 ♗e4   e6!
23 ♖d1?!

Now White is all over the shop, but what else? 23 dxe6 is perhaps more logical, though this only really succeeds in letting the black rooks into the game, and in any case the f3-pawn is a gonner.

23 ...	f5
24 gxf5	exf5
25 &d3	♘xf3
26 ♖e2	♘e5 (102)

Not so fast bucko! Needless to say this is the sort of position that Black would do well to aim for.

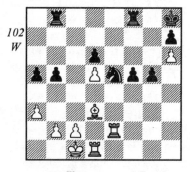

102
W

27 ♖f2	f4
28 ♖df1	♖f6
29 ♔d2	♖xh6
30 &f5	♖f6
31 &e6	♖bf8
32 ♖g2	h6
33 b3	♔g7
34 ♔c3	f3
35 ♖g3	g4
0-1	

In general losses by strong players in simultaneous displays result from a tactical oversight. In the end, this was not the case here, suggesting that the handling of the white pieces in these type of positions requires a good deal of thought even by the best. If indeed it was there to be found, such accuracy is lacking in the next game which sees Black improving his

position all of the time, until it is embarrassingly good.

Game 14
Müller-Khalifman
German Team Cup 1992

1 e4	c5
2 ♘f3	d6
3 d4	cxd4
4 ♘xd4	♘f6
5 ♘c3	g6
6 &e3	&g7
7 f3	0-0
8 ♕d2	♘c6
9 g4	&e6
10 0-0-0	♘xd4
11 &xd4	♕a5
12 a3	♖ab8!?
13 g5	

I suppose that White could also play 13 g5 against 12...♖fc8, but at the very least Black could transpose to this game.

13 ...   ♘h5!

More accurate than 13...♘d7?! when Black may receive problems down the h-file after 14 &xg7 ♔xg7 15 h4.

14 &xg7   ♘xg7 (103)

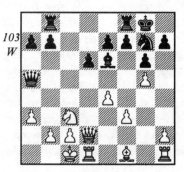

103
W

This is the first time that we have seen this recapture. Here Black is hoping that he will eventually find a vocation in life for his knight. As you will see, he does!

15 ♔b1

In Aseev-Khalifman, Erfurt 1991, White tried 15 h4 b5 16 ♘d5 ♕xd2+ 17 ♖xd2 ♗xd5 18 ♖xd5 and after 18...a6 (instead of the played 18...♘e6? 19 ♖xb5 ♖xb5 20 ♗xb5 ♘d4 21 ♗a6! ♘xf3 22 ♖h3± but ½-½ in 31) arguably has a small advantage. However Khalifman, who evidently has confidence in this line, has suggested an improvement in 15...♖fc8!?.

15 ...   ♖fc8
16 ♘d5

As is common, White has little faith in his own attacking prospects and doesn't want to hang around to be attacked himself. Although the words 'wimp' and 'bottle merchant' spring to mind, in all fairness White's decision is justified. The route to the black king is far from clear, whereas Black can double his rooks in preparation for a simple exchange sacrifice on c3 or launch his b-pawn with the rook behind it.

16 ...   ♕xd2
17 ♖xd2   ♗xd5
18 exd5

18 ♖xd5 is, I guess, playable, if somewhat unadventurous. However the imbalance of bishop vs knight is still present and Black would probably do well to put his knight on f4 and make the g5-pawn

a target. He can attack it with ...♖c5 and try to pave an entrance for his king with ...h6, which may also give him the h-file.

18 ...   ♘f5
19 ♗h3   ♖c4
20 ♖e1   ♔f8
21 ♖e4

Later White regrets not taking the knight, but after 21 ♗xf5 gxf5, although Black has doubled f-pawns, the e7-pawn is his only real weakness. In contrast White's d, f, g and h-pawns are all a little loose and will be searched out by Black's active c4-rook and his king, when it gets its act together. I am not trying to pull the wool over the readers' eyes, but at best White will be on the worse side of a draw.

21 ...   ♖bc8
22 c3   ♖8c7
23 ♖d3   h6
24 gxh6

Perhaps now White's best chance at activity lies with 24 ♗xf5 gxf5 25 ♖xc4 ♖xc4 26 gxh6 Δ ♖d4-c4 if 26...♖h4 with some exciting pawn racing in store.

24 ...   ♘xh6 (104)

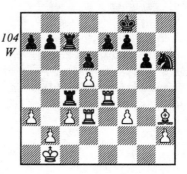

104
W

The black knight is temporarily on the rim, but it will certainly find its way back into the action. Meanwhile White's weak pawns will not go away (until they are taken!) and with little constructive to do, he must sit back and wait for Black to do his worst.

25	&c2	f5
26	Xed4	♘g8
27	b3	Xxd4
28	Xxd4	♘f6
29	&f1	

Although ...f5 originally conceded the e6-square, this was not important, and now the white bishop searches in vain for a better diagonal. In contrast the black knight has several good options.

29	...	&g7
30	h4	Xc5
31	c4	Xc8
32	&d2	♘d7
33	&e2	a5
34	&d1	

34 b4 merely succeeds in giving away the a-file.

34	...	&f6
35	&e3	Xh8
36	&c2	&e5
37	&d1	♘c5
38	a4	

A truly disgusting move. As White is rather tied up, he evidently fears a timely ...a4 and of course 38 f4+ forces the black king back, but at the cost of the h4-pawn.

| 38 | ... | ♘a6 |
| 39 | &c2 | ♘b4 |

40	&d1	♘a6
41	&c2	♘b4
42	&d1	b6 *(105)*

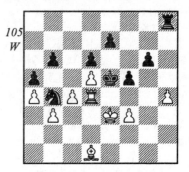

Black has obviously only been teasing White with the odd repetition in order to reach the time control. With great ease and simplicity, Black has manufactured this position from the previous diagrammed one. Yet, just as we are waiting to see how he will move in for the kill, White appears to go loopy with 43 h5. However a closer inspection reveals that he is extremely stuck for moves. King moves allow 43...&xd4, bishop moves (i.e. to e2!) allow 43...♘c2+, pawn moves all lose a pawn and 43 Xd2 is met by 43...Xxh4 (or 43...f4+ first). This leaves just 43 Xf4 which is adequately dealt with by 43...g5! 44 hxg5 Xh1 45 Xd4 (or 45 &e2 ♘c2+) 45...f4+, winning the bishop.

43	h5	Xxh5
44	f4+	&f6
45	Xd2	

Of course this little tactical jaunt still hasn't been successful for White as on 45 ♗xh5 ♘c2+ 46 ♔d3 ♘xd4 47 ♗d1 e5 is winning for Black.

45 ...　　　　♖h1

Now Black is 'in like Flynn', whilst White is still struggling to find moves. The game is effectively over.

46	♗f3	♖c1
47	♗d1	♖c3+
48	♔d4	♖h3

Zugzwang!

49	c5	bxc5+
50	♔c4	♖c4
51	♔b5	♖xf4
52	♔xa5	

In bishop vs knight endgames, the side with the long range power of the bishop will do well to seek out pawn races. Unfortunately for White, here he has just one passed pawn which the black knight is well placed to contain. Elsewhere the black pawns not surprisingly prove to be too much of a handful for the white bishop.

52	...	g5
53	♔b5	g4
54	a5	g3
55	a6	♘xa6
56	♔xa6	♖d4!
57	♖xd4	cxd4
58	♗f3	d3

0-1

The following thriller features the bishop vs three pawns endgame. Although such positions are undoubtedly good fun, they are certainly difficult to assess, most texts generally summarising them as 'unclear'.

Game 15

Marjanović-Velimirović

Yugoslavia 1983

1	e4	c5
2	♘f3	d6
3	d4	cxd4
4	♘xd4	♘f6
5	♘c3	g6
6	♗e3	♗g7
7	f3	♘c6
8	♕d2	0-0
9	g4	♗e6
10	0-0-0	♘xd4
11	♗xd4	♕a5
12	a3	♖ab8
13	h4	♖fc8
14	♘d5	♕xd2+
15	♖xd2	♘xd5 *(106)*

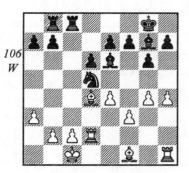

106
W

16 exd5

Unfortunately (as previously mentioned), here White can opt for a considerably less risky game with 16 ♗xg7. Then Black should recapture with his king, as any knight retreats provide White with the two bishops for bishop and knight advantage, in a nice open position. Also I would like to say a few words about 16...♘e3?!. I'm afraid that this is a misguided attempt at imbalancing the position. If after 17 ♗d4 ♘xf1 18 ♖xf1 b6, Black believes that he has winning chances but cannot lose due to it being an endgame with opposite-coloured bishops, then he is gravely mistaken. The reality of the situation is that due to White having the more dominant bishop (with the reminder to the reader that the dark-squared bishop nearly always plays the greater role), he can often drum up mating threats and as Black discovered in Short-Sax, Hastings 1983/84, the traffic is all one way: 19 g5 h5 20 f4 ♗h3 21 ♖ff2 ♖c6 22 f5 ♖e8 23 b3 ♗g4 24 ♔b2 a6 25 a4 b5 26 axb5 axb5 27 ♗c3 ♖c5 28 f6 ♖c6 29 ♖d5 exf6 30 ♗xf6 ♖xe4 31 ♖xb5 ♗c8 32 ♖d2 ♔f8 33 c4 ♔e8 34 ♖db5 ♖xh4 35 ♖xd6 ♖xd6 36 ♖xd6 ♗d7 37 c5 1-0. Returning to Black's best in 16...♔xg7, then after 17 exd5 ♗d7 the position is fairly equal as practical examples bear out:

a) 18 h5 h6! 19 hxg6 fxg6 20 ♗d3 ♖h8 21 ♖e2 ♖be8 22 ♔d2 ½-½ Nunn-Karlsson, Helsinki 1983.

b) 18 g5 h6 19 ♖d4 ♗f5 20 c3 ♖h8 21 f4 f6 22 gxf6+ exf6 23 ♖c4 ♖bc8 24 ♔d2= Gudmundsson-Karlsson, Reykjavik 1986.

c) 18 ♖d4 ♖c7 19 ♗d3 f6 20 b4 ♖c7 21 ♖e1 ♖c5 22 ♖b4 ♖c7 23 ♖e3 ♔f8 24 ♗e2 ♖ec8 25 ♗d3 ♖e8 26 ♗e2 ♖ec8= Agdestein-Hansen, Jerusalem 1987.

d) 18 ♗e2 like other moves: possible, but not exactly earth-shattering!

Incidently the reader will notice that despite having his rooks on b8 and c8, in this line particularly, Black tends to refrain from launching his a- and b-pawns. An attack is really out of the question and so any queenside pawn advancement on his part is more likely to be weakening.

16 ...   ♗xd5!?

Leading to a very interesting line, but now almost certainly best as 16...♗d7? simply loses a pawn to 17 ♗xa7 and 16...♗xd4 17 ♖xd4 ♗d7 leaves White a couple of tempi up on the variations above (leaving him better though far from won).

17 ♗xg7   ♗xf3
18 ♖h3   ♗xg4
19 ♖g3

Theory tends to take this obvious move for granted as it allows White to remain a piece up (well, for the odd pawn) but 19 ♗d4 looks like a different type of fun. Then after 19...♗xh3 20 ♗xh3 White will have two not-to-be-underestimated bishops for a rook and two pawns (once the a-pawn is bagged); or will he? Perhaps 20...♖c4 21 ♗xa7 (21 b3?! ♖c7 22 ♗xa7 ♖a8 △...♖xa3 seems good for Black) 21...♖xh4!? 22 ♗xb8 ♖xh3 reverting back to the 'usual' bishop for three pawns with White having a potential passed pawn and Black currently having four! But then again, what if White refuses to take the exchange with 22 ♗g2!? ♖a8 (22...♖c8 23 ♗xb7 ♖c7 24 ♗f2) 23 ♗f2 intending 24 ♗xb7. Although 23...♖b4!? 24 ♖xd6!? (not 24 axb4?? ♖a1 mate!) Anyone for a rook? 24...♖xb2!? No, take mine 25 ♖xg6+, I insist! Okay 25...hxg6 26 ♔xb2 and I guess Black is better, though no doubt there are improvements all round.

19 ...   ♔xg7
20 ♖xg4 *(107)*

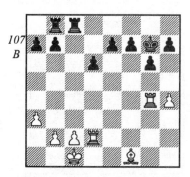

The last few Black moves have been forced with him correctly opting not to leave on the dark-squared and indeed both of the white bishops. Now how would

you continue? Well unless you happen to be *Deep Thought*, then analysing this position to the end is a little unfeasible. For Black, one would think that sound advice would be to get the kingside pawns rolling as soon as possible. However, due to problems which may crop up on the queenside, it appears that the most obvious move 20...f5 may not be best. For example: 21 ♖a4 a6 22 ♖b4 a5 (or 22...h6 23 a4!) 23 ♖b5! when the black rooks are a little tied up.

Hence probably the text is better, although 20...♖c7!? (a suggestion of Larsen's), intending to meet 21 ♖a4 with 21...b6, and 21 h5 with 21...f5, should certainly come into consideration.

20 ...   b6
21 ♗a6   ♖c7
22 ♖b4   ♖d8

Although the pushing of the big kingside majority requires a little care, certainly Black's plan is obvious. Unless Black slips up, White will not win any of these kingside pawns, nor indeed establish an adequate blockade. Therefore he must try to get something going for himself on the queenside.

23 a4   f5
The missiles are flying!
24 a5   bxa5
25 ♖b5   ♔f6
The black king will of course play its part in helping the pawns reach their destiny.
26 ♖xa5   e6 *(108)*

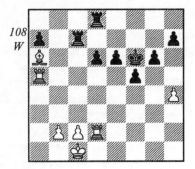

108
W

In accordance with endgame theory, Black instinctively advances his pawns on the same colour squares as the enemy bishop, in order to prevent a simple blockade.

| 27 ♗f1 | d5 |
| 28 ♖a6 | ♔e7 |

Getting out of the pin and as you will see, going backwards in order to go forwards.

29 ♖d4	♖d6
30 ♖a5	♔f6
31 ♔d2	h6
32 b3	♖dc6

White was preparing to meet 32...g5 with 33 c4!?, but in fact Black's last move, aimed at deterring this, should not put him off. Thus he should probably try 33 c4!? anyway, as an attempt at activity with ♖d8 to follow. Still, nothing is clear.

| 33 ♗d3 | ♖c5 |
| 34 ♖a6 | |

With no white passed pawns and the material still equal (i.e. three pawns for the bishop), it is in Black's favour to exchange rooks.

34 ...	♖5c6
35 ♖a5	g5
36 hxg5	hxg5
37 ♖da4	

Instead of drawing by repetition, Black decides to go for broke. His a-pawn is doomed, but his e-, f- and g-pawns remain on course for promotion.

37 ...	g4
38 ♖xa7	e5
39 b4	

For the first time it is White with the easier moves. He has just one pawn to push.

39 ...	e4
40 b5	♖xa7
41 ♖xa7	♖e6

Clearly played in preference to the more passive 41...♖c8.

| 42 ♖a6 | ♔e5! |

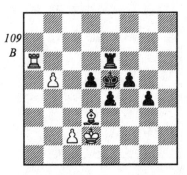

109
B

Definitely the best move, as neither 42...g3 43 ♗f1 ♔e5 (43... f4? 44 ♗h3!) 44 ♖xe6 ♔xe6, nor 42...exd3 43 b6 g3 (43...dxc2 44 b7

♖xa6 45 b8♕) 44 b7 g2 45 b8♕
♖xa6 (45...g1♕? 46 ♕h8+!) 46
♕h2 can possibly be better for
Black.

43 b6?

Now White makes what should
be the final mistake. Also bad was
43 ♖xe6? ♔xe6 44 ♗f1 (44 b6
♔d6 45 ♗b5 g3 46 ♔e1 f4 47 b7
♔c7 48 ♗c6 g2 49 ♔f2 f3 Δ...e3-
e2+-) 44...f4 45 c4 dxc4 46
♗xc4+ ♔d6 when the already
well advanced three connected
passed pawns would still prove to
be too much of a handful. Instead
White's best chance lies with 43
♗f1 f4 44 b6 (Δ 45 b7 ♖e8 46
♖a8) 44...♖e8 45 b7 ♖b8 46 ♖g6
g3 47 ♖g7 when at least his rook
is a better defender than Black's
is an attacker.

43 ...	**♖e8**
44 ♗b5	**♖b8**
45 ♗c6	**g3**
46 ♔e1	**f4**
47 b7	**g2?**

Things are certainly heating
up, but now Black repays the
error of move 43. Winning was
47...f3 48 ♖a8 e3! 49 ♖xb8 g2
50 ♖g8 (or 50 ♖e8+ ♔d4 51 c3+
♔c5!-+) 50...f2+ 51 ♔e2 f1♕+
52 ♔xe3 g1♕+. Fortunately as
we will see, he has time on his
side.

48 ♔f2	**♖g8**
49 b8♕+	**♖xb8**
50 ♔xg2	**f3+**
51 ♔f2	**♔f4** *(110)*

0-1

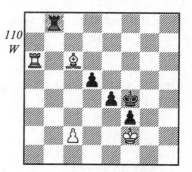

110
W

Sadly for White, here his flag
dropped. Things appear to be a little tricky for him as Black is threatening 52...e3+ followed by a rook
check on the eighth and an inevitable pawn promotion. However best
defence shows that White has actually lost on time in a drawn position. He should play 52 ♖a4!
pinning the e-pawn, and after
52...♖b2 53 ♗xd5 ♖xc2+ 54 ♔f1
♔g3 55 ♖xe4 ♖h2 56 ♔e1 ♖h1+
57 ♔d2 f2 58 ♗f1 (or 58 ♖e3+)
Black can try no more.

It is certainly not clear what the
correct result should be in this
15...♘xd5 16 exd5 variation, but
there is no doubt that in the limited
time of a game's duration, irrespective of the correctness, the
practical chances are immense.

The last two games in this system, starting with one of my
Dragon favourites, cover White's
most aggressive option 14 h5. Usually against direct play, a great deal
of accuracy is required. However,
what particularly strikes me here,

is the surprising number of very reasonable alternatives that are available to Black, which may explain why the majority of White 9 g4 players tend to run scared, seeking an early trade of queens.

Game 16
Plaskett-Watson
Brighton 1983

1 e4	c5
2 ♘f3	d6
3 d4	cxd4
4 ♘xd4	♘f6
5 ♘c3	g6
6 ♗e3	♗g7
7 f3	0-0
8 ♕d2	♘c6
9 g4	♗e6
10 0-0-0	♘xd4
11 ♗xd4	♕a5
12 a3	♖fc8
13 h4	♖ab8
14 h5	b5
15 h6 *(111)*	

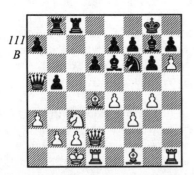

15 hxg6 is the main alternative, discussed in game 17, and it should

be noted that White has missed the boat regarding the early queen trade, i.e. 15 ♘d5? ♕xd2+ when 16 ♔xd2 will just lose a pawn and 16 ♖xd2 will fall prey to a bishop pin along the c1-h6 diagonal.

15 ...   b4!?

15...♗h8?! enables White to guarantee a slight advantage with 16 ♘d5 (arriving at an endgame that can be compared favourably with those reached in the previous game). However it is possible that the theoretical importance of the text may be reduced by the arrival of the more recent suggestion 15...♗f8. This move may well be deserving of one or even two exclamation marks, or then again it may not!

It is true that whilst the bishop has moved to a rather silly square, White has blocked the h-file with Black still having the b-file to attack down. Sapi and Schneider now consider 16 ♗xf6 b4!! 17 ♗d4 (17 ♘b1 exf6 18 ♗d3 ♕a4 19 axb4 d5! 20 ♖h2 ♗xb4 21 c3 d4 ∓) 17...bxa3 18 b3 ♗xb3! 19 cxb3 (19 ♗d3 allows the neat little combination 19...a2 20 ♔b2 a1♕+! 21 ♖xa1 ♗c4+ with mate or heavy material loss inevitable, whilst 19 ♕d3 is met by 19...e5 20 ♕a6 ♕b4 21 ♖d3 exd4 22 ♘d5 ♕e1+ mating) 19...♖xb3 20 ♗d3 a2! 21 ♔c2 ♕a4 22 ♗c4 ♖xc4-+. Whether or not any significant improvements can be found for White, only time will tell, although this should not prevent readers from conducting their own investigations.

16 hxg7

16 axb4? loses to the common theme of 16...♕a1+ 17 ♘b1 ♗a2 and 16 ♘d5 ♗xd5 17 exd5 ♗f8!? 18 ♗xf6 exf6 △ 19...♕a4∓, but depending on the validity of 15...♗f8, the position arising after the alternative 16 ♘b5!? ♖xb5 17 ♗xb5 ♕xb5 18 hxg7 bxa3 *(112)* may be critical.

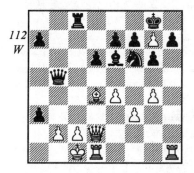

112
W

Things are a little messy. White is the exchange for a pawn up, but whilst it is true that Black is only a few moves away from being mated, it is still his own king that is the more exposed. Now a few of White's possibilities are as follows:

a) 19 ♗xf6 when Black can at least draw with 19...a2 20 ♕h6 a1♕+ 21 ♔d2 ♖xc2+ 22 ♔e3 ♕e2+ 23 ♔f4 ♕c1+ 24 ♖xc1 ♕d2+ 25 ♔g3 ♕g2+ 26 ♔f4 ♕d2+ etc, or try for more perhaps with 19...exf6!?.

(b) 19 bxa3?! ♕a4 20 ♖h2? (20 ♕d3 ♗c4 21 ♕c3 ♗a6 22 ♕b2 ♗e2 23 ♖d2 ♗xf3 leaves Black notching up the pawns, yet not relieving the pressure on the white king) 20...♕xa3+ 21 ♗b2 ♕xf3 22 ♖f2 ♕xe4 23 ♗xf6 exf6 24 ♕xd6 ♔xg7 25 ♕e7 ♕e3+ 26 ♖fd2 ♖c5 0-1 Bezemer-Sehner, Amsterdam 1986. A truly grim position, and, yes, also winning but unnecessary was 26...♖xc2+ 27 ♔xc2 ♗b3+.

c) 19 ♕d3 axb2+ (amongst others 19...♕g5+ seems quite interesting) 20 ♗xb2 ♗c4 21 ♕e3 (or 21 ♕c3!? ♖c6!?) 21...♗e2! 22 ♖de1 (if 22 ♖d2 ♖b8!) 22...♗d3 23 ♖h2 ♕b3∓ Shirov-Golubev, Latvian Junior 1985, as after 24 ♖ee2, either 24...♗xc2 or 24...a5!? are fine.

16 ...   bxa3!
17 ♕h6

The most obvious in view of 17...axb2+ and 18...♕a1 mate. Nevertheless 17 ♘d5?! was tested in Fernandez-Gonzalez, Barcelona 1985, but bearing in mind the outcome after 17...axb2+ 18 ♗xb2 ♖xb2! 19 ♘xe7+ (19 ♕xa5?? ♖cxc2 mate) 19...♔xg7 20 ♕h6+ ♔h8 21 ♘xc8 ♕b4 0-1, it is unlikely to see the light of day again (at least not by Mr Fernandez!).

17 ...   axb2+
18 ♔d2

White needed to evacuate his queen to give his king this flight square. What is incredible about this position is that with 19 ♗xf6 △

♕xh7 mate a giant threat, it is not surprising that for quite a while the assessment was '+-'. However after Black's brilliant riposte, it is likely that this judgement should be reversed to '-+'! An excellent example of how theory comes and goes.

18 ...   ♗xg4!! *(113)*

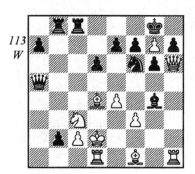

This is, I believe, a suggestion of English Grandmaster Jonathan Mestel, which certainly puts a bit of a dampener on White's opening preparation.

19 ♗xf6

As we will see, Black's light-squared bishop is set for a simple defensive task, whilst the major pieces get on with the attacking. However, if it is removed with 19 fxg4, White is faced with 19...e5! after which:

a) 20 ♕e3 exd4 21 ♕xd4 ♖xc3! 22 ♕xc3 ♘xe4+ is curtains, and

b) 20 ♔d3 exd4 21 ♘d5 ♕b5+ 22 ♔d2 (22 ♔xd4 ♕c5+ 23 ♔d3 ♕xc2+ 24 ♔d4 {24 ♔e3 ♘xg4+

-+} 24...♕xe4 mate) 22...♖xc2+ 23 ♔xc2 (23 ♔e1 ♕a5+ -+) 23...b1♕+ 24 ♖xb1 ♕xb1+ 25 ♔d2 ♖b2 is mate.

19 ...   ♗h5

The point! The h-file is now firmly blocked and as far as White is concerned his g7-pawn is very much in the way.

20 ♗d4

White has a few alternatives to this move, but nothing that really helps:

a) 20 ♗h3 exf6 21 ♗xc8 ♖xc8 22 ♕e3 ♕b4. White is somewhat tied up and Black is simply threatening ...a5-a4-a3-a2. But if 23 ♖h4 (Δ 24 ♖dh1 and 25 e5) Black has 23...d5! (Δ...d4) 24 exd5 ♕xh4 25 d6 ♕h2+ 26 ♔e1 ♕xc2 27 d7 ♖d8 28 ♕e8+ ♔xg7 29 ♕xd8 ♕xc3+ 30 ♔f2 ♕xf3+ -+.

b) 20 ♖xh5 ♕xh5! (20...gxh5 is possibly also winning but the text is the easiest) 21 ♕xh5 gxh5 22 ♗xe7 ♖xc3 23 ♔xc3 b1♕ 24 ♖xb1 ♖xb1 when with the black king tucked safely away (from awkward bishop checks) his three(!) passed rooks' pawns will win him the day, e.g. 25 ♗d3 a5 26 ♗xd6 h4 27 ♔d2 h3 28 ♔e2 ♖g1 (Δ...h2) 29 ♔f2 ♖g2+ 30 ♔f1 ♖g6 31 ♗e5 a4 32 c4 a3 33 c5 a2 Δ ...h2-+.

c) 20 ♔d3 (Δ 20...exf6? 21 ♘d5!) 20...b1♕! when both 21 ♖xb1 ♖xb1 22 ♘xb1 ♕b5+ 23 ♔e3 ♕xb1 and 21 ♘xb1 exf6 leave White with his king still in a lot of danger and his pieces very uncoordinated.

d) 20 ♔e3 ♖xc3+! 21 ♗xc3 ♕xc3+ 22 ♗d3. Once again, a word of warning here for anybody who flicks through sidelines such as these with no recourse to analysis, accepting assessments without question. Here numerous texts supply 22...a5-+ implying that although Black is a rook down, White can do nothing but sit back and wait for ...a4-a3-a2 etc. But is this really the case? It seems to me that in desperation White would surely try 23 ♖xh5 gxh5 24 e5 ♕xe5+ 25 ♔f2 but then what? Okay, the answer seems to be 25...♕d4+! (and not 25...f5? 26 ♗c4+ d5 27 ♖xd5!+-) 26 ♔e2 (or else 26...♕xg7) 26...f5 (rather than 26...♕xg7? 27 ♖g1!+-) when Black is probably winning as 27 ♗xf5 is met by 27...♕xd1+ 28 ♔xd1 b1♕+ when the new black queen will check its way back to an adequate defensive post. Nonetheless it goes to show that sometimes, even in apparently 'winning' positions, care must be taken and here, had 22...a5 not worked out, Black would have had to work out if there was time for 22...e5!?, and if not, perhaps rethink the whole line!

20 ...   e5
21 ♖xh5

Desperation? Well Black is threatening to capture on d4 and c3 in succession, and Plaskett, in his usual energetic style, wants to do something.

21 ...   gxh5
22 ♕g5

Temporarily at least pinning the e-pawn. After 22 ♕xh5 both 22...♕b4 and 22...b1♕ do the business.

22 ...   ♕b4
23 ♗d3   ♕xd4
24 ♘d5 *(114)*

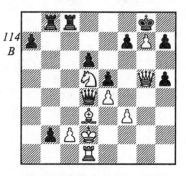

114
B

White has finally created a threat, but now he loses by force.

24 ...   ♕f2+
25 ♗e2   ♖xc2+!
26 ♔xc2   ♕xe2+
27 ♔c3

Or 27 ♕d2 b1♕+ -+.

27 ...   ♕xf3+
28 ♔c4

White now walks into a mate in one, but retreating the knight is hopeless as ...b1♕ will always follow and 28 ♔d2 (or 28 ♔c2) can be met by 28...♕xd1+ 29 ♔xd1 b1♕+ with mate or winning of the queen or both(!) forthcoming.

28 ...   ♕b3 mate.

Game 17
Waitzkin-Jirovsky
Oakham 1992

1	e4		c5
2	♘f3		d6
3	d4		cxd4
4	♘xd4		♘f6
5	♘c3		g6
6	♗e3		♘c6
7	f3		♗g7
8	♕d2		0-0
9	g4		♘xd4

Again quite commonly played, but maybe less accurate than 9...♗e6.

10	♗xd4		♗e6
11	0-0-0		♕a5
12	a3		♖fc8
13	h4		♖ab8
14	h5		b5
15	hxg6 *(115)*		

This move is perhaps the most testing in the whole of the 9 g4 lines, yet Black appears to be more than holding his own.

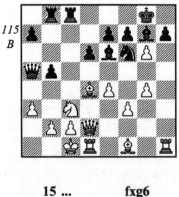

115
B

15 ...   fxg6

A safe (though once considered bad) response which may not suit everybody. For this reason I will give the two critical alternatives:

a) 15...b4?!. Unfortunately in light of all the evidence to date, I'm afraid that I have to imply that this move is a little dubious although I would love to see it rehabilitated. In order to explain, let me start with the 1987 correspondence game Laplaza-Copié which continued 16 gxh7+ (16 gxf7+?! ♗xf7 17 ♘b1 ♗b3 18 axb4 ♕a1 19 ♗d3 ♗a2 20 c3 ♖xb4 left Black with a reasonable attack in Matulović-Vuletić, Ljubljana 1955) 16...♔h8 17 ♘d5 ♗xd5 18 g5! ♕a4 19 gxf6 ♗xf6 20 ♗xf6 exf6 21 ♗d3 (21 ♖g1!? is an aggressive-looking alternative but 21 exd5? is really too risky in view of 21...bxa3) 21...bxa3 22 ♕g2 (Not 22 ♕h6?! as 22...♕d4! defends and attacks at the same time, e.g. 23 bxa3 ♗a2 24 ♖hg1 ♖b1+ 25 ♔d2 ♖xc2+ -+) 22...♕a5 (although I'm not entirely convinced that Black can't just play 22...axb2+ 23 ♔d2 ♕a5+ 24 ♔e2 ♗a2 {or 24...♗e6} and if 25 ♖(d or h)g1 then 25...♕g5) 23 bxa3 ♗a2 24 ♕g8+! ♖xg8 25 hxg8♕+ ♔xg8 26 ♖dg1+ ♔f8 27 ♖h8+ ♔e7 ♖xb8 and a draw was agreed several moves later.

A while later it was suggested that White has a big improvement on the above with 18 exd5(!) ♕xd5 19 g5 (19 ♔b1?! bxa3! 20 ♗xf6 ♗xf6!-+) 19...♕a2 20 ♕e3 e5 21 gxf6 ♗xf6 22 ♖g1 (Δ ♕h6) 22...bxa3 23 ♕xa3±.

However then Arkell and Arkell put this into question with 22...exd4! supplying the analysis of 23 ♕h6 ♖xc2+!! (rather than the mousey 23...♗e5 24 ♗d3 bxa3 25 ♖g8+!+-) 24 ♔xc2 ♖c8+ 25 ♔d3 ♕c4+ 26 ♔e4 (White is mated after 26 ♔d2 ♕c2+ 27 ♔e1 ♖e8+) 26...♕e6+ 27 ♔f4 (or again 27 ♔d3 ♕f5+ 28 ♔d2 ♕c2+ -+) 27...♗e5+ 28 ♔g5 ♗f4+ -+.

The big problem for Black seems to be the appearance of the clever finesse 16 ♘d5! (replacing 16 gxh7+), first played in Zso.Polgar-Lindemann, Vienna 1991. Although Black lost this game with 16...♗xd5 17 g5 e5 18 gxf6 ♗xf6 19 gxh7+ ♔h8 20 ♖g1 exd4 21 ♕h6 ♖xc2+ (21...♗e5 22 ♗d3 Δ ♖g8+ as well as exd5) 22 ♔xc2 ♕a4+ 23 ♔d2 ♗e5 24 ♗b5, the obvious plus for White when compared with all of the above is that White's pawn remains flexible on g6 and instead of a later gxh7+ which allows the black king to hide on h8, White retains the option of the more deadly ♕h6. Black's rather surprising difficulty is in creating threats quickly enough, an example being 17...♗b3 (instead of 17...e5) 18 gxf6 fxg6 19 fxg7 ♗xc2 (Alas, 19...♖xc2+? 20 ♕xc2 ♗xc2 21 ♗c4+ is pretty terminal!), when after 20 ♕h6, it is hard to see anything concrete.

b) 15...hxg6. Although I have a feeling that we haven't seen the last of the enterprising 15...b4, the alternative involves a straight choice between recapturing with the f- or h-pawn. Indeed we have already discovered that the latter is possible and often even preferred with White's bishop on d4 (i.e. unable to zap quickly to h6) but, 15...hxg6 did have a dicey reputation due to 16 ♕g5!, pinning Black's b-pawn and preparing ♖d2-h2 followed by ♕h6 or such like. For this reason 16...a6?! really isn't so hot, but 16...♗xg4! as played in Fogaraši-Antal, Budapest 1986 certainly throws the cat amongst the pigeons. The game continued 17 fxg4 (Conceding the dark squared bishop is always dangerous and here is no exception, e.g. 17 ♗xf6?! ♗xf6 18 ♕xg4 ♖xc3! 19 bxc3 ♗xc3 20 ♖d5 ♕xa3+ 21 ♔d1 ♕a1+ 22 ♔e2 ♕e1+ 23 ♔d3 ♕d2 mate) 17...e5 18 ♗f2 ♖xc3! (by now this move should come naturally to the reader, Black being more eager to give, than White is to accept a shattered queenside) 19 ♗e1 ♖xc2 20 ♔xc2 ♕a4+ 21 ♔c1 ♖c8+ 22 ♗c3 ♘xe4 23 ♕e3 ♘xc3+ 24 bxc3 ♕xa3+ (bringing the 'dark one' into the game with ...e4!? now or next go also looks more than adequate) and Black has very good compensation (in terms of dark squares, piece activity and pure pawns) for the rook.

16 g5

Can this move really be wrong? If so, what else? 16 ♘xb5? as ever is rather foolish, losing two pieces for a rook and a pawn, and sure to be devastating for White as rooks are generally poor defenders. 16 ♘d5 is of course possible, laying a course for a familiar type of ending but, as Black has the '...♖a8 and ...b4' trick at his disposal after 16...♕xd2+ 17 ♖xd2, the a7-pawn is immune, giving him a pleasant choice of 17...♘(or ♗)xd5.

Meanwhile Black is ready to continue attacking with 16...b4.

16 ...   ♘h5!

It is somewhat incredible that theory only considers 16...♘e8(?!) when 17 ♗xg7 ♘xg7 18 ♗h3! is '±'. The text, blocking the h-file and eyeing up a later re-entry into the game via f4 or g3, appears much more natural.

17 ♖xh5?!

Perhaps a little ambitious, yet no obvious plan stands out. This move prevents ...♘xg7 but no doubt Black intended meeting 17 ♗xg7 with 17...♔xg7 anyway! Probably 17 ♘d5 is the safest though Black's position remains comfortable.

17 ...   gxh5
18 ♗xg7   ♔xg7
19 ♕d4+   ♔f7

There is a lot of space around the black king, but there are no available white pieces to fill it.

20 ♘d5   ♕a4!

It seems unfair that when Black sacrifices the exchange, he nearly always has compensation, but when White does likewise he is often simply material down. Still, I guess that's just the way it goes!

21 ♕d2

Back she comes with her tail between her legs, but a trade of queens is of course unthinkable.

21 ...   b4

Now back to business. 22 ♘xb4? is of course impossible due to 22...♖xb4!, bearing in mind the mates on a1 and c2.

22 ♕h2   bxa3
23 ♕xh5+   ♔f8 *(116)*

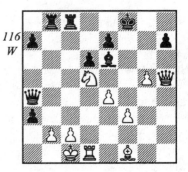

The black king can run to d7 if necessary, but the future of the white king is in rather more doubt.

24 ♗d3   ♖xb2
25 ♕h6+   ♔e8
26 ♔d2   ♗xd5
27 exd5   ♕f4+

0-1

System 2:
9...♗e6 with
10...♘e5

The main aim behind 10...♘e5 after the usual 10 0-0-0 is to try to win White's key dark-squared bishop by first offering a trade of light-squared bishops on c4. The point is of course that should, as a result of this trade, the black knight wind up there, White will be forced reluctantly to relinquish his prized bishop in favour of keeping his queen!

Game 18
Zapata-Miles
Brussels 1986

1	e4	c5
2	♘f3	d6
3	d4	cxd4
4	♘xd4	♘f6
5	♘c3	g6
6	♗e3	♗g7
7	f3	0-0
8	♕d2	♘c6
9	g4	♗e6
10	0-0-0	

As well as 10...♘xd4, a good reply to 10 ♗e2?! is 10...♖c8, the game continuation in Balashov-Enklaar, Wijk aan Zee 1973, being 11 h4 ♘e5 12 ♘xe6?! fxe6 13 h5 ♕a5 14 hxg6 hxg6 15 ♘b5?! ♕xb5 16 ♗xb5 ♘xf3+ 17 ♔d1

♘xd2 leaving Black already a pawn to the good and with more to follow.

The big question though must be whether 10 ♘xe6 is a good idea. Whilst this move gains a bishop for a knight and it could be argued weakens the Black pawn structure, the answer must still be 'No' (and note in contrast to 9 0-0-0 ♗e6?! 10 ♘xe6!). The problem is that Black obtains a firm grip on d5 and also now has the use of the f-file, to amongst other things pressurize the severely weakened f3-pawn. After 10 ♘xe6?! fxe6 two practical examples are:

a) 11 ♗c4 d5 (11...♕c8!? Δ...♘e5 or ...♘a5) 12 exd5 ♘e5 13 ♗e2 ♘xd5 14 ♘xd5 exd5 15 0-0-0 e6∓ Varga-Piriši, Hungary 1992. White has the two bishops and less pawn islands. However Black has two very useful half-open files, and as b2 will soon come under pressure as well, it is him with the edge.

b) 11 0-0-0 ♘e5 12 ♗e2 ♖c8 13 ♘b5 (played to prevent ...♕a5, e.g. 13 h4?! ♕a5 14 h5 ♘fxg4! 15 fxg4 ♘f3! 16 ♗xf3 ♖xc3 when the hanging white bishop on f3 helps give extra weight to a strong attack) 13...♕d7!? (Δ 14...♘xf3) 14 ♘a3 b5! 15 ♖hf1 (or 15 ♗xb5?! ♕b7 16 ♗e2 when greed is punished nicely by 16...♘xf3! 17 ♗xf3 ♘xe4! 18 ♗d4 ♖xf3 and Black is a pawn up with a superb position) 15...♘c4 16 ♘xc4 bxc4 17 c3 (or else this move would

soon have been on Black's agenda)
17...♛a4 18 ♚b1 ♜c6 and White is
in big trouble; Sveshnikov-Van der
Wiel, Sochi 1980.

10 ...   ♜c8

Although I am actually advocating 10...♞e5 here, the text is eminently playable and this game in
particular demonstrates a few extra
available ideas for Black, should
White make an early capture on e6
(i.e. ♞xe6).

11 g5   ♞h5
12 ♞xe6   fxe5
13 ♝h3   ♛d7
14 f4 *(117)*

Played to prevent ...♞e5 which
would have threatened both
...♞xf3 and ...♞c4.

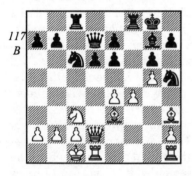

117
B

14 ...   ♝xc3!?

As Black has some space around
his king, and the h-file remains
firmly blocked, he can afford to
concede his pride and joy. In fact
White finds this move fairly hard
to handle. However, the same cannot be said of the natural
14...♞a5?! which enables White to

utilize the slightly awkward pin on
the e6-pawn (one of the few things
going for him) with 15 ♛d5!.

15 ♛xc3

After the ugly 15 bxc3, Black
would do well to prepare ...♞a5
with a move like 15...♜c7!?.

15 ...   ♞xf4

The point behind Black's last
move is clear. Not only has he won
an important pawn, but his knight
is now very much in the action.

16 ♝g4   ♞d8

Satisfactory although 16...b6!?
△...♞a5 also has a certain appeal.

17 ♛b3   ♛c6
18 ♜d4

White rejects a chance to regain
his pawn with 18 ♝xf4 ♜xf4 19
♝xe6+ ♞xe6 20 ♛xe6+ ♚g7! as
Black, with better piece activity
and a superior pawn structure, remains clearly better.

18 ...   ♚g7
19 ♜hd1   e5
20 ♜a4   ♜c7
21 ♜xa7   ♛xe4
22 ♝b6   ♜c4
23 ♝xd8   ♜xd8
24 ♝f3   ♜d4!
25 ♜xb7

The black queen stays dominant,
Black's clever last move ensuring
that 25 ♝xe4?? ♞e2+ 26 ♜xd1 is
mate.

25 ...   ♚f8?!

A slight inaccuracy which
should have let White off the hook.
Correct was the trade of rooks first
with 25...♜xd1+ 26 ♝xd1 and then

26...♔f8. White could now have played 26 ♖xd4 ♕xd4 27 ♕b6!, where in an endgame his bishop and outside passed pawns will be of more use. Fortunately White returns the favour.

    26 a4?!   **♖xd1+**
    27 ♗xd1   **♖c8**

Threatening amongst other things ...♘d3+ followed by ...♘c5.

    28 ♖b8   **♖xb8**
    29 ♕xb8+   **♔f7**
    30 ♕b3+   **d5** *(118)*

Theory tells us to control the centre and to centralize one's pieces, and then any wing play is often easily crushed. The sceptics amongst you would no doubt prefer to see this than to believe it. What is clear here is that while White's best hope is an a-pawn sprint, Black (with piece centralization!) is not only attacking with the most deadly force (queen and knight), but he also has a handy passed pawn of his own.

    31 a5   **♕e1!**
    32 c3

Necessary to prevent both 32...♘e2+ winning the house and 32...♕xa5.

    32 ...   **e4**
Intending simply ...e3-e2.

    33 ♕a4   **♘d3+**
    34 ♔b1   **e3**
    35 ♕b3   **♘f4**
    36 ♔a2   **e2**
    37 ♗xe2   **♕xe2**
    38 ♕b6

White would put up more resistance with 38 ♔a3, but really time is the only variable in question here as the result is in no real doubt.

    38 ...   **♕c3+**
    39 ♔a3   **♘e6**
    40 a6   **♘c5**
    41 b3   **♕xa6+**
        0-1

Game 19
Rytkonen-Ward
Gausdal 1993

    1 e4   **c5**
    2 ♘f3   **d6**
    3 d4   **cxd4**
    4 ♘xd4   **♘f6**
    5 ♘c3   **g6**
    6 ♗e3   **♗g7**
    7 f3   **0-0**
    8 ♕d2   **♘c6**
    9 g4   **♗e6**
    10 0-0-0   **♘e5**
    11 ♔b1

Both 11 h3 and 11 g5 are covered in game 20, with 11 ♗e2 appearing in game 21, but here I would like to discuss the other obvious alternative to the text in 11 h4. While maintaining the attacking option, this move prepares to meet 11...♗c4 with 12 ♗h3 and then 12...♗a6 (△...♘c4), with 13 b3. There is nothing particularly wrong with Black's position then, but instead I would like to concentrate on 11...♕a5!?. This is a favourite of mine, not least because I have had several games like the following which took place in the same tournament six years earlier, Fossan-Ward, Gausdal 1987: 12 ♔b1? *(119)* (12 ♘xe6?! fxe6 13 ♗e2 b5!? 14 a3 ♖ab8 15 h5 b4! 16 ♘a2 ♕a4 17 ♘xb4 a5 18 ♘a6 ♖xb2! 19 ♗d4 {or 19 ♔xb2 ♘xe4 △ 20...♘xc4+ is crushing} 19...♗h6 was easily winning for Black in the quickplay game A.Jackson-Ward, Highbury 1990. Really White should play 12 a3, though this is a weakness and I have then had a lot of success with both 12...♖ac8 and 12...♖fc8, but not 12...♗c4 yet {i.e. a plan to hold back on} as it loses a piece to 13 f4 ♗xf1 14 fxe5 dxe5 15 ♘b3 △ 16 ♖hxf1 or 16 ♖dxf1.)

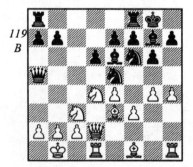

119
B

12...♘xf3!! 13 ♘xf3 ♘xe4! (When White's position looked so solid, and Black had no rooks in play, it is almost hard to believe that such sacrifices can work) 14 ♕d3 (They do though, as Black is still attacking with queen and two bishops, whose diagonals have just been opened. Sure enough, 14 ♘xe4 falls foul of 15...♕xa2+ 16 ♔c1 ♕a1 mate) 14...♘xc3+ 15 bxc3 (15 ♔c1 does not help as on top of 15...♘xd1, Black has 15...♘xa2+ 15 ♔b1 ♘c3+ 16 ♔c1 ♕a1+ 17 ♔d2 ♕xd1 mate) 15...♗xc3 0-1 *(120)*.

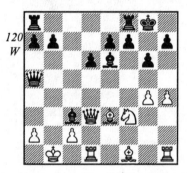

120
W

Yes, unlike a beginner always going for Fool's Mate, I'm quite proud to say that I have finished at this very stage on a few occasions, where several mates are threatened and for example 16 ♕b5 meets its end with 16...♗xa2+ 17 ♔c1 ♕a3+ amongst others.

The text move has been suggested to prevent 11...♕a5, in view of the 12 ♘d5 trick but ...

11 ...   ♕a5!?

Played anyway, although also consistent is 11...♗c4 (intending to win White's dark-squared bishop with 12...♗xf1 and 13...♘c4) 12 ♗d3 when one game of interest continued 12...♖c8 (better than the slightly premature 12...d5?! 13 g5 ♘h5 14 f4 ♗xd3 16 cxd3 ♘c6 16 e5±) 13 h4 b5 14 h5 ♕a5 15 a3?! (15 ♘b3 is the suggested improvement accompanied with the usual assessment of unclear) 15...b4 16 axb4 ♕xb4 17 ♘d5 ♘xd5 18 exd5 ♕xd2 19 ♖xd2 ♘xd3 and Black will be a pawn up and have the two bishops advantage to boot; Savereide-Kudrin, London Lloyds Bank 1984.

12 ♘d5

Obviously 12 ♘b3 loses a pawn to 12...♗xb3 Δ 13...♘xf3 (we have already seen that it is due to this f3 pawn being loose, that keeps a white knight on d4, thus reducing the interest in ♘xe6), whilst 12 g5, as indeed 12 h4?, can be met by 12...♘xf3!! Δ 13...♘xe4! as above.

12 ...   ♕xd2

Off-hand, it looks as though Black has just fallen for one of the oldest tricks, at least in this book. However although I certainly do not consider myself over the hill yet (in 1993!) as a player, it may sound that way when I say that in fact I had waited a long time to get this variation, having prepared it seven years earlier!

13 ♘xe7+

Bearing in mind the game's outcome, perhaps White should try to bale out here with 13 ♘xf6+ ♗xf6 14 ♖xd2, but then the advanced white kingside pawns are more of a weakness than a strength and 14...♘c4 secures Black the two bishops.

13 ...   ♔h8
14 ♖xd2   ♖ae8
15 g5

15 ♘d5 would be treated in the same way as 16 ♘d5.

15 ...   ♘h5
16 ♘d5

Forced as after 16 ♘ef5 gxf5 17 exf5, both 17...♘c4 and 17...♗d5 Δ 18...♘xf3, leave Black significantly up in material.

16 ...   ♗xd5
17 exd5   ♘xf3!

The point. These liquidations leave Black with the more active pieces and the vastly superior bishop.

18 ♘xf3   ♖xe3
19 ♗e2   ♘f4
20 ♗d1   ♘h3! *(121)*

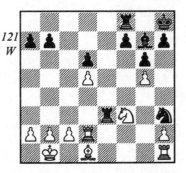

Whilst clearly better here, Black has not lost sight of the fact that the bishops are of opposite colour. For this reason in preventing 21 h4, Black targets the g5-pawn (rather than the far less relevant d5-pawn, which gets in White's way) with the aim of ultimately creating a big kingside majority.

21 ♖g2

Though grovelling around, White is trying to orchestrate some exchanges to relieve the pressure. Unfortunately for him, Black is not so obliging and continues to improve the position of his pieces, whilst preventing any White activity.

21 ...   ♖fe8
22 c3   ♖d3

White's last move was really necessary to avoid back rank mate problems, help blunt the a1-h8 diagonal and to give his bishop some options. However, whilst still not particularly interested in the d5-pawn, Black sees this move as a concession and another square for infiltration.

23 ♗a4   ♖ee3
24 ♖e1   ♖xe1+
25 ♘xe1   ♖e3

Again forsaking an unwanted pawn in order to limit activity, though 25...♖xd5 couldn't be bad.

26 ♘c2   ♖e5

Finally securing the g5-pawn with White's pieces still not exactly at their best.

27 ♘d4   ♘xg5

Just in case White is able to create a passed pawn on the queenside, Black chooses to keep the rooks on (his, of course, still dominating the only open file).

28 ♘b5   ♘e4
29 ♘xa7   f5

Black continues to select the simple option, although it could be argued that more accurate play might have involved capturing the d5-pawn on one of the many occasions (including now) that it was available. The argument though is hardly important as the text method of winning appears to be sufficient.

30 c4   ♘c5
31 ♗d1   ♖e1
32 ♔c2   ♗xb2
33 ♔xb2   ♖xd1 *(122)*

0-1

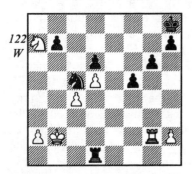

122
W

In this position White lost on time, having used up the allocated two hours, but with still seven moves left to play. Probably White wouldn't resign just yet, but with Black's pawn majority far more effective, it is clear that by playing on, he would be fighting a losing battle.

Game 20

Zso.Polgar-Sosonko

Match, Aruba 1991

1 e4	c5
2 ♘f3	d6
3 d4	cxd4
4 ♘xd4	♘f6
5 ♘c3	g6
6 ♗e3	♗g7
7 f3	♘c6
8 ♕d2	0-0
9 g4	♗e6
10 0-0-0	♘e5
11 h3 *(123)*	

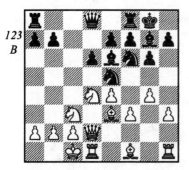

123
B

In playing this move, White signals her intention to change her pawn structure. However, whilst the expected 12 f4 undoubtedly helps control the centre, it is also less aggressive as the most direct route to the black king must be down the h-file. Similar positions to this game can be reached with the slightly more committal 11 g5 ♘h5 12 f4 ♘c4 when, keen (as always) to preserve the dark-squared bishop, White has:

a) 13 ♘xe6 (a rather unambitious move, but probably best if he is playing for a draw!) 13...♘xd2 14 ♘xd8 ♘xf1 15 ♖hxf1 when now the choice is Black's. Does he play safe with 15...♖fxd8= or does he mix things up a little with 15...♗xc3 (a move annotated as '!' by some and '?!' by others)? Then one outing runs 16 ♘xb7 (perhaps White should forget ironing out his pawns and play more dynamically with 16 bxc3 ♖fxd8 17 f5) 16...♗xb2+ 17 ♔xb2 ♖ab8 18 ♖d4 (again maybe 18 ♖d3 is more accurate) 18...♖xb7+ 19 ♔c3 ♖c8+ 20 ♖c4 ♖xc4+ 21 ♔xc4 ♖b2, when Black's active rook and White's weak pawns give him the edge in the endgame; Velimirović-Kudrin, Titograd 1984.

b) 13 ♗xc4 ♗xc4. Here Black should be planning to open up some lines and bring his knight back into play with ...e5, as the temporarily weakened d6-pawn is of little consequence (plus it is likely to be transferred to e5), when weighed up against the counter-play that will be obtained elsewhere. For this reason 14 f5 seems logical (on 14 b3, Black may choose to retreat his bishop to, say, e6, but I quite like the look of opting for complications with

14...e5!?) though this concedes the e5 square, e.g. for the later occupation of the black bishop, in order to both facilitate a knight re-entry, and to reduce the force of f5-f6 break, should it ever come. After 14 f5 I suppose Black should consider 14...♖c8 (14...♖fe8 is solid as it protects e7, dissuades f5-f6 and perhaps prepares an e-pawn push), one idea being 15 b3 ♕a5!? (Δ 16 bxc4 ♕a3+ 17 ♔b1 ♖xc4 with the odd threat!), or even 14...♕a5 and on 15 b3 ♗a6 (or ♖ac8!? or ♖fc8!?). The choices are endless though I agree it is not yet clear as to how many are good!

11 ...	♖c8
12 f4	♘c4
13 ♗xc4	

This confrontation was game one in a six game match. In game five of this match White's improvement of 13 ♘xe6 was (sadly!) sufficient to achieve a draw in 23 moves after 13...fxe6 14 ♗xc4 ♖xc4 15 e5 ♘e8, but with Black's a7-pawn always out of bounds in view of ... b6, Black was never in danger of losing. However this line is not completely dead and both sides must be a little careful with practical chances still remaining.

| 13 ... | ♗xc4 |
| 14 g5 | |

Always when played, this move has its pros and cons. Certainly White stakes a claim for more control over the often key d5-square,

but the g7-bishop is unleashed and this knight on the rim isn't so dim and inevitably makes a re-appearance (often crucial as in this game).

| 14 ... | ♘h5 |
| 15 f5 | b5!? |

Black starts his queenside attack actively, though with ...♘g3 always an option, this aggressive pawn thrust isn't even really a sacrifice.

16 b3	b4
17 ♘b1	♗a6
18 ♕xb4	♕c7
19 c4	

The holes are appearing around the white king, but even with 19...♗xd4 Δ 20...♕xc2 mate the threat, White has absolutely no right to attempt to set up a bind. However with 19...d5 possible against 19 ♖h2 and once again bearing in mind ...♘g3, there is little else.

| 19 ... | ♘g3 |
| 20 ♘c3 (124) | |

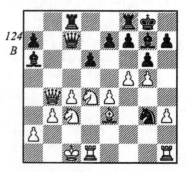

With central control and there being no open files, White is more

than willing to get out of this mess
by giving up the exchange but ...

20 ...	♗xc4!
21 bxc4	♕xc4
22 ♕xc4	♖xc4
23 ♔d2	

If 23 ♔b2 then 23...♖b8+ is even
worse for White.

23 ...	♗xd4
24 ♗xd4	♖xd4+
25 ♔e3	♖c4
26 ♔d3	♖xc3+
27 ♔xc3	♘xe4+
28 ♔d4	♘f2

It must be infuriating for White
to have these pawns removed and
still end up losing the exchange,
but nonetheless with her king so
centralized, she knows that Black
has still a little work to do in order
to convert the whole point.

29 f6	♖e8!

With the black king on the back
rank, a white pawn on f6 could be
a real thorn and so Black wisely
maintains the tension and keeps his
options open.

30 ♖he1	♘xd1
31 fxe7	*(125)*

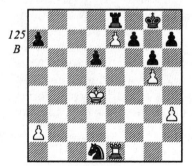

125
B

If 31 ♖xd1, then 31...exf6 32
gxf6 and 32...♖e6, when this pawn
will inevitably drop. Surely then,
the text is White's best try. From
here on in it can be seen just how
cumbersome a creature the knight
can be in endings. Nonetheless
Black takes his time and with a
little bit of care he gets there in the
end.

31 ...	♘f2
32 ♔d5	f5
33 gxf6	♔f7
34 ♖e3	h5
35 ♖f3	♘d1
36 h4	♘b2
37 ♔xd6	♘c4+
38 ♔d5	♘b6+
39 ♔c6	♘c4
40 ♔d5	♖c8
41 ♖f4	♘e3+
42 ♔d6	♘g4
43 ♖a4	♘xf6
44 ♖xa7	♘e8+
45 ♔d5	♖c2
46 a4	♖h2

0-1

The final game in this chapter
is intended to supply the reader
with a few more ideas in this
9...♗e6 and 10...♘e5 system. It is
particularly interesting, not just
because Black wins comfortably,
but because White is guilty of trying to stay solid, and not really
doing anything constructive himself.

Game 21
Yang Xian-Mestel
Lucerne OL 1982

1 e4	c5
2 ♘f3	d6
3 d4	cxd4
4 ♘xd4	♘f6
5 ♘c3	g6
6 ♗e3	♗g7
7 f3	♘c6
8 ♕d2	0-0
9 g4	♗e6
10 0-0-0	♘e5
11 ♗e2	*(126)*

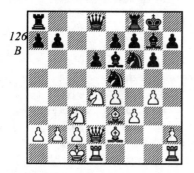

126
B

A cautious move. White over-protects his f3-pawn, so that he is able to move his d4-knight if need be. It also looks as though he may be questioning the security of a knight on h5 (e.g. g5 △ f4), but this is doubtful as White's light-squared bishop must always keep guard on c4.

| 11 ... | ♖c8 |

12 ♔b1	♗c4
13 ♘b3	♕c7
14 ♗d4	♖fd8
15 ♖he1	b5!

Of course this pawn is immune as White's f3-pawn is always hanging. It appears that White has 'set out his stall', with the message of 'Come and get me'. So Black has started the process of chiselling away, and this aggressive outburst provokes a reaction of a rare weakening move (in terms of squares conceded). However White's c3-knight is a little pushed for space.

16 g5	♘h5
17 ♘d5	♕d7!?

Black appreciates that he can handle a white knight on d5 for the moment and so refrains from exchanging it off until another concession is made.

18 f4	♗xd5
19 exd5	♘c4
20 ♕c1	

White would like to claim that it is his turn now to hold back purposefully from 20 ♗xc4, but in fact this move would put him in hot water due to 20...bxc4 intending a timely ...c4-c3. Note 20... ♖xc4 would also be good for Black, as the weak points c2,d5 and f4, outweigh the one on e7.

| 20 ... | ♕h3! *(127)* |

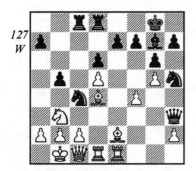

The black queen protects the h5-knight and threatens to wreak havoc on the white kingside, whilst being easily transferable to the attack on the queenside.

21	♗xh5	♕xh5
22	♗xg7	♔xg7
23	♖xe7	♖e8

White jumped at the chance to win a pawn, indeed making the e7-rook White's only active piece. Black now offers to trade it for his only inactive piece, knowing only too well that further greed on White's part would allow a significantly more dangerous penetration of the seventh rank. i.e. 24 ♖xa7?! ♖e2 with both ...♘e3 and ...♕xh2 threatened. A lot has been said about Black's manoeuvring of a

knight to c4, in order to gain a white bishop and facilitate the doubling of the black rooks. However perhaps not enough has been mentioned of the attacking power of this knight should it get to stay there. Generally in all openings c4, c5, f4 and f5 are terrific squares for knights and if White didn't know that before this game, you can rest assured that he does now!

24	♖de1	♖xe7
25	♖xe7	♕xh2
26	a3	♔f8
27	♖e1	

Once more 27 ♖xa7 is just not on, this time in view of 27...♕f2! △ 28...♖e8-e1.

27 ...		♕f2

Turning the screws. For White now, non-losing moves are not easy to come by.

28	♖h1	♘e3
29	♘d4	♕xf4
30	♕d2	♖c4

0-1

The pressure on both c2 and d4 is too much. For example 31 c3 ♕e4+ −+ and 31 ♖e1 ♖xd4 32 ♕xe3 ♖d1+ 33 ♔a2 ♕c4+ 34 b3 ♕xc2 mate.

7   Yugoslav Attack 9 0-0-0

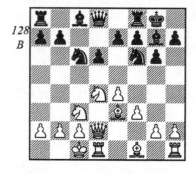

128
B

Although 9 ♗c4 is probably White's most popular choice, 9 0-0-0 certainly seems to me to be the most natural continuation. I mean, why should White fiddle around with other moves when he knows that he is going to castle queenside? The answer to this may lie with 9...d5!?, a move which I couldn't believe at first but over the years have slowly come around to consider as the best. Simple analysis tells us that it is a gambit (though rarely accepted) and several variations are analysed in system 1.

A not unreasonable alternative is 9...♘xd4 Δ 10 ♗xd4 ♗e6, which provides similar positions to those seen in chapter 6 (system 1), and is covered in some detail under system 2.

System 1: 9...d5!?

As mentioned above, the most pertinent observation on this rather brash move (first introduced by the Russian master Alexander Konstantinov, possibly after a few pints!) is that immediately a pawn is offered to the cause. The first encounter shows that this is only the first of the sacrifices played, if White is brave (or stupid?) enough to take up the challenge.

Game 22
Anelli-Lotti
Corr. 1983-85

1	e4	c5
2	♘f3	d6
3	d4	cxd4
4	♘xd4	♘f6
5	♘c3	g6
6	♗e3	♗g7
7	f3	♘c6
8	♕d2	0-0
9	0-0-0	d5!? (129)

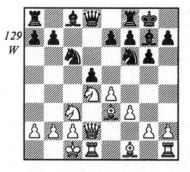

129
W

10 exd5

10 h4?!, ignoring the central rumblings, and 10 ♕e1!? are covered in game 27. Assuming that Black is simply threatening to weaken White's pawn structure with 10...dxe4, I guess the only other real alternative is 10 ♘xc6. Then after 10...bxc6, 11 ♗h6 is discussed in the 'cowardly' ♗h6 game (number 23), whereas an attempt to transpose to the text with 11 exd5?! can (if preferred) possibly be exposed as inaccurate by 11...♕a5!?, a favourable example of this being the juicy game Voitsik-Rusinkevich, Riga 1954 which continued 12 dxc6?! (pushing his luck, 12 ♗c4 being the safer option) 12...♗e6 13 a3 ♖fd8 14 ♕e2 ♖xd1+ 15 ♕xd1 ♖d8 16 ♕e2 ♘d5 17 ♘xd5 ♕xd5 (with White's pieces out of play and Black's not, a storm is brewing!) 18 c7 ♗xb2+! (*voilà!*) 0-1.

10 ...   ♘xd5
11 ♘xc6   bxc6
12 ♘xd5

With the pressure building up on c3 as well as e3, White chooses to de-isolate the black c-pawn (for which compensation was present in terms of a half-open b-file). Although the black knight is well posted on d5, many regard this move as a cop-out and look to 12 ♗d4 (the subject of games 24-26) to search for an advantage.

12 ...   cxd5
13 ♕xd5?! (*130*)

A bit greedy, but at this stage 13 ♗h6 (see game 23) is White's only playable alternative. I say this because Black is preparing to do a lot of damage to White's queenside, and with 13 h4?! △ h5 being far too slow, he would be wise to seek exchanges.

13 ...   ♕c7

Trading queens would be completely dumb, but the reader will no doubt observe that there appears to be a rook *en prise* in the corner! On 14 ♕xa8?! Black has 14...♗f5 when bearing in mind the mate on c2, the white queen is lost. Nonetheless after 15 ♕xf8+ ♔xf8, if we get all materialistic, we could say that White is two 'points' up. In practice, though, the white rooks are no match for the black queen (when as here accompanied by two bishops) and even with best play, Black's chances remain the better (whilst poor defence will prove fatal), e.g. 16 ♖d2 (or 16 ♗d3? ♕e5 is not far off winning for Black)

16...h5!? 17 ♗e2 (again 17 ♗d3? ♕e5!) 17...♕b8 (perhaps 17...♔g8!? is a worthwhile precaution) 18 b3 (if 18 c3 ♗xc3! and similarly if 18 c4 ♗c3!) 18...♗c3 19 ♖d5 ♗e6 20 ♖c5 ♕b4 21 ♔b1 ♗f6 and with 22...♕a3 a threat, Black maintains the initiative.

14 ♕c5

White must tread carefully as he will soon be attacked by two rooks, two bishops and a queen!

14 ... ♕b7!

15 b3

Undoubtedly the most instinctive response, advancing the b2-pawn out of danger, though creating the odd hole. As this is a fairly critical position, it seems only reasonable to consider White's defensive alternatives:

a) 15 ♕b5?!. A move deemed as pretty bad by 'old' theory, but as we can see in this respect history has a habit of repeating itself. 15...♕xb5 16 ♗xb5 ♖b8 17 ♗c4 ♗xb2+ 18 ♔d2 ♗f5!? 19 ♗xa7 ♖bc8 20 ♗b3 ♖c7 21 ♗e3 ♖fc8 and Black has the advantage in the endgame which in Van Riemsdijk-Kir.Georgiev, Manila IZ 1990 he duly converted into a win in 78 moves!

b) 15 c3? opens up another crucial diagonal and hence encourages some lovely combinations. For example 15...♗f5 16 ♕b5 ♕c7 17 ♕c4 (not 17 ♕c5?? ♕xc5 18 ♗xc5 ♗h6+ –+) 17...♕e5 18 ♗d2 ♖fd8 19 f4 ♕a5 20 ♗e2 ♖ac8 21 ♕b3 (or 21 ♕a6? ♗xc3+! 0-1 Byvshev-Beilin, Leningrad 1955; 22 ♕xa5 ♗xd2 is mate and 22 bxc3 ♖xc3+ 23 ♔b2 ♖c2+ 24 ♔b3 ♖b8+ soon will be) 21...♖b8 22 ♕c4 ♕a3!! 23 bxa3 ♖b1 mate.

c) 15 ♗d4?! is a natural attempt to block out the Dragon bishop, but there just isn't the time and now Black's moves practically play themselves. 15...♗f5 16 ♗d3 ♖fc8 17 ♕a3 ♗xd4 18 ♗xf5 ♖c3!! 19 ♗e4 (19 ♕a4 will at least leave White a piece down after 19...♗e3+ whilst 19 bxc3 ♗e3+ 20 ♖d2 gxf5 21 c4 f4 leaves him in a horrendous pin from which not even Houdini could escape) 19...♕b6 20 ♕xe7 (if 20 bxc3 now then 20...♗e3+ 21 ♖d2 ♖b8! 22 ♕b3 ♗xf2+ 23 ♔xf2 ♕f2+ is winning) 20...♖xc2+!! 21 ♗xc2 (as 21 ♔xc2 ♕xb2+ 22 ♔d3 ♕c3+ 24 ♔e2 ♕e3+ 25 ♔f1 ♕f2 is mate) 21...♕xb2+ 22 ♔d2 ♕c3+ 23 ♔c1 ♖c8 24 ♕e4 (the only move as 24 ♖d2 allows 24...♕a1 mate) 24...♕a3+ 25 ♔d2 ♖xc2+!! (again absolutely beautiful) 26 ♔e1 ♕c3+ 0-1 Tolnai-Perenyi, Budapest 1981.

d) 15 ♕a3! is the only correct defence after which if White doesn't stray from the straight and narrow, he might be able to get a draw! Black's most active is probably 15...♗f5 when 16 ♗a6! is forced (e.g. 16 ♗d3 ♖fb8!? 17 c3 ♗xc3!) after which follows 16...♕c7 17 ♕c5 (alas this bugging queen move really forces a swap, but it can be on favourable grounds) 17...♕b6! 18 ♕xb6 axb6 19 ♗c4 ♖fc8 20 ♗b3 ♖xa2! 21 ♖d8+! (21 ♗xa2?? meets a familiar fate: 21...♖xc2+ 22 ♔b1 ♖xb2+ 23 ♔a1 ♖d2+ 24 ♗d4 ♗xd4 mate) 21...♖xd8 22 ♗xa2 ♖a8 23 ♖d1! (again the only move as 23 ♔b1 allows 23...♗xc2+! leading to a very good and probably winning endgame for Black) preparing to meet 23...♖xa2?? with 24 ♖d8+ ♗f8 25 ♗h6+-. White has a queenside majority and the b6-pawn is a little weak, but Black's pressure on the queenside balances things up and he should consider 23...h5 and 23...b5.

15 ...   ♗f5
16 ♗c4

Trying to post the bishop actively, whilst blocking off the c-file. 16 ♗d3 is the other move that springs to mind when a couple of moves down the line Black has a brilliancy at his disposal: 16...♖ac8 17 ♕xa7 ♕b5!! 18 ♗xf5 (18 ♗xb5? ♖xc2+ 19 ♔b1 ♖c4+! 20 ♖d3 ♗xd3 mate and 18 c4 ♕e5-+) 18...♕xf5 and Black has an excellent position due to his dual threats 19...♕xc2 mate and 19...♖a8 Δ 20...♖xa2.

16 ...   ♖ac8
17 ♕d5 *(131)*

17 ♕xa7? is punished by 17...♖xc4! 18 ♕xb7 (18 bxc4 allowing 18...♕b2+ also looks pretty hopeless) 18...♖xc2+ 19 ♔b1 ♖c6+! 20 ♖d3 ♗xd3 mate.

17 ...   ♖xc4!

Played anyway, with 18 ♕xb7? losing as above.

18 ♕xc4   ♖c8
19 ♗c5   h5!

Dissuading g4, securing h6 if need be for the bishop and above all freeing the rook from back rank duties.

20 ♖he1   e5

The a1-h8 diagonal is not blocked for good, the text move merely providing the option of ...♗f8.

21 ♖e2   a5!

With his c2-pawn now defended White planned 22 ♕b4. The text prevents both this and b3-b4.

22 a3   ♗e6
23 ♕c3   ♕b5!

0-1

Here White called it a day, but it appears somewhat prematurely as he should continue with 24 ♖xe5!. Evidently he didn't quite appreciate the chances that can be drummed up when Black is without his dark-squared bishop. For example 24...♗xe5 25 ♕xe5 ♕xc5?? 26 ♖d8+ +-. Instead Black should try 25...♗xb3! Δ 26...♗xc2-+ and after 26 ♗d4 ♖xc2+ 27 ♔b1 ♕xe5 28 ♗xe5 f6 29 ♗xf6 ♖xg2 he has the superior ending as his king will be the more active; if 30 ♖d7 then 30...♗c2+! Δ 31 ♖xh2∓.

The next game features some lines in which White appears to 'chicken out' and seeks an early exchange of bishops with ♗h6. I suppose bearing in mind how effective the long a1-h8 diagonal can be for Black, White cannot be blamed even if his play is a bit boring. In fact even without the dark duo it is surprising just how much excitement can be generated, although perhaps not when we remember that 'coming at us' down the h-file is the usual ploy and this is the fastest route into the attack for the white queen.

Game 23
Kuijf-Rechlis
Beersheva 1987

1	e4	c5
2	♘f3	d6
3	d4	cxd4
4	♘xd4	♘f6
5	♘c3	g6
6	♗e3	♗g7
7	f3	0-0
8	♕d2	♘c6
9	0-0-0	d5!?
10	exd5	

The other main ♗h6 variation is 10 ♘xc6 bxc6 11 ♗h6 when 11...♗xh6 12 ♕xh6 ♕b6!? is critical. Obviously Black is not afraid of sacrificing the d5-pawn, when previously he had offered it to a white queen (not a rook) which could more easily return to defensive duties. The big question then, is whether the white queen is out of play or very much in play! 13 e5 logically removes a key defender and then 13...♘d7 14 h4 gets on with it. However, as can be seen Black can take on e5, as he still has the odd trick up his sleeve. e.g. 14...♘xe5 15 h5 ♗f5 16 g4 f6! *(132)*

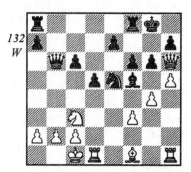

132
W

(The point. If now 17 gxf5? g5 and the white queen is not only out of play, but in view of ...♘f7, is unlikely to be on the board for much longer! Now in addition to being surrounded by potential defenders, the black king could also run away in the unlikely event of it coming to that.) 17 ♕f4 ♖ab8 18 b3 ♗d7 19 hxg6 ♘xg6 20 ♕h6 ♖f7 21 ♗d3 ♖g7 and Black is now solid on the kingside and hence free to continue working on the queenside and in the centre.

    10 ...   **♘xd5**
    11 ♘xc6   **bxc6**
    12 ♘xd5   **cxd5**
    13 ♗h6 *(133)*

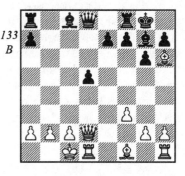

133
B

    13 ...   **♗xh6!**
    14 ♕xh6   **♕a5**
    15 ♔b1   **e5**

No doubt the reader may wonder whether now (in light of the ferocious attacking about to evolve) is the right time for Black to be simply putting his pawns in the centre. The real purpose for this move will soon be disclosed and the very sensible 15...♖b8 will transpose to the text.

    16 h4   **♖b8**
    17 h5

Not hanging around. More recently though in Podlesnik-Justin, Yugoslavia 1989, White was a little more subtle in trying to prevent Black's next move with 17 ♗d3. Then came 17...e4 18 fxe4 ♕b4 19 b3 dxe4 20 ♗e2 ♕c5! 21 h5 g5 22 ♖hf1?! (22 ♕f6 ♖b6 23 ♕d4 ♕xd4 24 ♖xd4 f5 leads to some interesting pawn races) 22...♖b6 23 ♖f6 (the problem is that with this queen and rook alignment, White has trouble in drumming up threats fast enough) 23...♗e6! 24 c4? (bad, but there is now little that White can do about the rapidly growing pressure on b3) 24...♕e3 (threatening 25... ♖xb3+ 26 axb3 ♕xb3+ 27 ♔a1 ♕a3+ 28 ♔b1 ♖b8+ 29 ♔c2 ♕b2 mate) 25 ♗d3 exd3 26 ♖df1 d2 27 ♖g6+ hxg6 28 hxg6 ♖xb3+ 0-1.

    17 ...   **♗f5**

Not for the first time we see this 'aggressive' defensive move called in to guard against a mate on h7. Note now that 18 g4? is just asking for 18...♗xc2+! 19 ♔xc2 ♖xb2+! 20 ♔xb2 (20 ♔c1 ♕c3 mate and 20 ♔d3 ♕a3 mate) 20...♖b8+ 21 ♔c2 ♕xa2+ 22 ♔d3 ♖b3 mate.

    18 ♗d3   **e4**

The idea behind 15...e5. Black keeps the bishops on, hence maintaining a latent attack on the c2-pawn, whilst still covering h7. With all that said and done, 18...♕c3 also looks fairly handy as it seems to force 19 ♕c1 (19 b3?!

e4 20 fxe4 dxe4 21 ♗e2 ♖fc8 22
♖c1 e3 and Goodnight Charlie!)
when after 19...e4 again it is Black
doing all of the pressurizing.

19 hxg6   ♗xg6
20 ♗e2   ♖fc8

It has to be said that things aren't
exactly looking rosy for White as
Black is taking full advantage of
the two half-open files, donated to
him by his opponent in the opening.

21 ♕e3   ♖c3

Making White feel the pain and
holding back on ...exf3.

22 ♕d4   ♕a3
23 b3 *(134)*

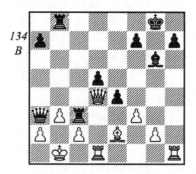

23 ...   ♖xc2!
24 ♔xc2   ♕xa2+
25 ♕b2

On 25 ♔c1 ♖xb3 △...♖b1 mate
is just one way to guarantee the
win.

25 ...   e3+!

A nice touch before the finale.
Now after 26 ♗d3, 26...♖c8 is actually mate!

26 ♔c1   ♖c8+
27 ♗c4   ♖xc4+!
            0-1

Beautiful and leading to a forced
mate in two.

Although I am going to refrain
from passing judgement on the two
less mainstream twelfth move
Black alternatives covered in the
next game, I consider including
them as a useful exercise, if only as
food for thought. However if indeed the reader prefers either
12...♗xd4 (an old move with a bad
reputation, but recently resurrected) or 12...♘xc3 (a newish idea
that leads to a position of which the
assessment seems to be constantly
changing and certainly isn't unfavourable to Black this week!) to the
move I am suggesting, 12...e5 (see
games 25 and 26), then so be it.

Game 24
I.Gurevich-Rogers
London Lloyds Bank 1992

1 e4	c5
2 ♘f3	d6
3 d4	cxd4
4 ♘xd4	♘f6
5 ♘c3	g6
6 ♗e3	♗g7
7 f3	♘c6
8 ♕d2	0-0
9 0-0-0	d5!?
10 exd5	♘xd5
11 ♘xc6	bxc6
12 ♗d4 *(135)*	

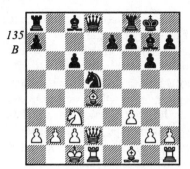

135
B

12 ...   ♗xd4

This move played in this position certainly appears to be a little illogical. Black trades off what is often his trump card while centralizing the white queen at the same time. As always Black has the half-open b-file as a useful tool for attack, but simple exchanges must favour White as he clearly has the superior pawn structure. Indeed Black might easily be made to suffer in a basic endgame because of his isolated a- and c-pawns.

The most recent well-documented outing with 12...♘xc3 was in the game Fernandez-Tolnai, Komotini 1992 which continued with 13 ♕xc3 ♗h6+ 14 ♗e3 ♗xe3+ 15 ♕xe3 ♕b6 (This pawn sacrifice is currently a popular Dragon topic, the views on which I am sure will switch between ∓ or ∓ to ± or ± a few more times before a general consensus of opinion is reached) 16 ♕xe7 (16 ♕c3 is playable, but 16 ♕xb6?!, iron-

ing out Black's pawns, is no problem) 16...♗e6 17 ♕f6 (17 ♕a3 is another commonly played queen retreat while 17 ♗d3 should certainly come into the reckoning) 17...♗xa2 18 b3 (critical but hardly forced with 18 ♗d3 being a sensible option) 18...a5!? (quite possibly preferable to the main alternative 18...♗xb3) 19 ♗c4 ♖a7 20 h4 a4 21 h5 axb3 22 cxb3 (On 22 h6?, the mate on g7 can be stopped with the advantage after 22...b2+ 23 ♔d2 ♖d8+ 24 ♗d3 ♕d4) 22...♕e3+ 23 ♔b2 ♕f2+ 24 ♔c3?! ♗xb3! 25 ♗xb3 ♖b7 26 ♕d6 ♕b6 27 ♕a3 ♖fb8 28 ♖b1 ♕e3+ 29 ♔c2 ♕e2+ 30 ♔c1 ♕xg2 31 ♗xf7+ (Black is now very much on top and 31 ♖d1 ♕xf3 leaves things no different) 31...♔xf7 32 hxg6+ ♕xg6 33 ♕a2+ ♔f6 34 ♕a1+ ♔f5 35 ♖xb7? ♕g5+! 36 ♔d1 ♖xb7 37 ♕a5+ ♖b5 38 ♕a2 0-1. Here White's flag dropped in a lost position (after, say, 38...♖d5+). Bearing in mind the time limit for most of the games in this book is forty moves in two hours, followed by twenty moves in one hour (and only then perhaps some sort of quickplay finish, though with a minimum of half an hour extra added), the reader may be surprised at how often one side may lose on time. It is of course true that many of the opening moves are 'theory' but when players do eventually reach a position that is new to them, there is usually so much to be considered and indeed so many vital decisions to be made that time trouble is not uncommon.

13 ♕xd4   ♕b6
14 ♘xd5

Back in Voroshilovgrad in 1955 this whole Black idea was written off after the game Suetin-Vasiukov in which White played the apparently stronger 14 ♘a4 and was clearly better after 14...♕a5 15 b3 ♖b8 16 ♕c5 ♕xc5 17 ♘xc5 ♖e8 18 ♖d2 ♔f8 19 ♗d3, the pawn structure remaining as his key advantage. However Rogers argues that the counterplay missing can be obtained with 15...♗f5! as on 16 ♕c5 there is 16...♕xc5 17 ♘xc5 ♘c3 and if 16 g4 Black has 16...♗e6 17 ♕c5 ♕c7 or even maybe 16...♗xc2!?.

14 ...   cxd5
15 ♕xd5?! *(136)*

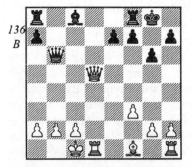

As White was only really in need of a draw here due to his Grand-master norm aspirations, he would no doubt have been better off with say 15 ♕xb6 axb6 16 a3 when I suppose '=' is a fair assessment. As it is, he grabs a risky pawn and as a result has his queen booted all over the place, whilst his kingside has no time to develop.

15 ...   ♗e6
16 ♕d4   ♕a5
17 a3?!

Missing a rare chance to bring a piece out, but 17 ♗c4 ♖ad8 18 ♕h4 ♗xc4 19 ♕xc4 ♕g5+ 20 ♔b1 ♕xg2 leaves Black slightly better as this time it is him with the better pawn structure.

17 ...   ♖fd8
18 ♕b4   ♕g5+!

Black doesn't let up, with the obvious 19 f4 being met by 19...♖xd1+ 20 ♔xd1 ♖d8+ 21 ♔c1 ♕d5, keeping an eye on the g2-pawn whilst threatening mate on d1 and an invasion on a2.

19 ♖d2   a5

How frustrating for White. If only he had time for ♗d3.

20 ♕c3   ♖ac8
21 h4   ♕f4
22 ♔d1? *(137)*

A reflex action losing by force, but hoping to grovel on after 22...♖xc3 23 ♖xd8+ ♔g7 24 bxc3∓. One alternative, 22 ♕xa5, still left Black very much in the driving seat after 22...♗b3 23 ♔d1 ♗xc2+.

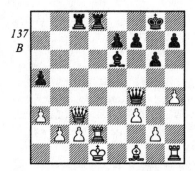

137
B

22 ...   ♗d5!!

Grandmasterly play from a Grandmaster! Mr Rogers has got better things to do than hang around trying to win some fiddly queen vs two rooks endgame.

23 ♕xa5   ♗xf3+
24 ♔c1   ♗e4

Threatening the crushing 25...♖xc2+.

25 c4   ♗xg2!
26 ♗xg2   ♖xc4+
27 ♔d1   ♖xd2+

0-1

28 ♕xd2 ♖d4 just about wraps things up.

Game 25
Dolmatov-Schneider
Budapest 1982

1 e4	c5
2 ♘f3	d6
3 d4	cxd4
4 ♘xd4	♘f6
5 ♘c3	g6
6 ♗e3	♗g7
7 f3	0-0
8 ♕d2	♘c6

9 0-0-0	d5!?
10 exd5	♘xd5
11 ♘xc6	bxc6
12 ♗d4	e5

Black, who is keen on keeping the dark-squared bishops on, temporarily blocks his own in. However he is well aware that if he correctly times ...e5-e4 then he may 'free the beast' with a devastating effect.

13 ♗c5   ♗e6 *(138)*

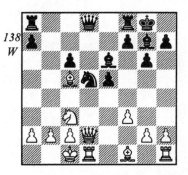

138
W

If he has not already done so, then certainly by the end of these next few games the reader will have got the impression that Black is only too happy to trade a rook for a white bishop. First of all, let me stress that I do not want you to get carried away. Even in this opening, rooks are still those pieces which in endgames do zap impressively around the board, capturing enemy pawns on light-squares and dark-squares alike. However in these type of Dragon middlegames, bishops do appear to have a certain charm and their dual attacking and defensive qualities often go some way to ensuring that an endgame is never reached or that it is reached with material balance at least re-established.

Although I definitely believe in 13...♗e6, I found it particularly interesting when not so long ago, two Dragon experts clashed. As both players played 1 e4, a Dragon was inevitable and indeed a 9 0-0-0 Yugoslav Attack arose with 13...♖e8 rather than 13...♗e6. The reason that I don't like this move is that after 14 ♘xd5 cxd5 15 ♕xd5 ♕xd5 16 ♖xd5 ♗e6, all that Black can realistically hope for is a draw. However instead of 14 ♘xd5, the game in question, Tiviakov-Ernst, Gausdal 1992, continued 14 ♘e4 f5 15 ♘d6 ♗f8 16 ♘xe8 ♗xc5 17 c4 ♕b6 18 ♔b1 ♘e3 19 ♘f6+ ♔f8 20 ♕d7 ♘xd1 21 ♘xh7+ ♔g8 22 ♘f6+ ♔f8 23 ♘h7+ ½-½. Afterwards, International Master John Emms observed that a quick glance at clock times (1.45-0.09!) shows us who spent their energy at the board, and who had been burning the midnight oil. The amusing story behind all this is that Grandmaster Thomas Ernst (known to many as 'The Hit Man') emerged from the *post-mortem* grinning and exclaimed "The Dragon, it's always a draw!". Now I wouldn't have told you this if I hadn't later that day opened up my latest *Informator* only to see a convincing

Dragon victory with Ernst having the white pieces!

14 ♘e4

Back to the point in question which here is 14 ♗xf8?!. After 14...♕xf8 (when Black is incidentally immediately threatening 15...♗h6), White might for example try:

a) 15 ♔b1 a5 (or 15...♖b8!? is maybe even more to the point) 16 ♘xd5 cxd5 17 ♗b5 ♕c5 18 ♗a4 e4 and if 19 ♗b3 e3∓.

b) 15 ♘xd5 cxd5 16 ♕a5 (hoping to prevent Black's attack from flowing freely) 16...♕e7 17 ♖d3 (attempting to transfer the rook to where it might reduce the force of Black's queen, rook, and two bishops) 17...e4 18 ♖b3 d4 19 ♖b5 d3!? 20 cxd3 ♖c8+ 21 ♔b1 exf3 22 gxf3 ♗f5 23 ♖xf5 (being so tied up, this is necessary, hence re-iterating the power of the bishops) 23...gxf5 24 d4 ♗xd4 25 ♗a6 ♖b8 26 b3 ♗g7 (△ 27...♕f6) 27 ♕xf5 ♕a3 and White could have resigned here in Tokarov-Gufeld, Odessa 1957.

At best a transposition into (b) above would occur after 14 ♘xd5?!, as after 14...cxd5, how else could White justify giving Black a beautiful centre, other than by snatching the exchange with 15 ♗xf8 (or 15 ♗b5 ♖b8)?

The text move of 14 ♘e4 sees White ignoring the hanging f8-rook, whilst removing the temptation of the weak ♘xd5. Instead White prevents a possible ...♕a5, perhaps prepares to expel the black knight with c4, and certainly whilst temporarily stopping ...e4, ultimately looks to take up d6 or g5 as residence for the knight. Probably White's only sensible alternative to this is 14 ♗c4 after which Black has two interesting possibilities:

a) 14...♕h4!? 15 ♗xd5 cxd5 16 ♗xf8 (we now know that White should be more wary of this materialistic option) 16...♖xf8 17 g3 ♕c4 18 ♕d3 d4 (something else that shouldn't go unmentioned is just how good two bishops can be in the endgame) 19 ♕xc4 ♗xc4 20 ♘e4 ♗e2 21 ♖d3 (and White, aware of the potential avalanche of black pawns, opts to return the exchange) 21...f5 22 ♘d2 ♗xd3 23 cxd3 ♔f7. Black's bishop for knight advantage might be enough for the win and, in Zapata-Diaz, Capablanca Memorial 1988, indeed was in 83 moves!

b) 14...♘xc3 (a safe and solid alternative) 15 ♕xc3 ♕g5+ 16 ♗e3 (on 16 ♔b1? e4 is perfectly timed) 16...♕xg2 17 ♗xe6 fxe6 when due to the weak points f3 and c2, the chances in practice favour Black, e.g. 18 ♖hf1?! (better is 18 ♕xc6 ♖ac8 when 19 ♕xe6+?! ♔h8 is ∓ and 19 ♕e4! ♖xf3 20 ♖hf1! is dynamically equal) 18...e4 19 ♕xc6 exf3 20 ♕xe6+ ♔h8 21 ♖f2 ♖ae8 22 ♕d5 ♕g4 23 ♗xa7 ♖e2 24 ♕b3 ♖c8! 25 ♖xe2 fxe2 26 ♖e1 ♕f4+ 27 ♗e3 ♕f1 28 ♕b4 ♖d8 0-1 Tu-murhuyag-Schneider, Ulan Bator 1982.

14 ...   ♖b8!? *(139)*

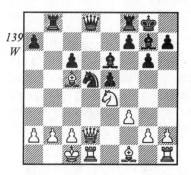

The main alternative 14...♖e8 remains very playable, but the text brings a rook quickly into the attack. As usual Black loses no sleep over 15 ♗xf8 after which one line of play might be 15...♕xf8 16 ♕a5 f5!? 17 ♘c5 e4 18 c3 (18 ♘xe6 ♗xb2+ 19 ♔d2 ♕h6+ 20 f4 ♗c3+ -+) 18...♗xc3! 19 bxc3 ♕h6+ 20 ♖d2 ♖b1+ 21 ♔xb1 ♕xd2 22 ♘a4 (22 ♕d8+ ♔g7 23 ♘a4 ♘xc3+ -+) 22...♘e3 23 a3 ♕c2+ 24 ♔a1 ♕c1 mate. In addition, it is very unlikely that White will be seeking an exchange of a-pawns with 15 ♗xa7? ♖a8.

15 g4

The object of this move is to try to discourage ...f5 whilst possibly hoping to prevent it for good with 16 g5. Both 15 c4 and 15 ♗c4 are looked at in game 26, but for the time being I would like to supply the reader with a nice demonstration of how to handle the black pieces. Here White opts for the other aggressive kingside pawn thrust: 15 h4 f5 (15...♛c7!? preparing 16...♖fd8 is also sensible) 16 ♘g5 e4 (straight to the point, with 16 ♘xe6?? losing to 16...♗xb2+ 17 ♔b1 ♗c3+ 18 ♔d2 ♖b1+! 19 ♔xb1 ♛b8+ 20 ♔c1 ♛b2 mate) 17 ♗d4 e3 18 ♛d3 ♛d7 19 a3 f4 20 ♘xe6 ♛xe6 21 ♗xg7 ♔xg7 22 ♛d4+ ♔h6! 23 ♗d3 c5! 24 ♛c4 ♖xb2!! *(140)*

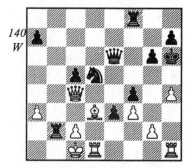

25 h5 (Play after 25 ♔xb2 might run 25...♛e5+ 26 c3 ♖b8+ when both 27 ♔c2 e2 △...♘e3+ and 27 ♔c1 ♘xc3 △ 28...♘xd1, 28...♘a4 or 28...♘e2+, are winning) 25...♖fb8 26 hxg6 ♔g7 27 c3 e2 (△ 28...♛e3+) 28 ♗e4 exd1♛+ 29 ♖xd1 ♖b1+! 30 ♗xb1 ♛e3+ 31 ♔c2 ♛f2+ 32 ♔d3 ♖e8 33 ♛a2 c4+! 34 ♔xc4 ♛xa2+ 35 ♗xa2 ♘e3+ 0-1 Zagrebelny-Khalifman, Sochi 1984.

15 ...   f5!

Black knows what he wants and not even the prospect of an open g-file stops him going for it. Evi-

dently White's ploy was unsuccessful!

16 gxf5   gxf5
17 ♖g1

Attempting to fight fire with fire. A now not unfamiliar theme might arise after 17 ♘g5 e4 18 c3 (18 ♘xe6?? ♗xb2+ etc, etc!) 18...♖xb2!! (also 18...♛a5!? △ 19 ♘xe6 ♛xa2 looks pretty dangerous) 19 ♔xb2 (or 19 ♛xb2 ♛xg5+ 20 ♛d2 e3 when Black's compensation for the exchange could hardly be better) 19...♛a5 20 ♗d4 ♗xd4! 21 ♛xd4 (the game would finish with all of Black's pieces in the attack after 21 cxd4 as well, e.g. 21...♘b4 22 a3 ♖b8-+) 21...♖b8+ 22 ♔a1 ♘b4! with mate being very much on the cards. What appears consistent is that White is forever (which generally isn't that long!) fending off the black forces and his own counterplay never quite seems to get under way. Hence the text move.

17 ...   fxe4

It may seem somewhat unfair that Black can, on one hand, apparently sacrifice to his heart's content, yet on the other confidently accept any offerings coming his way. But, well, who's complaining?

18 ♛h6   ♛f6
19 ♖xg7+   ♛xg7
20 ♛xe6+

White cannot have his cake and eat it. If 20 ♗xf8 ♔xf8! 21 ♛xe6 ♛g5+ 22 ♖d2 (else 22...♘c3+)

22...♖d8! and White is powerless to prevent 23...♕xd2+ followed by a knight move discovering check and winning the white queen.

20 ...   ♔h8
21 ♗xf8   ♕g5+
22 ♔b1

After 22 ♖d2 ♖xf8, White is pinned all over the place. Besides, Black doesn't intend taking up 22...♘c3+ 23 ♔a1 ♘xd1 in view of 24 ♗h6! when everything will have gone horribly wrong!

22 ...   ♖xf8 *(141)*

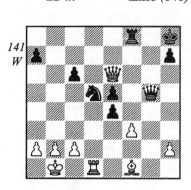

141
W

23 ♕xc6

23 fxe4? loses a piece to 23...♘e3 whilst 23 ♖e1 exf3 24 ♖xe5 ♘c3+! 25 bxc3 ♖b8+ might not force mate, but certainly guarantees a winning queen endgame after 26 ♗b5 ♖xb5+ 27 ♖xb5 ♕xb5+.

23 ...   ♘e3
24 ♖e1   ♘xf1
25 ♖xf1   exf3

The material is level but with black's passed pawns so far advanced, the major piece ending is

just a formality. Ironically the presence of a big queenside majority currently leaves White unable to take the f3-pawn, in view of the back-rank mate.

26 ♕e4   f2
27 c4   ♖f4
28 ♕d3

The black king has no trouble finding shelter after 28 ♕a8+ ♔g7 29 ♕xa7+ ♔g6 and the a7-pawn isn't exactly the issue here!

28 ...   e4
29 ♕c3+   ♖f6
30 ♔c2   e3
31 ♔d3   ♕f4
32 b3   ♔g7

0-1

Clearly White had no desire to torture himself further.

Game 26
Gruneveld-De Palma
Corr. 1989/90

1 e4	c5
2 ♘f3	d6
3 d4	cxd4
4 ♘xd4	♘f6
5 ♘c3	g6
6 ♗e3	♗g7
7 f3	♘c6
8 ♕d2	0-0
9 0-0-0	d5!?
10 exd5	♘xd5
11 ♘xc6	bxc6
12 ♗d4	e5
13 ♗c5	♗e6
14 ♘e4	♖b8
15 c4	

White is naturally only too eager to oust the black knight from d5, but he is in line for a shock. As this move, along with both 15 h4 and 15 g4, apparently gets White nowhere (and often Black quite some distance!), it may be that with these alternatives, White is adopting the wrong approach. Therefore instead of trying to force Black's hand, which often seems to rebound, perhaps he should complete his development and keep things 'tight at the back'. Hence a prime candidate for the best move here must be 15 ♗c4. To illustrate this option I would like to show what might have been in the game Popović-Sax, Subotica IZ 1987: 15 ♗c4 ♖e8 16 h4 a5 17 ♗b3 h6 18 g4 ♖a8 19 a4 ♕c7 20 g5 h5 21 ♕f2 ♖fd8 22 ♖d3 ♖ab8 23 ♖hd1 ♖d7 24 ♗a3 ♗f5 25 ♗xd5? cxd5 26 ♖xd5 ♖xd5 27 ♖xd5 ♕c4 28 ♖xa5 ♕a2 29 ♘d6 e4 30 ♖b5 ♖d8 31 fxe4 ♗c3!! *(142)*

left him with a completely winning position. The threat is 32...♕a1 mate, whilst 32 bxc3 is met by 32...♕xa3+ 33 ♔b1 (33 ♖b2 ♕xd6-+) 33...♖xd6. As another mate threat makes the f5-bishop immune, Black will be a piece up.

Up until White cracked under the pressure with 25 ♗xd5?, there was a very tense middlegame struggle in progress. Although 15 ♗c4 attempts to bolster up the queenside, with no clear way forward, it is easy to see why many impatient Yugoslav Attack players may not favour this line. As for improvements, well, White should probably have tried to remain cool with 25 ♔b1, when no doubt more jockeying for position would occur. As for Black, if he is unhappy with the course of events, then a couple of alternatives worth considering are 15...a5!? and 15...f5 16 ♘g5 ♗h6!?.

15 ...   ♕c7!? *(143)*

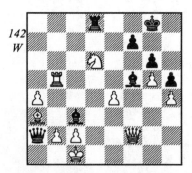

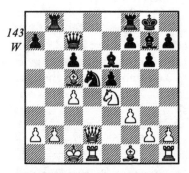

Sadly Black didn't play this beautiful move which would have

It has to be said that 15...♖e8!?, at least preserving the rook, has also scored well for Black at the highest level, but on encountering this rather casual move, White immediately puts it to the test by grabbing all available material.

16 &xf8?!

16 ♘g5 receives the usual treatment of 16...e4! and if White is not feeling quite so greedy, after 16 &d6 ♛b6 17 c5 ♛b7, having rejected the knight, he can take his pick of the black rooks:

a) 18 &xf8 &xf8 19 ♘d6 &xd6 20 cxd6 ♘b4 21 d7 ♜d8 22 b3 ♛b6!?.

b) 18 &xb8 ♜xb8 19 ♘d6 ♛e7!?.

In both instances Black remains the exchange down but has reasonable compensation due to the vulnerability of the white king and the inactivity of the white rooks.

16 ...   &xf8

17 cxd5.

We have already learnt that White is not exactly 'winning' the exchange when his dark-squared bishop captures the black rook on f8, but I guess if he is satisfied with his current material plus then he might consider not taking on d5. Nonetheless after, say, 17 ♔b1 &b4 17 ♛d3 ♘f4, it is clear that Black's piece activity and dark-square domination leave him with more than sufficient compensation.

17 ...   cxd5+

18 ♛c3

Returning a piece now with 18 ♔b1 is foolhardy, e.g. 18...fxe4 19

fxe4 &b4 20 ♛e3 ♛a5 and everything is pointing towards the white king.

18 ...   ♛e7

19 ♛xe5

19...♜c8 as well as 19...dxe4 was threatened.

19 ...   ♜c8+!?

20 ♘c3   ♗h6+!

An improvement on previous games in this line. The point behind this check is that White's forced next move restricts his choice of queen retreats.

21 f4

If 21 ♔b1 then 21...&f5+ and if 21 ♜d2 then 21...d4 22 ♛xd4 (necessary or else all hell will break loose) 22...♜d8. In both cases, Black winds up with a clear plus.

21 ...   &g7

22 ♛e3   ♛b4 *(144)*

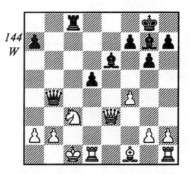

144
W

Now the threat is simply 23...&xc3.

23 ♜d3   d4

24 a3   ♛a4

25 ♛e4

25 ♕d2 is not much better. For example 25...dxc3 26 ♖d8+ ♖xd8 27 ♕xd8+ ♗f8 and White has no defenders with his kingside undeveloped, whilst Black's attack is still apparent.

25 ...	♗f5
26 ♔b1	♖xc3
0-1	

Game 27
Morozevich-Savchenko
Moscow 1991

1 e4	c5
2 ♘f3	d6
3 d4	cxd4
4 ♘xd4	♘f6
5 ♘c3	g6
6 ♗e3	♗g7
7 f3	♘c6
8 ♕d2	0-0
9 0-0-0	d5
10 ♕e1!?	*(145)*

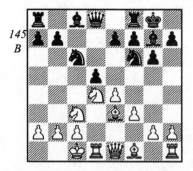

This move, which effectively places the black queen in the firing line of the white rook, has recently been gaining in momentum. Although it was originally considered to be quite bad, it has been resurrected by the likes of Kramnik and in my view until it is 'refuted', its popularity will continue to rise. One of the reasons for this is that whether or not Black's options discussed in game 24 are any good, as with the 'main line', 10 ♕e1!? avoids them.

A few words first though on the aggressive 10 h4?! which Black does well to neutralize with 10...dxe4 11 h5 ♘xd4!:

a) 12 ♗xd4 e5 13 ♗xe5 ♕xd2+ 14 ♖xd2 exf3 15 hxg6 fxg6 16 ♗c4+ ♔h8 17 gxf3 ♗f5.

b) 12 h6 ♗h8 13 ♗xd4 exf3 14 ♗c4 e5 15 ♗xe5 (15 ♗c5 ♗g4! 16 ♗xf8 ♕xf8 leaves Black two pawns and a bishop for a rook up!) 15...♕xd2+ 16 ♖xd2 fxg2 17 ♖xg2 ♗e6.

In both instances Black has the better endgame prospects, either due to the structural advantage or the extra pawn.

10 ... **e6**

With this move Black reinforces his d5-pawn, but I would like to tell the far from obvious story of the more natural 10...e5. Not wanting to allow ...d5-d4 White has two exchanges forced upon him. But after 11 ♘xc6 bxc6 12 exd5, how should Black continue? It may surprise you to learn that probably best is 12...♘xd5 when after 13 ♗c4 ♗e6 14 ♘e4, a position is arrived at that is not dissimilar to those covered in games 25 and 26. The problem with 12...exd5 is 13 ♗g5 ♗e6 and now not 14 ♕xe5? allowing strong counterplay as in the text with 14...h6, but 14 ♗c4!. Then 14...h6 drops a pawn to 15 ♗xd5 whilst 14...♕c7 15 ♗xf6 dxc4 16 ♗xg7 ♔xg7 17 ♕e3 is slightly better for White.

11 g4

With this White seeks to exert more pressure on d5 via a timely g4-g5. Being a relatively new variation I am sure that plenty of new possibilities for both sides will soon come to light. For now though White's main alternative seems to be 11 h4. Black has then come back with 11...♕e7 and 11...♖e8 which incidently are both eminently playable against 11 g4, but again I feel that there is room for innovation.

11 ...   e5!?

Very deep! Black seeks to highlight White's last move as a weakness.

12 ♘xc6   bxc6
13 exd5   cxd5
14 ♗g5

Even now 14 g5 can be met by 14...d4, e.g. 15 gxf6 ♕xf6 16 ♘e4 ♕xf3∓.

14 ...   ♗b7
15 ♕xe5?!

This seems to walk straight into trouble, but with f3 weak, 15 ♗c4 is no longer the solid alternative.

15 ...   h6

16 ♗h4

Naturally 16 ♗xf6 ♗xf6 is unappealing to White, who even by preserving his dark-squared bishop is unable to neutralize the Black counterpart in the forthcoming tactics.

16 ...   g5
17 ♗e1 *(146)*

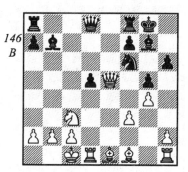

146
B

17 ...   ♘xg4
18 ♕g3   ♘e3
19 ♖d2   ♕a5

Everything is proceeding like clockwork and although it looks as if White puts up about as much fight as a wet dishcloth, a close inspection of the position leads one to the conclusion that there is in fact little to be done.

20 ♕f2   ♗xc3!
21 ♔b1

Instantly losing, though it is possible that only now did White realize that 21 ♕xe3 is swiftly dealt with by 21...♕xa2.

21 ...   ♕b4
0-1

System 2:
9...♘xd4
10 ♗xd4 ♗e6

The main difference between the lines covered here and those discussed in system 1 of chapter 6 is that White gets in the move ♔b1 for free.

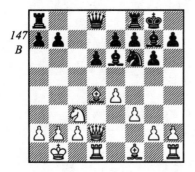

147
B

The reason for this is that after 9...♘xd4 10 ♗xd4 ♗e6 11 ♔b1(!), in the resulting position illustrated above, Black is unable to play 11...♕a5 due to 12 ♘d5. Then 12...♕d8 would be hopeless, whilst 12...♕xd2 simply loses a pawn to 13 ♘xe7+! ♔h8 14 ♖xd2. Hence instead Black should embark on the manoeuvre 11...♕c7 △ 12...♖fc8 and only then 13...♕a5, i.e. when ♘d5xe7+ can be met by ...♔f8 winning a piece. Thus since Black's queen has taken two moves to get its active post on a5, White has gained ♔b1. The ques-

tion then remains as to exactly how useful this is to White.

Game 28
Morris-Berg Hansen
Gausdal 1992

1 e4	c5
2 ♘f3	d6
3 d4	cxd4
4 ♘xd4	♘f6
5 ♘c3	g6
6 ♗e3	♗g7
7 f3	♘c6
8 ♕d2	0-0
9 0-0-0	♘xd4
10 ♗xd4	

By the way, ♗xd4 is nearly always taken for granted, as ♕xd4 runs into a discovered attack from the g7-bishop. Here 10 ♕xd4? would be met very well by 10...♘d5 although 10...♘g4, simply gaining White's dark-squared bishop, is more than sufficient.

10 ...	♗e6
11 ♔b1	

11 ♘d5 (which could also be played on move 12) similarly prevents 11...♕a5 but is no real problem. The reader may wish to compare its appearance here with the ninth move notes to game 12. Now play might, and indeed has, continued 11...♗xd5 12 exd5 ♕c7 13 g4 ♖ac8 14 c3 ♕a5 15 g5 ♘h5 16 ♗xg7 ♘xg7 17 ♔b1 e5 18 dxe6 fxe6 19 ♗h3 ♖xf3 when Black had the better side of the

draw in Timman-Sosonko, Wijk aan Zee 1978.

11 ...   ♕c7

12 g4

For 12 h4 intending 13 h5 (13 g4 would transpose − see games 29 and 30) see game 31. Other than this, nothing else really impresses and, besides, Black's plan is the usual ...♖fc8, ...♕a5, ...♖ab8 (or ...♖xc3 if it wins!), ...b5-b4 etc. Of course it does pay to keep an eye on what White is doing, as no doubt some annoying opponent hoping to catch you on autopilot is bound to try 12 ♘b5. In such an instance with sensible play, the last laugh will be with you; e.g. 12...♕c6 13 h4 (Not 13 ♘xa7? ♖xa7! 14 ♗xa7 ♕a4, when one white rook is absolutely no match for two black minor pieces) 13...♖fc8 14 g4 a6 15 ♘c3 b5 16 h5 (bad, but how else is White to progress?) 16...b4 17 ♘e2 ♗h6! (trying to deflect the queen from c2) 18 ♕d3 ♗c4-+.

12 ...   ♖fc8

13 g5

White opts for a line that was once considered to bring him a slight advantage. However in light of more recent developments it would appear that 13 h4 (see games 29 and 30) is more critical.

13 ...   ♘h5

14 ♗xg7   ♘xg7

One of my favourite Dragon players, Grandmaster Kiril Georgiev, has since demonstrated that 14...♔xg7 is also fine for Black for the same reason as in the text.

15 ♘d5   ♕d7!

The point! The old response 15...♗xd5 enabled the white bishop to materialize quickly on the h3-c8 diagonal, from where it could also control the black knight with ♗g4 (whilst contemplating h4-h5). With 15...♕d7! Black realizes that the d5-knight, though well posted, is not too hot to handle. Rather Black intends to remove it on his terms.

16 f4

White seeks to enhance his light-squared bishop and obtain some control on the dark-squares.

16 ...   b5

This is my only quibble with this game. Possibly 16...♖c5 is preferable first as it removes the option of 17 ♗xb5 ♕xb5 18 ♘xe7+ (which was not taken up in this game).

17 ♗e2   ♖c5

18 ♗f3   ♖ac8

19 ♖c1

White understandably does not wish to make the concession of 19 c3, but as you will see, the target pawn on c2 is a real problem for him throughout the game.

19 ...   ♗xd5

20 exd5   ♕f5

21 ♖hf1   ♘h5

22 ♗xh5

Before 21...♘h5 the knight was the only one of the black pieces that needed improving. Now it is reluctantly exchanged off, but White had little choice as pressure was mounting on f4 and if 22 ♗g2 then 22...♖c4.

22 ...   **gxh5** *(148)*

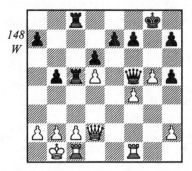

148
W

Although one might pinpoint h5 and e7 as potential white targets, a glance at the position tells us that White's pieces are all defending and are in no position to do any attacking. Meanwhile both the pawns on d5 and f4 are weak and something is destined to drop.

23	♖f2	♖xd5
24	♕e2	e6
25	♕xh5	♖d4
26	♕f3	d5
27	b3	b4
28	♕e3	♖e4
29	♕xa7	♖xf4

The last few moves have seen the white queen dashing around like a headless chicken. White has scooped the somewhat irrelevant a7-pawn and Black dominates the centre of the board.

30	♕b7	♖xf2

31 ♕xc8+   **♔g7**

In view of what follows, it is difficult to believe that at this stage, Black isn't even a pawn up!

32	h4	♖h2
33	♕c5	♖xh4
34	♖g1	♖h2
35	♖c1	

Very sad, but White opts to have his rook rather than his queen tied down. For Black now though, the way home is clear.

35	...	♕f4
36	♕g1	♖h5
37	♖f1	♖xg5
38	♖xf4	♖xg1+
39	♔b2	e5
40	♖xb4	e4
41	♖b7	h5
42	♖d7	e3
43	♖e7	d4
44	c3	d3

0-1

Game 29
Ostermeyer-Sosonko
Mannheim 1975

1	e4	c5
2	♘f3	d6
3	d4	cxd4
4	♘xd4	♘f6
5	♘c3	g6
6	♗e3	♗g7
7	f3	♘c6
8	♕d2	0-0
9	0-0-0	♘xd4
10	♗xd4	♗e6
11	♔b1	♕c7
12	g4	♖fc8

13 h4   ♛a5
14 a3
14...♖xc3 was a familiar threat and 14 ♗xf6 ♗xf6 15 ♘d5 ♛xd2 16 ♘xf6+ ♚g7! leaves Black with a comfortable endgame.
14 ...   ♖ab8
15 h5
Again, having 'weakened' his kingside, there seems little else for White to do but press on with his attack. Note also that often the more tedious attempts have a habit of backfiring. After 15 ♗xf6 ♗xf6 16 ♘d5 ♛xd2 17 ♘xf6+ ♚g7 18 ♘e8+ ♖xe8 19 ♖xd2 h6 20 g5 ♖h8 21 ♖dh2 ♖bc8 22 ♗d3 ♖c5∓ White went on to lose in 78 moves, in Kuczynski-Perenyi, Saint John Open 1988.
15 ...   b5
16 h6 *(149)*

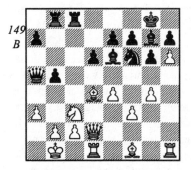

It may seem like a strange decision by White to seal off the h-file. Certainly it is not a very profitable one, but then again 16 hxg6, covered in game 30, is probably no better.

16 ...   ♗h8
Interesting here is an inconsistency between theory and practice. After 16...b4 (!, !?, ?! or ?) 17 ♘d5 ♘xd5 18 hxg7 ♘c3+ 19 ♚a1 f6! 20 ♖e1 (if 20 ♖c1 then 20...bxa3) 20...♘b5 21 ♗xb5 ♛xb5 22 ♖h2 bxa3 23 b3 ♛b4, two fairly recent games continued:
a) 24 ♗xa7 ♛xd2 25 ♖xd2 ♖a8 26 ♗d4 h6! 27 ♚a2 ♚xg7 28 ♖e3 ♖a4! Hellers-Kir.Georgiev, Haifa 1989.
b) 24 ♛e3 a5 25 ♖eh1 a4 26 ♖xh7 axb3 27 cxb3 (27 ♖h8+ leads nowhere) 27...g5 28 e5?! (28 ♖h8+ ♚f7 29 ♖1h7 ♖g8∓) 28...dxe5 29 ♗xe5 ♛xb3 30 ♖h8+ ♚f7 Ponce-Ravelo, Puerto Padre 1990.
In both cases these clear advantages for Black were converted into wins, yet although all of the players might be forgiven for not knowing that 22 b3 is supposed to be good for White, why not 17 axb4 initially? This is what theory recommends White brush aside 16...b4 with, but I would hazard a guess that certain Dragon players have one or two ideas up their sleeve!
17 ♗xf6?
White should always be 100% sure before playing this move. Either he wasn't, or else his analysis was wrong. On 17 g5?! (hoping after 17...♘d7 to liquidate with a timely ♘d5 to some approximately equal ending!), after 17...b4! the complications will favour Black, as it is not his king in the firing line!

Therefore it is fairly clear that 17 ♘d5 is best when after 17...♕xd2 18 ♖xd2, Black has the familiar choice of trading either a bishop or a knight for the white d5-knight. Either way when compared to the more common endgames like this that we have seen, it then becomes a question of whether the white h6-pawn is a hinderance to Black or a weakness for White (probably both!).

17 ...   ♗xf6
18 ♘d5

Obviously White is hoping for 18...♕xd2 19 ♘xf6+ exf6 (As 19...♔g7 is illegal) 20 ♖xd2, when the isolated d6-pawn weakness will be fatal. However Black is not about to oblige.

18 ...   b4!
19 axb4?!

White is eager to block the b-file and 19 ♘xb4 fails (as it should do with a queen, two rooks, and two bishops attacking!) to the beautiful 19...♗c3!. 20 bxc3 is forced but then after 20...♕xa3, mate or vast material gain is not far off, e.g. 21 ♕d4 f6 22 ♗d3 ♖xc3-+.

Amongst other things, the rather cheeky 19...♗xd5 20 exd5 bxa3! 21 ♕xa5 ♖xb2+ is threatened and so 19 ♘xf6+ exf6 is advised, when while the b4-pawn is pinned, White will have one move (before 20...♕a4) to do something constructive. However it is very unlikely that this is time enough.

19 ...   ♕a4
20 b5

20 c3 is also no use as Black tears away this flimsy cover with 20...♗xd5 21 exd5 ♗xc3! 22 bxc3 ♕b3+ 23 ♔a1 ♖xc3-+.

20 ...   ♗xd5
21 exd5   a6 *(150)*
0-1

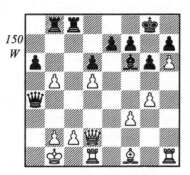

150
W

Often I hear people suggesting that in chess generally, the light-squared bishop seems to be the more dominant. This is the sort of position that makes me wonder what exactly they are going on about! White has just resigned in the above position, a pawn up and with no weaknesses. However he has no good plan of his own and he will soon be defenceless on the dark squares around his king, making it inevitable that he will be mated down the a-, b- or c-file. Now might be a good time to reiterate that in the Dragon, it is the dark-squared bishops that tend to dominate.

The following game, which introduces a whole new attacking dimension, is another one of my favourites.

Game 30
Sisniega-Fernandez
Havana 1984

1 e4	c5
2 ♘f3	d6
3 d4	cxd4
4 ♘xd4	♘f6
5 ♘c3	g6
6 ♗e3	♗g7
7 f3	0-0
8 ♕d2	♘c6
9 0-0-0	♘xd4
10 ♗xd4	♗e6
11 ♔b1	♕c7
12 h4	♖fc8
13 g4	

For 13 h5 see game 31.

13 ...	♕a5
14 a3	♖ab8
15 h5	b5
16 hxg6	hxg6

With reference to the h- or f-pawn recapture explanation given in chapter 5, 16...hxg6 is fine as White's dark-squared bishop is too far from h6. 16...fxg6 is also playable as 17 ♗xf6? ♗xf6 18 ♕h6 would be tantamount to suicide, e.g. 18...♖xc3! 19 ♕xh7+ ♔f8-+.

17 ♕g5

White holds up Black's attack by utilizing a sneaky pin. Meanwhile Black has no wish to hang around

and not fearing the line-opening 18 ♗xb5, unpins immediately.

17 ...	♕c7
18 e5 *(151)*	

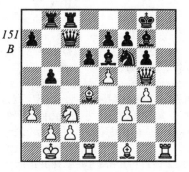

For White, trebling his major pieces on the h-file would be nice. However this is somewhat impractical and instead (facing 18...b4) he tries either to remove Black's defensive knight or skewer the queen and rook. He achieves the former, but probably not how he expected to!

18 ...	♘e4!
19 fxe4	

Forced, as 19 ♘xe4?? walks into 19...♕xc2+ 20 ♔a1 ♕xd1+ mating and 19 ♕h4 dxe5 is also rather undesirable.

19 ...	dxe5
20 ♗f2	b4
21 axb4	♖xb4
22 ♕e3	

22...♕xc3 was the immediate threat which had to be dealt with. Note that now 22...♕xc3? allows 23 ♕xc3 ♖xc3 24 ♗e1+-.

22 ...	♕a5

The idea is the simple 23...♕a3.

23 ♘d5

If 23 ♕xa7?, then 23...♖xb2+! is crushing.

23 ...	♖a4
24 c4	♗xd5
25 ♖xd5	♖a1+
26 ♔c2	♕a4+
27 ♔c3	e6

Not being a personal friend of Señor Fernandez, I couldn't tell you whether he overlooked the more than satisfactory possibility of 27...♖xf1 28 ♖xf1 ♕xc4+ 29 ♔d2 ♕xf1. Later a few repetitions indicate time trouble, but, well, anyway 27...e6 certainly provides more entertainment!

28 ♖c5	♖b8
29 ♖b5	♖xb5
30 cxb5	♗f8!

In come the troops.

31 b3	♕a5+
32 ♔d3	♕d8+
33 ♔c3	♕a5+
34 ♔d3	♕xb5+
35 ♔c2	♕c6+
36 ♔b2	

It must be frustrating for White to have his kingside there, but unavailable due to the pin of his f1-bishop. Interposing the queen is also going to be generally off limits with 36 ♕c3 here losing to 36...♖c1+.

36 ...	♖c1!
37 ♕d3 (152)	

After 37 ♕xc1 ♗a3+ 38 ♔xa3 ♕xc1+ either the pawns, the rook or the f2-bishop will fall to a check.

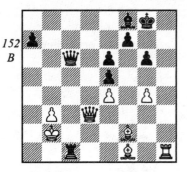

152
B

37 ...	♗a3+!
38 ♔a2	

Forced. If 38 ♔xa3 then 38...♖a1+ 39 ♔b2 (39 ♔b4 a5 mate) 39... ♕c1 mate.

38 ...	♗f8
39 ♔b2	♗a3+
40 ♔a2	♗e7
41 ♔b2	♕c7!
42 ♖h2	♗a3+
43 ♔a2	♖c2+
44 ♕xc2	

Or 44 ♔a1 (44 ♔b1 ♖b2+ 45 ♔a1 ♕c1+) 44...♗c1 45 ♔b1 ♖b2+ 46 ♔a1 ♕a5 mate.

44 ...	♕xc2+
45 ♔xa3	♕c1+
46 ♔b4	♕xf1
47 ♗xa7	♕e1+
48 ♔b5	♕g3!

0-1

White will soon be severely lacking in pawns.

The final game of the chapter tackles what I consider to be the real acid test of this Black system.

Game 31
Van der Wiel-Sax
Plovdiv 1983

1 e4	c5
2 ♘f3	d6
3 d4	cxd4
4 ♘xd4	♘f6
5 ♘c3	g6
6 ♗e3	♗g7
7 f3	♘c6
8 ♕d2	0-0
9 0-0-0	♘xd4
10 ♗xd4	♗e6
11 ♔b1	♕c7
12 h4	♖fc8
13 h5!	

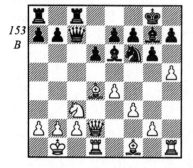

153
B

Leaving out 13 g4 as now 13...♘xh5? is refuted quite impressively by 14 ♗xg7 ♔xg7 15 g4 ♘f6 16 ♕h6+ ♔g8 17 e5! dxe5 18 g5 ♘h5 19 ♖xh5 gxh5 20 ♗d3+-.

13 ...	♕a5
14 hxg6	

The correct move. The inaccurate 14 a3?! can be punished by 14...♘xh5! 15 ♗xg7 ♔xg7 16 g4 ♖xc3! 17 ♕xc3+ (or 17 gxh5 ♖c5/+) 17...♕xc3 18 bxc3 ♘f4 and Black has good compensation for the exchange.

Once again though 14 h6 rears its ugly head. It is however not too much to worry about as after 14...♗h8 15 a3 ♘d7 (avoiding 16 ♗xf6 Δ 17 ♘d5) 16 ♗xh8 ♔xh8 17 ♘d5 ♕xd2 18 ♖xd2 there are no great shakes. Also 15...♘e8!? is a suggestion of Levy's, though it is not clear where this knight is heading.

14 ...	hxg6
15 a3	♖ab8
16 ♗d3!	

16 g4?! b5 would transpose to game 30 and despite 16 ♘e2 looking fairly dull, it brought about a nice finish in Tamas-Sergyan, Keszthely 1982: 16...♕a4!? 17 g4 b5 18 g5 b4!? 19 gxf6 bxa3 20 fxg7? (20 b3! exf6 is not so clear) 20...♖xb2+! 21 ♗xb2 ♗a2+ 22 ♔xa2 axb2+ 23 ♔xb2 ♖b8+ 0-1.

16 ...	b5?!
17 ♕g5	♕c7
18 e5	dxe5
19 ♗xe5	♕c5
20 f4	♖b7
21 ♗xg6!	fxg6
22 ♕xg6	♗f7 *(154)*

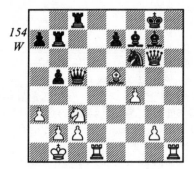

154
W

23 ♖h8+!   1-0

Play might continue 23...♔xh8
24 ♕xf7 ♖g8 25 ♖h1+ ♘h7 26
♕h5 which really is the end!

You are probably thinking 'Why
on Earth has this game been included', or 'Perhaps I'll stick to the
French Defence after all!'. The
point was not only to demonstrate
how White wins can look almost as
brilliant as Black wins, but rather
to remind the reader of the danger.
Overall this was a very tidy game
by White, but as far as improve-

ments for Black are concerned, I
have some 'food for thought':

a) 16...b5?! is careless and Black
should probably try 16...♗c4!?.
Then 17 ♗xc4 ♖xc4 (△ 18...♘xe4)
18 ♗xf6 ♗xf6 19 ♘d5 ♕xd2 20
♖xd2 ♔g7 was drawn ten moves
later in Marjanović-Mesing, Bela
Crkva 1984. Both 17 f4 and 17 g4
can be met actively by 17...b5
whilst on 17 ♗e3 (△ 18 ♗h6),
Black has 17...♘d7 if all else fails.

b) 14...hxg6 is solid and taken for
granted, but what of the unmentioned 14...fxg6 (interesting in a
dubious sort of way!)? The light-
squared bishop could always drop
back to f7 or g8 to defend (if need
be) and 15 ♗xf6? (which if played
later intending a ♘d5 follow-up,
might be met by ...exf6!?) appears
to lose to 15...♖xc3! 16 ♕xc3
♕xa2+ 17 ♔c1 ♗xf6 18 ♕a3 (18
♕e3 ♕xb2+ is also extremely
good for Black) 18...♗g5+.

8   Classical Dragon

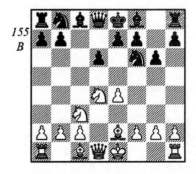

155
B

This Classical Dragon chapter is the most difficult for me to write and hence probably the most difficult for the reader to get to grips with. The problem is the amount of transpositions that can occur. Although at first I considered these to be rather a nightmare, I believe that I have now managed to isolate certain relevant subtleties between variations. Consequently, as you will soon see, I have supplied a quick reference menu for those wanting to get stuck straight into the nitty gritty.

The Yugoslav Attack is the most critical line against the Dragon, but it is not everyone's cup of tea. I have recognized the 'Classical' to be basically anything involving an early ♗e2 (most likely 6 ♗e2, but different move orders are a consideration). Amongst the 'quieter' White 1 e4 players, the Classical is a very popular choice. Although it is of course very possible for Black to lose, the move 6 ♗e2 is not especially fearsome to Dragon (and indeed most Sicilian) players. To expand on this, and to confuse the reader a little more; Classical Sicilian players often choose to transpose into the Classical Dragon! i.e. 1 e4 c5 2 ♘f3 d6 3 d4 cxd4 4 ♘xd4 ♘f6 5 ♘c3 ♘c6 6 ♗e2 (as we saw in chapter 3, both 6 ♗g5 and 6 ♗c4 prevent the Dragon) 6...g6 is a very common move order.

From the positions in the next two diagrams, there are several plans which Black can adopt, though much may depend on the stance that White takes. Queenside expansion is a frequent option, with ...a6 and ...b5 featuring regularly. Very playable, but not dwelled upon in this chapter, is ...a5 (when the white knight has retreated to b3), intending ...a4-a3. Nearly always this is met by a4, when the relative weaknesses of the b4- and b5-squares must be weighed up. Usually Black's light-squared bishop vacates the c-file to go to e6, where it eyes up the c4-square. This can be followed up by ...♕c8 (slowing down White's f4-f5). However my own recommendation is that this square should be preserved for a rook. Possibilities of an exchange sacrifice on c3 then occur, whilst an occupation of the c4-square with a knight or bishop is facilitated.

Through a lack of experiencing anything different, in my earlier Dragon days, I believed the real starting position of the Classical Dragon to be as below.

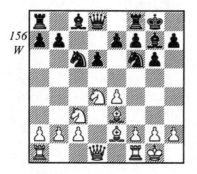

156
W

Black has played all of the normal Dragon moves, and now threatens the thematic 9...d5. If allowed, this pawn break will open up the Dragon bishop's diagonal, and the new lines created may expose White's centrally posted pieces. White is well advised to take preventative measures, but his main alternatives make concessions of their own:

Game 32: **9 f4**. For the unprepared, possibly the most obvious continuation. White is ready to meet 9...d5? with 10 e5!. However he is now temporarily vulnerable

along the a7-g1 diagonal, making the reply 9...♕b6! very attractive.

Game 33: **9 ♕d2**. Not strictly speaking completely stopping 9...d5, but the idea that ♖ad1 may soon follow is a deterrent.

Nevertheless the queen has in moving relinquished some control over the g4-square. Hence Black can strike while the iron is hot with 9...♘g4!?.

Game 34: **9 ♘b3**. A sensible retreat, the only drawback being that this knight no longer controls the e6-square. This means that Black's only undeveloped minor piece now has at its disposal an active post, and so 9...♗e6 is a highly satisfactory response. A couple of other White tries do not look stupid, but fail to deal with the matter at hand:

a) **9 ♔h1?!** d5! and now:

a1) 10 exd5 ♘xd5 11 ♘xd5 ♕xd5 12 ♗f3 ♕a5 13 ♘xc6 bxc6 14 c3 ♖b8 15 ♕c1 ♕c7 16 ♖d1 ♗f5 17 ♗d4 e5 18 ♗c5 ♖fd8 19 ♖xd8+ ♖xd8 20 ♕e3 ♖d3 21 ♕e2 ♕d7 (threatening both 22...♖d2 and 22...e4) 22 ♕e1 ♖xf3!! 23 gxf3 ♕d5 24 ♕e3 ♗h6! 25 c4 (25 ♕xh6 ♕xf3+ 26 ♔g1 ♗e4+ leads to mate) 25...♗xe3 26 cxd5 ♗xc5 27 dxc6 ♗b6 and with a rather easy task, Black went on to win the ending (Pesotsky-Ward, Kiev 1990).

a2) 10 ♘xc6 bxc6 11 e5 ♘e4!? 12 ♘xe4 dxe4 13 ♕xd8 ♖xd8 14 ♖fd1 ♗e6 15 ♗d4 f5 16 a4 ♔f7 17 a5 ♖xd4! 18 ♖xd4 ♖b8! 19 f4 exf3 20 ♗xf3 ♗xe5 21 ♖d3 ♖xb2 22

♖e1 ♗d6 23 ♗xc6 ♖xc2 24 ♗d5
♗xd5 25 ♖xd5 ♖a2 26 g3 ♗b4 27
♖b1 ♖xa5 and Black capped a brilliant display by cruising to victory
(Adams-Khalifman, Las Palmas
1993).

b) **9 h3 d5!** 10 exd5 ♘xd5 11
♘xd5 ♕xd5 12 ♘xc6 (In the same
fashion as the previous line, 12
♗f3 ♕a5 13 ♘xc6 bxc6 gets White
nowhere. Black has an isolated c-
pawn, but is well compensated for
this by the pressure against White's
queenside. However after 14
♗xc6?! ♖b8, White will lose his
pawn, resulting in a similar isolated c-pawn, but minus the compensation.) 12...♕xc6 13 c3 e5 14
a4 ♗e6 15 ♕c2 f5 16 f3 a6 and
Black's kingside space advantage
gives him a slight edge (Rizvi-
Ward, London Lloyds Bank 1991).

As time progressed and I began
looking closer at text books and
strong players' games, I began to
realize that my concept of the Classical was somewhat narrow. Indeed it appears that most
diversions start from the position
below.

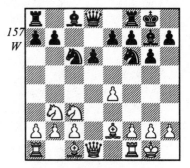

157
W

White has retreated his knight to
b3 in order to give his dark-squared
bishop more scope. Of course **9
♗e3** is still possible (and transposes directly into game 34), but
alternatively with nothing to support on d4, it may venture further
to g5, ultimately to pressurize the
e7-pawn. The other popular choice
is to leave it on c1 temporarily, in
order to keep the options open. Although again one must take into
consideration various move orders
(e.g. 8 ♗g5 ♘c6 9 ♘b3), basically
a summary of White's possibilities
(and my suggested responses)
from here are:

Game 35: 9 ♗g5 a6!?
Game 36: 9 ♔h1 ♗e6 10 ♗g5
Game 37: 9 ♔h1 ♗e6 10 f4

In comparison to the above lines,
9 f4 is a little premature as it allows
the immediate 9...b5!. This is
based on the premise that 10
♗xb5?! is very favourably met by
10...♘xe4! 11 ♗xc6 ♕b6+. Instead then play may continue with
10 ♗f3 b4 11 ♘d5 (if 11 ♘a4?!,
then 11...e5! 12 a3 a5 13 ♗e3 ♗a6
14 ♖e1 ♗b5 makes White's pieces
look a little uncoordinated)
11...♘xd5 12 exd5 ♘a5, when
either 13 ♔h1 ♘c4 or 13 ♘xa5
♕xa5, leave Black with a comfortable position. The f-pawn would
rather be back on f2, where it
would keep the king covered and
not obstruct the c1-bishop.

Unfortunately a rather tedious
White idea has more recently en-

tered the fray; it starts with the move **9 ♖e1**. This heralds the beginning of a super-solid plan, which has hopefully been nipped in the bud by the game Zagrebelny-Serper, Tashkent 1992. This continued with 9...a6 10 ♗f1 b5 11 ♘d5 ♘d7! 12 c3 (if 12 a4!?, then perhaps 12...♖b8!?) 12...e6 13 ♘e3 ♘b6 14 f4 ♗b7 15 ♘g4 ♘c4 16 ♘d2 ♕b6+ 17 ♔h1 ♘xd2 18 ♗xd2 f5!?. Black has managed to liven things up a little and certainly stands no worse. If this Black plan doesn't catch the club player's fancy (or fails to impress in the time ahead), then my only other advice is to stay off the alcohol. Stick to black coffee to avoid drowsiness and you should be okay! To let the reader into a little secret, I have recently noticed that it is against such systems that top Dragon players have occasionally been known to develop their b8-knight to d7. This is in conjunction with ...a6 and ...b5, the idea being to fianchetto on b7. As there can be no way of knowing for sure that the abovementioned plan is going to be adopted, it must be that 9 ♖e1 players let off some sort of vibes. These evidently are often sufficient for ...♘c6 to be delayed (i.e. in favour of ...a6). Clearly this means that if suspicions were wrong, then transposing back into other lines may not be possible. However I have already stated

that in the Classical, ...a6 and ...b5 would not look out of place.

Finally game 38 is different from the above two diagrams altogether. Nevertheless it covers not uncommon, but slightly uncharacteristically aggressive lines in which White foregoes the usual 0-0, in favour of a very early pawn storm on the black king. I understand that the reader may have been a little confused with what they have read in this chapter up to now. Do not worry, so have I at times! Do read on, but never lose sight of the fact that you should always try to play your own game. Put into practice all of the ideas, but avoid bashing out pre-learnt, but miscomprehended moves in case of memory lapses. You may not grasp all of the Classical transpositional features at first. If you do, then all the better, but if you don't, just remember some ideas and revisit the intricacies later.

Game 32
Javarone-Poli
Italian Ch 1991/92

1 e4	c5
2 ♘f3	d6
3 d4	cxd4
4 ♘xd4	♘f6
5 ♘c3	g6
6 ♗e3	♗g7
7 ♗e2	♘c6
8 0-0	0-0
9 f4	♕b6! *(158)*

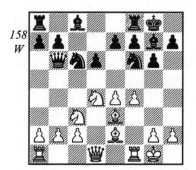

158
W

As the e3-bishop is unprotected, Black can afford to play this extremely clever move. Its two threats can be highlighted by looking at two instinctive, but bad, White responses:

a) 10 ♕d2? ♘xe4! 11 ♘xe4 ♗xd4 winning a pawn for nothing.

b) 10 ♘f5? ♕xb2! 11 ♘xg7 ♕xc3. White may have won the Dragon bishop, but Black will soon have won a piece.

10 ♕d3

The only solid move, after which 10...♕xb2? 11 ♘cb5 is very dodgy for Black and 10...♘xe4? loses to 11 ♘xc6. If the reader is not as yet too confident in his powers of analysis, then at this point he would do very well to pay close attention to the 'Zollner Gambit' initiated by 10 e5?!. Although straying from the correct path can be fatal, with best play Black can expose this as simply a bag of tricks:

10...dxe5 11 fxe5 ♘xe5 12 ♘f5 ♕xb2! 13 ♘xe7+ ♔h8 14 ♗d4 ♕b4! 15 ♗xe5 (15 ♘ed5 ♘xd5 16

♘xd5 ♕xd4+! 17 ♕xd4 ♘f3+ −+ or 15 ♘xc8 ♖d8!) 15...♕xe7 16 ♕d4 ♘h5 17 ♗xg7+ ♘xg7 18 ♗d3 ♗e6∓ Hazelton-Ward, London Lloyds Bank 1985. I recall that at the time, winning this game was an extremely satisfying achievement. It was the first time that I had come across this variation, yet I could remember having played over the line in a Dragon textbook. The point was that despite using up a lot of time on the clock, I had managed logically to reconstruct the theory. Okay, perhaps in a way I was doing what I have told you not to (i.e. recalling in a parrot fashion), but what the hell, it worked! Certainly my opponent had learnt a lesson. He confessed that he had 'hoped' that I wouldn't know it and besides even if I did, the position after move 18 had been assessed as 'probably a bit better for Black'. However, after the game we both agreed that although White has a little pressure along the d4-h8 diagonal, this is negligible. Meanwhile Black is already one pawn up and in contrast to White, has no weak pawns. With three splendid files available to him, he will have no trouble improving his position and evidently I didn't!

10 ...   ♘g4

11 ♘d5

After 11 ♗xg4 ♗xd4 12 ♗xd4 ♕xd4+ 13 ♕xd4 ♘xd4 14 ♗xc8 ♖axc8 15 ♖f2, it is probably fair to say that because the c2-pawn is weaker than the d6-pawn (i.e. comparing the pawns on the half-open files), Black is on the slightly better side of a not very exciting endgame.

11 ...   ♗xd4! (159)

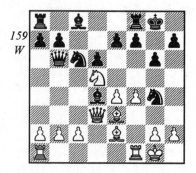

159
W

12 ♘xb6?

Although taking the queen is very tempting, in fact it is a mistake. Here White should opt for 12 ♗xg4 ♗xe3+ 13 ♕xe3 ♕xe3+ 14 ♘xe3. Compared to the notes to White's 11th move, his knight is better placed. The position is even and I might have said dull, if it weren't for Grosar-Ward, Bern 1992 which livened up with 14...♗xg4 15 ♘xg4 ♖ac8 16 ♘e3 f6 17 ♖ad1 ♘a5 18 ♖f2 ♔f7 19 e5 dxe5 20 fxe5 ♖fd8 21 ♖df1 f5 22 e6+ ♔xe6 23 g4 fxg4 24 ♖e2. Despite this flutter of activity, the game later ended in a draw, with the players' assessments being 'unclear' rather than 'equal'.

12 ...   ♗xe3+
13 ♔h1

It is too late for White to try to bale out with 13 ♕xe3 ♘xe3 14 ♘xa8 ♘xf1 15 ♗xf1, as 15...f5! leaves White's pawns vulnerable and his knight looking silly in the corner.

13 ...   ♗xb6
14 ♗xg4   ♗xg4 (160)

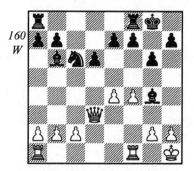

160
W

Black's pawn structure is excellent as always. The white queen has nowhere good to go, but Black's equivalent material can be in three places at once!

15 c3

Ideally White would like to trap the bishop on g4 with 15 f5, but this concedes the e5-square to the black knight. Then the light-squared bishop could escape (from h3 and g4) either via e2 or with the help of ...f6 (and a pawn trade on f5).

15 ...   ♗e6
16 b4

Again 16 f5 would be no better, with 16...♘e5 17 ♕g3 ♗c4 being very nice for Black.

16 ...   ♖ac8

17 h3	♖fd8
18 ♕g3	♗c4
19 ♖fe1	d5

White must go for an attack, but will have difficulty in enlisting support for his queen. Black's bishops already control a lot of squares, and now he is trying to open up the position for his rooks.

20 f5	d4
21 e5	dxc3
22 fxg6	hxg6
23 e6	

It is pointless White taking time out with 23 ♕xc3, e.g. 23...♗e6 24 ♖ad1 ♖d4 25 ♖xd4 ♘xd4 26 ♕d2 ♖c2 27 ♕d3 ♗d5 28 ♖g1 ♖xa2, when he is completely passive, with no hope whatsoever. Therefore he decides to throw in everything bar the kitchen sink. Unfortunately for him that doesn't amount to much!

23 ...	♘xb4
24 ♕f4	f6
25 ♕h6	♗d3
26 ♖ad1	

Hoping to get in 27 ♖xd3, when a perpetual check would be there for the taking.

26 ...	♗f5
27 ♖d7	♘d5!

And not 27...♖xd7?? 28 exd7 ♖d8 29 ♖xe7, when the tables are completely turned.

28 g4	♗d3
29 g5	fxg5
30 ♕xg5	♗f5
31 ♖xd8+	♖xd8
32 ♖e5	

White has finally managed to get a rook in the general direction of the black king. However even with the threat of 32 ♖xf5, this is a very extreme case of too little too late.

32 ...   ♗e3! *(161)*

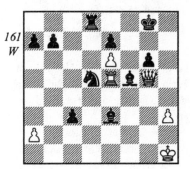

161 W

0-1

White must play 33 ♖xe3, but after 33...♘xe3 34 ♕xe7 ♗e4+ 35 ♔g1 (or 35 ♔h2 ♖d2+ 36 ♔g1 ♖g2+ 37 ♔h1 ♖g3+ 38 ♔h2 ♘f1 mate) 35...♖f8 36 ♕c5 ♖f1+ 37 ♔h2 ♘f5, mate is inevitable.

Game 33
Illescas-Gulko
Leon 1991

1 e4	c5
2 ♘f3	♘c6
3 d4	cxd4
4 ♘xd4	♘f6
5 ♘c3	d6
6 ♗e2	g6
7 0-0	♗g7
8 ♗e3	0-0
9 ♕d2 *(162)*	

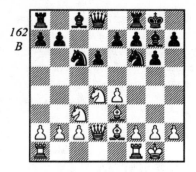

162
B

With this move it is White's intention to keep a grip on the centre and to strive for a minimal advantage.

9 ... ♗d7

At this point, the reader may wonder what has happened to my logical recommendation. Do not worry, the text is merely a sensible alternative. After 9...♘g4!?, White must preserve his dark-squared bishop and so 10 ♗xg4 ♗xg4 is forced, when a few practical examples are:

a) 11 f4 ♘xd4 12 ♗xd4 e5! 13 ♗e3 exf4 14 ♖xf4 (Not 14 ♗xf4?! ♕b6+ 15 ♔h1 ♕xb2, leaving White with insufficient compensation) 14...♗e6 15 ♖f2 ♖ac8 16 ♗d4 ♗e5 (S.Jackson-Ward, British Championship 1988). Black is sitting comfortable with his two bishops, but White has a useful outpost for her knight.

b) 11 ♘xc6?! bxc6 12 ♗h6 ♗xh6 13 ♕xh6 ♕b6 14 ♖ab1 ♗e6 15 ♖fd1 f5! 16 ♖f2 ♖f7 17 b3 f4 18 ♘e2 ♕b4 19 ♖d4 ♕c5 20 ♖d2 ♕e5 (P.H.Nielsen-Tiviakov,

Gausdal 1993). White, by his own admission, has played rather wimpishly and Black clearly has the upper hand.

c) 11 ♘d5!? (the most enterprising move – White has conceded a bishop for a knight, but wants to obtain a bind on d5) 11...♖c8!? (11...♗d7 12 c4 ♘e5 13 b3 e6 14 ♘c3 ♕a5 15 h3 a6 {15...f5!?} 16 a3 b5!? was finely balanced in Read-West, John Kellner Memorial Corr. 1989/91) 12 c4 (12 ♖c1 is more cautious) 12...♘xd4 13 ♗xd4 ♖xc4!? 14 ♗xg7 ♔xg7 15 ♘e3 ♖xe4! 16 f3 ♗xf3 17 ♖xf3 ♕b6 18 ♔h1 ♕d4 19 ♕f2 f5 (Stoica-Vera, Timisoara 1987). Black has three good pawns for a knight, giving both sides practical chances.

10 f4

The more solid and less aggressive move is the non-committal 10 ♖ad1. With the text, White prefers to be more testing.

10 ... ♘xd4
11 ♗xd4 ♗c6
12 ♗f3 *(163)*

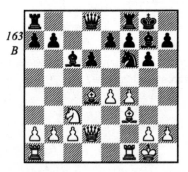

163
B

12 ...   **e5!**

A perfectly timed central thrust which leaves White with an isolated e-pawn.

13 fxe5

After 13 ♞e3?! exf4 14 ♞xf4, both 14...♜e8 and 14...♕b6+ look good for Black.

13 ...	dxe5
14 ♞e3	♕xd2
15 ♞xd2	♜fd8
16 ♜ad1?!	

Probably 16 ♞e3, preventing Black's next, is more accurate.

16 ...   **♜d4!**

A strong square for the black rook. However now 17 ♞e3 would merely nudge it on to another good square, e.g. 17...♜c4 when 18 ♞e2 can then be met well by 18...♜b4.

17 ♞g5	h6
18 ♞xf6	♞xf6
19 ♜xd4	exd4
20 ♘d5	

It is clear that already it is White who is playing for the draw.

20 ...   **♞g5** *(164)*

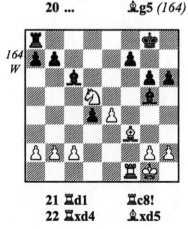

164
W

21 ♜d1	♜c8!
22 ♜xd4	♞xd5

Black reluctantly concedes one of his two bishops. Nevertheless he still finds himself in a favourable rook and opposite-coloured bishops ending.

23 ♜xd5

And not 23 exd5?? ♞e3+.

23 ...	♜xc2
24 ♜d7!	

White must stay as active as possible. 24 ♜b5 b6 25 a4 ♞e3+ 26 ♔f1 a6 27 ♜b3 ♞d4 28 ♜b4 ♞c5 29 ♜b3 a5 (intending ...♞d4 and/or ...♜c4 to follow), for example is inadequate.

24 ...	♜xb2
25 e5	♜xa2
26 ♞d5!	

Again trying to get materialistic at this point doesn't help. e.g. 26 ♞xb7 ♞e3+ 27 ♔f1 ♜f2+ 28 ♔e1 ♜f5 29 ♞d5 ♞f4 30 g3 ♜xe5 31 ♞e4 (31 ♜xa7?? ♞c3+) 31...♜f6 32 ♜xa7 ♞xg3+! 33 hxg3 ♜e6-+.

26 ...	♞e3+
27 ♔f1	♜f2+
28 ♔e1	b5
29 g4	♜f4
30 ♜d8+	♔g7
31 ♜d7	

Threatening 32 e6.

31 ...	♔f8
32 ♜d8+	♔e7
33 ♜b8	♞b6
34 ♜b7+	♔e8
35 ♜b8+	♔d7
36 ♜b7+	♔c8
37 ♜xf7	

Black didn't want to lose his f-pawn nor exchange rooks, but in order to make progress these concessions have been forced upon him.

37 ...	♖xf7
38 ♗xf7	g5
39 ♗e8	a6
40 e6	♗d8 *(165)*

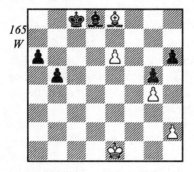

165
W

41 e7?

White believes that if he is going to be able to draw, then his bishop must be able to travel freely from one side of the board to the other. Therefore he opts to jettison this obscuring pawn. However the reality of the situation is that he needs this pawn as a potential diversion, to have any chances. Now Black finishes very competently.

41 ...	♗xe7
42 ♔e2	♔c7
43 ♔d3	♔d6
44 ♗g6	♔c5
45 ♗f5	♔b4
46 ♗c8	a5
47 ♗d7	♗d6
48 ♔c2	

Or 48 h3 ♔b3 49 ♗xb5 a4 is also winning.

48 ...	♗xh2
49 ♗e8	a4
50 ♗d7	♗e5
51 ♗e8	♔a5
52 ♗c6	b4
53 ♔d3	b3
54 ♔c4	h5

0-1

The white bishop will never be able to cope with the three passed pawns.

The following game, a Classical favourite of mine, is characterized by a very familiar idea.

Game 34
Pisa Ferrer-Ochoa de Echagüen
Andorra 1986

1 e4	c5
2 ♘f3	♘c6
3 d4	cxd4
4 ♘xd4	♘f6
5 ♘c3	d6
6 ♗e2	g6
7 ♗e3	♗g7
8 0-0	0-0
9 ♘b3	♗e6
10 f4	♖c8! *(166)*

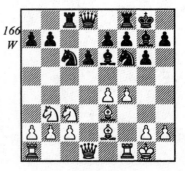

166
W

A few years ago, 10...♘a5 would have been my suggestion. The point is that then Black can meet 11 f5 (11 ♘xa5 ♕xa5 leaves the black queen helping to prevent this f4-f5 push) with 11...♗c4. Then if 12 ♘xa5 (probably 12 ♗d3!? is best) 12...♗xe2 13 ♕xe2 ♕xa5 14 g4, Black has the perfect response to this so-called 'Stockholm Attack' with 14...♖ac8 15 g5 ♖xc3!. Very bad for White would then be 16 bxc3?! ♘xe4, but the alternative 16 gxf6 ♖xe3 17 ♕xe3 ♗xf6 leaves Black with a pawn and good positional compensation for the exchange.

The above is very playable, but as it seems that 11 f5 is not to be feared, the text is even better.

11 f5

White played 10 f4 with the eventual intention of this move, but now, it may not be best. However, if White puts it off with, for instance, 11 ♔h1, then Black can return favourably to the above plan with 11...♘a5, though on 12 f5, perhaps even 12...♘c4!?.

11 ♗f3 is a typical Classical Dragon move, but here it causes few problems, and after 11...♗c4 12 ♖f2, Black has been successful with both 12...b5!? and 12...e5!?.

11 ...   ♗d7

Black must always have a good follow-up if he is to justify exchanging this bishop for the comparatively redundant knight on b3. The main problems with

11...♗xb3?! 12 axb3 are that Black has lost control over both d5 and c4, White has a half-open a-file, and the white queenside pawns would not be shattered by an exchange sacrifice on c3.

12 g4

The natural continuation. White seeks to squash Black to a pulp with g4-g5 and later perhaps even f5-f6 (White having the freedom of the d5-square). Little does he know that his plan of kingside expansion will soon backfire.

12 ...   ♘e5

13 g5 *(167)*

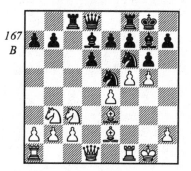

167
B

In retrospect, it is very easy to criticise this move. However, it would appear that even solid moves do not help White much:

a) 13 ♗d4 ♖xc3! 14 bxc3 ♘xe4 15 ♕e1 ♗c6 16 ♘d2 ♘xd2 17 ♕xd2 ♕a5 18 ♔f2 ♕d5 19 ♕f4 a6 20 ♖g1 ♖c8 21 h4 ♗b5 22 ♗xb5 ♕xb5 23 a4 ♕b2 24 ♕e4 ♘xg4+! and White resigned shortly in Letay-Szalanczi, Hungary 1986.

b) 13 ♘d2 ♖xc3!? 14 bxc3 ♗c6 15 ♗f3 d5!. White's king is exposed, and he has several weak pawns. He may be a whole exchange up but rooks will not be figuring prominently in the near future.

13 ...   ♖xc3!

The saviour and the killer.

14 bxc3

Forced as after 14 gxf6 ♖xe3 15 fxg7 ♔xg7, with ...♕b6 at Black's disposal, there is no chance of trapping the black rook.

14 ...   ♘xe4
15 fxg6

Also excellent for Black was 15 ♘d4 ♘xc3 16 ♕e1 ♘d5 in Eales-Ward, Kent County Cup 1990.

15 ...   hxg6
16 ♕e1

Not effectively defending the c3-pawn, but 16 ♗d4 has its drawback in 16...♘xg5.

16 ...   ♘xc3!
17 ♗d4

17 ♕xc3?? loses the queen to 17...♘f3+.

17 ...   ♘xe2+
18 ♕xe2   ♗h3

This game is fairly short and sweet. Nevertheless it has to be said that perhaps even more appealing was 18...♗c6 (that's what I call a diagonal!).

19 ♖f2   a6

A few words about this pawn. Rarely is it possible for White's dark-squared bishop to take it, without being trapped by ...b6. Although here it is not necessarily the most relevant pawn ever seen, Black has plenty of time and so uses some to safeguard it.

20 ♕e4   ♕c8
21 ♖e1   ♕g4+

Very simply, Black decides that with a vastly superior pawn structure, his task in the endgame will be easy.

22 ♕xg4   ♗xg4
23 ♔g2   ♖c8
24 ♖b1

White pinpoints Black's only potential weakness, the b7-pawn.

24 ...   ♗e6
25 h4   ♘g4
26 ♖d2   ♗xd4
27 ♘xd4   ♗xa2 *(168)*

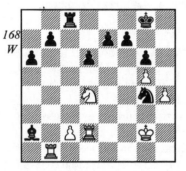

Black is currently three pawns for the exchange up, and as 28 ♖xb7?? is not possible in view of 28...♗d5+, he may as well end his suffering. In effect he does!

28 ♖b2?   ♘e3+!
0-1

Black's next move would be 29...♘c4.

Game 35
Basanta-Tolnai
Saint John 1988

1 e4	c5
2 ♘f3	d6
3 d4	cxd4
4 ♘xd4	♘f6
5 ♘c3	g6
6 ♗e2	♗g7
7 0-0	♘c6
8 ♗g5	0-0
9 ♘b3	a6 (169)

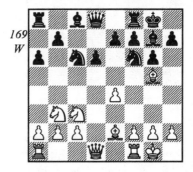

There is nothing wrong with the consistent 9...♗e6 (when 10 ♔h1 would transpose to game 36), but I am including the text for a little diversity.

10 f4

White must decide on whether he wants to prevent 10...b5. If he does, then 10 a4 is the obvious candidate, when a comparison with game 36 (and to a lesser degree, game 37) should be made. A favourable continuation for Black was: 10...♗e6 11 f4 ♖c8 12 ♔h1 ♘a5 13 ♘xa5 ♕xa5 14 ♗f3 ♖c5

15 ♖b1 ♕c7 16 ♗h4 ♖c8 17 ♖e1 ♖c4 18 ♗f2 ♕a5 (Ramirez-Hernandez, Mexico 1984). However I suspect that 14 ♗d3!? is more to the point.

Leaving a little to be desired is 10 ♔h1, which would transpose into V.Knox-Ward, British Ch (Eastbourne) 1991. In this game White's dilly-dallying soon got him into hot water: 10...b5 11 a3 ♗e6 12 f4 ♖c8 13 ♗d3 ♖e8 14 ♕e1 h6 15 ♗h4 ♗c4 16 ♖d1 ♕c7 17 ♗f2 e5!? 18 fxe5 ♘xe5 19 ♘d4 d5! 20 ♗g3 ♕b7 21 ♗h4 ♘xe4 22 ♘xe4 dxe4 23 ♗xe4 ♕b6 24 ♖f4 g5-+.

10 ...   b5
11 ♗f3!?

Stronger than the more passive 11 a3.

11 ...   b4! (170)

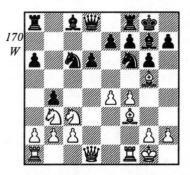

Although the black c6-knight looks loose, it is worth remembering that in fact at present it is indirectly defended via a check on b6.

12 ♘d5

This is probably another case of the most obvious move not being the best move. Surprisingly, a better reputation has 12 ♘a4!?, when the question is which of 12...♗d7 or 12...♕c7 is Black's best response. Giving the benefit of the doubt to the former, some practical examples are:

a) 13 a3 ♖b8 14 axb4 ♘xb4 15 e5 ♘e8 16 c3 ♘c6 17 ♗h4 ♕c7 Wilder-Petursson, Belgrade GMA 1988. The position is dynamically equal.

b) 13 ♖f2 ♕c7 with:

b1) 14 a3 ♖ab8 15 axb4 ♘xb4 16 c3 ♘c6 17 ♘d4 ♘a5 18 f5 ♘c4 19 b3 ♘e5 20 c4 h6 21 ♗e3 ♗xa4 22 ♖xa4 g5 23 ♖xa6 g4 24 ♗e2 ♘xe4 25 ♖f4 ♕b7 26 ♖a5 h5 27 ♘b5 ♖a8 28 ♖xa8 ♖xa8 29 ♕b1 ♘f6 30 ♗d4 ♗h6 31 ♖f1 ♘e4 32 ♕b2 f6 33 ♖a1 ♖xa1 34 ♕xa1 ♘d2 35 ♕d1 ♕e4 36 ♗b6 ♗e3+ 37 ♗xe3+ ♗xe3 38 ♔h1 ♘xb3 39 h3 gxh3 40 ♗xh5 hxg2+ 41 ♔xg2 ♕d2+ 42 ♕xd2 ♘xd2-+. i.e. A messy middlegame turned into a winning endgame by a random time scramble! (Gallagher-Ward, Haringey 1988).

b2) 14 e5?! ♘e8 15 ♖d2 ♖d8 16 exd6 ♘xd6 17 ♘bc5 ♖fe8 18 ♔h1?! ♗c8 19 ♗e2 ♘f5 20 ♖xd8 ♖xd8 21 ♕e1 h6 22 ♗h4 ♕xf4 23 ♗f2 ♘cd4 24 ♗d3 ♗e5 25 ♗g1 ♘f3! 26 ♕f1 ♕h4 27 ♗xf5 ♘xh2 28 ♗h3 ♘xf1 0-1 Simpson-Ward, Glorney Cup 1986.

c) 13 ♕e1 ♖b8 14 a3 ♕c7 15 ♕d2 a5 16 ♗h4 ♗e6 17 ♗f2 ♘d7 18 ♖fc1 ♗c4 19 ♘d4 ♘xd4 20 ♗xd4 ♗xd4+ 21 ♕xd4 e5!∓ Andrijević-Petursson, Belgrade GMA 1988.

What is clear, is that a lot of the positions arising after 12 ♘a4!? are unclear!

12 ... ♘xd5
13 exd5 ♘a5 *(171)*

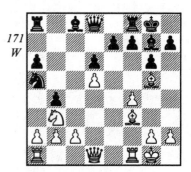

171
W

14 ♘xa5

Fearing that the black knight will eventually reach c4, White takes the easy way out. The main features of this position are that White has a poor bishop on f3 and the a7-g1 diagonal is a bit drafty too. Indeed the f4-pawn is also a hinderance to White's other bishop. White's queenside pawns are (as proved in this game) vulnerable, whilst Black's main weakness is his now exposed e7-pawn.

Instead of the text, White has other moves to consider:

a) 14 ♕e2! ♗xb2 15 ♗xe7 ♕b6+ 16 ♕f2 ♕xf2 17 ♔xf2 ♗xa1 18 ♗xf8 ♔xf8 19 ♖xa1 ♘c4 20 c3! with a draw the likely outcome.

b) 14 ♖b1?! ♘c4 15 ♕e2 ♕c7! Zapata-Miles, Thessaloniki OL 1984. Black has the better structure and the more active position.

c) 14 ♘d2?! ♕c7 15 ♔h1 ♗f5 16 ♘e4 ♘c4 17 ♕e2 ♖ac8 18 g4 ♗xe4 19 ♗xe4 ♘xb2 Kristiansson-Petursson, Scandinavian Cup 1981. It is *Black* who has compensation for his extra pawn!

14 ...	♕xa5
15 ♔h1	

Trading the e7-pawn for the b2-pawn clearly favours Black and once again the d6-pawn is immune because of ...♕b6+. Hence 15 ♗xe7?! ♖e8 is bad, and not much better is 15 ♕e1 ♗f5.

15 ...	♖e8!

On the face of it, a slightly passive move. However Black puts a stop to 16 ♗xe7, while preparing to muscle in on White's queenside pawns.

16 ♖e1	♗xb2
17 ♖b1	♗c3

Actually, there is not much to this tidy game. Black sets about showing that White's pawns are weaker than his. He does so by taking them and then winning in style.

18 ♖xe7	♖xe7
19 ♗xe7	♕xa2
20 g4	

Preventing 20...♗f5, which would have met 20 ♗xd6 nicely.

20 ...	♗b7
21 f5	

Rather desperate, but 21 ♗xd6 ♖d8 22 ♗xb4 ♗xd5 23 ♗xd5 ♖xd5 24 ♕c1 ♖b5 loses anyway.

21 ...	♕c4
22 ♗xd6	♖d8
23 ♗e7	*(172)*

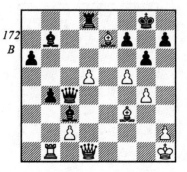

23 ...	♖xd5!
24 ♕f1	

If White captures the rook, then he gets caught in a fatal crossfire, i.e. 24 ♗xd5 ♗xd5+ 25 ♔g1 ♗d4+.

24 ...	♕xf1+
25 ♖xf1	♖d1!

Exquisite!

26 ♗xb7	♖xf1+
27 ♔g2	♖a1

0-1

Game 36
Kuzmin-Khalifman
USSR Ch 1990

1 e4	c5
2 ♘f3	d6
3 d4	cxd4
4 ♘xd4	♘f6
5 ♘c3	♘c6
6 ♗e2	g6
7 0-0	♗g7
8 ♘b3	0-0

9 ♗g5   ♗e6
10 ♔h1 *(173)*

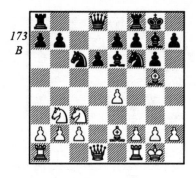

173
B

10 ...   ♘a5

Black immediately sets out to occupy the c4-square. Another idea worth mentioning is 10...h6 11 ♗h4 g5 12 ♗g3 d5. Although this is fairly logical, I have to admit that having played it before, I'm not too keen on it. Black has some active play, but after 13 ♘c5, his position is a little loose.

11 f4

Having prepared this move with ♔h1, it seems inconsistent not to follow up this way. Nevertheless it must be said that 11 ♘d5 is a less rash alternative (if 11 f4 can really be described as 'risky'). Then after 11...♗xd5 12 exd5 ♖c8 13 c3 ♘c4, the position is finely balanced. Black has the c-file and some pressure against White's queenside pawns. White has the e-file, bringing promise of some play against Black's e7-pawn.

11 ...   ♘c4

The most direct move, bearing in mind that White will not want to concede his bishop yet with 12 ♗xc4?!, giving Black the run of the light squares.

One flexible-looking alternative is 11...♖c8 (threatening 12...♖xc3 with ...♘xe4 to follow), a practical example being: 12 f5 ♗d7 13 fxg6 hxg6 14 ♘d5 ♘xd5 15 exd5 ♗xb2 16 ♖b1 ♗e5 17 ♘xa5 ♕xa5 18 ♖xb7 ♗a4 19 ♗d3 ♕xd5 and the players somewhat prematurely halted the proceedings by agreeing a draw, in Hebden-Yakovich, Copenhagen 1992.

12 f5 *(174)*

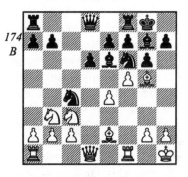

174
B

We can now see another reason for White putting his bishop on g5, rather than e3. It is safe from the clutches of the black knight on c4. Although it sacrifices a pawn, the text is therefore not only possible, but best. Taking time out to defend the b-pawn is too passive, so instead White goes 'all-in'.

12 ...   ♘xb2
13 ♕e1

The last chance for caution is the materialistic 13 ♕c1, attempting to win the trapped black knight. Indeed it does, but at the cost of three good pawns after 13...♗c4 14 ♕xb2 ♗xe2 15 ♘xe2 ♘xe4 16 f6 ♘xf6. Interesting is that this game's Dragon player deviated from the above path with White, with 14 e5?! ♗xe2 15 ♘xe2 ♘e4 16 f6 exf6 17 exf6 ♖e8! (Khalifman-Savchenko, USSR 1984). The standing of White's position evidently convinced him that he would be more than happy to change colour!

13 ...   ♗d7

If 13...♗c4?! then 14 ♗c1! leaves the knight in trouble.

14 ♕h4

The essence of the whole idea. White seeks play for his lost pawn and weakened queenside, in the form of a kingside attack.

14 ...   ♘a4

Black immediately extracts his knight, though 14...♖c8 is a very sensible alternative.

15 ♘xa4   ♗xa4
16 ♘d4

White starts to rustle up the troops. Unfortunately for him, he is unable to take advantage of his queen being on the same rank as Black's light-squared bishop. e.g. 16 e5 ♗xb3 17 exf6 exf6 18 fxg6 fxg6 19 axb3 fxg5 and though they are perhaps not the greatest, Black still remains two pawns up.

16 ...   ♖c8

17 ♗d3   ♗d7!

Black brings back his bishop, ready to help paper over any cracks.

18 ♖ab1   ♕c7
19 ♖f3

Very predictable. White prepares to slide the rook over to h3 with threats of mate. The problem with this plan is that his back rank is vulnerable and so Black quickly activates his queen.

19 ...   ♕c5
20 ♘e2   ♕a5
21 ♖h3   h5

The aggressive way of meeting the threat of 22 ♗xf6 ♗xf6 23 ♕xh7 mate.

22 ♘f4   ♕xa2
23 ♖f1 *(175)*

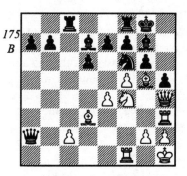

23 ...   ♖xc2!

The light-squared bishop looks like a big pawn, but without it, White's position will fall apart.

24 ♘xh5!?

It appears that White is really going for it, but he has no choice. Besides removing Black's h-pawn is the only way for him to make headway.

24 ...	♘xh5
25 g4	f6!

Sealing off his bishop, but also preparing to seal off the only lines to his king.

26 ♗e3	♕b3

Forcing White to take the exchange, when he will be extremely weak along the c6-h1 diagonal.

27 ♗xc2	♕xc2
28 gxh5	♗c6

Delaying ...g5 for a move, as now 29 hxg6 ♗xe4+ 30 ♖hf3 ♖c8 might be winning, and 29 ♕xe4+ is a safe alternative.

29 ♖g3	g5
30 ♕g4	♕xe4+
31 ♕xe4	♗xe4+
32 ♔g1	♔f7

Black's Dragon bishop is rather untypical at present, but he has sufficient compensation for this in a lot of extra pawns. Although the text offers the a-pawn, it reduces the impact of 33 h4 and from here onwards, Black comfortably proceeds to win the endgame.

33 ♖g4	♗d3
34 ♖f2	♖h8
35 ♗xa7	♖xh5
36 ♗b6	d5
37 ♖b4	♗e4
38 ♗c5	g4
39 ♖xb7	♗f8
40 ♖f4	♖g5!
41 ♔f2	♗xf5
42 ♖a4	♖h5
43 ♔g2	♗e4+

44 ♔g3	f5

0-1

White can't bear the thought of facing up to four passed pawns, and there is always the possibility of 45 ♖aa7 ♖h3+ 46 ♔f4 ♗h6+ 47 ♔e5 ♗f7+ 48 ♔f4 ♖f3+ 49 ♔g5 ♗f6+ 50 ♔h5 ♖h3 mate.

In the following game, it has to be said that Black takes a while to get his act together. However it will be seen that when he does, White's days are numbered.

Game 37
J.Sørensen-Watson
Herning 1991

1 e4	c5
2 ♘f3	d6
3 d4	cxd4
4 ♘xd4	♘f6
5 ♘c3	g6
6 ♗e2	♗g7
7 0-0	0-0
8 ♔h1	♘c6
9 ♘b3	♗e6
10 f4 *(176)*	

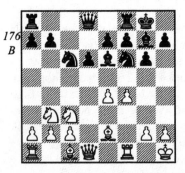

176
B

10 ...   ♜c8

The usual provocative move, doing nothing to dissuade 11 f5. Again, though I will not dwell on it, the cautious 10...♛c8, and 10...♞a5, facilitating 11...♝c4, are both playable.

11 f5

White for his part, does not hang about, but has little else new to offer. 11 ♝e3 would return to the realms of game 34, but one slightly offbeat though interesting example is: 11...♞a5 12 f5 ♞c4 (12...♝c4 is the logical alternative) 13 ♝d4 ♝d7 14 ♝xc4 ♜xc4 15 ♛d3 ♜c8 16 ♝xa7 b6 17 ♛a6 b5! 18 ♝b6?! ♛e8 19 ♛a5 (Thipsay-Watson, Kuala Lumpur 1992). Now Black, who already has adequate compensation for the pawn, could have gained the upper hand with 19...♞g4!, opening up the Dragon bishop, and intending to embarrass the white queen with ...♞e5-c4(or c6).

Another more solid move that we have seen before is 11 ♝f3. Then Black should choose between 11...♝c4 12 ♜e1 e5!? or 11...♞a5 e.g. 12 ♜e1 (and note if 12 e5 then 12...♞e8 and not 12...dxe5??, losing a piece to 13 ♛xd8 and 14 ♞xa5 i.e. it is worth remembering not to fall into this trap!) 12...♞c4 13 ♞d5 ♝d7 14 ♞e3 b5 15 c3 ♛c7 16 ♞xc4 bxc4 17 ♞d2 e5! leaving Black's position slightly preferable; Olafsson-Petursson, Reykjavik 1985.

11 ...   ♝d7

12 ♝g5

This move demonstrates a similarity between this game and the last. Previously the black knight travelled to c4 via a5, but here it has the e5-square at its disposal.

If White has his heart set on a caveman approach, then I would suggest that there might not be a better time than now for 12 g4!? (or ?!). The plus point of it is that Black does not have available the saving (and usually winning) exchange sacrifice. i.e. 12...♞e5 13 g5 ♜xc3? 14 gxf6! (gaining a whole piece, as there is no bishop on e3 for Black to take with his rook). Hence Black must find some other way of exploiting this early pawn sortie. Two candidates for the job are 12...♞e5 13 g5 ♞e8 (hoping that White has over extended), and 12...h6!? (so that after 13 h4, intending 14 g5, Black has the h7-square for his knight), when Black hopes that White's weaknesses will be worse than his (note that posting a knight on e5 always helps).

12 ...   ♞e5

13 fxg6

This is the move which needs to be brought into question. The short-term gains are self evident. White opens up the f-file for his rook(s). Nevertheless his pawn structure is now significantly worse and White's h-pawn cannot be compared with Black's f-pawn, as this game eventually shows. Obviously White also says goodbye to any hope of ever achieving f5-f6 and for this reason Gallego-G.Martin, Pontevedra 1986 saw 13 ♗d3!? ♘c4 14 ♗xc4 ♖xc4 15 ♕d3 b5 16 ♖ad1 (16 hxg6?! hxg6 17 e5 ♘h7!∓) 16...♗c6 17 ♘d5 ♗xd5 18 exd5 ♘e4! 19 ♗c1 ♕d7 with equal chances.

13 ...   **hxg6**
14 ♘d5 *(177)*

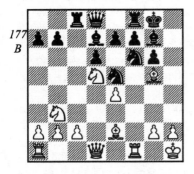

14 ...   **♘xd5**

Also played to good effect in Lobron-Cebalo, Zagreb/Rijeka 1985 was 14...♗e6!?, the game continuing with 15 ♘xf6+ exf6 16 ♗h4 d5! 17 exd5 ♕xd5 18 ♕xd5 ♗xd5 19 c3 ♘c4 20 ♗xc4 ♗xc4 21 ♖fe1 ♖fe8 22 ♔g1 f5 23 ♗f2 a6 24 ♘c5? ♖xe1+ 25 ♖xe1 ♗xa2. Needless to say with an extra pawn and the advantage of the two bishops in an open position, Black converted the whole point.

15 exd5   **♗f5!?**
16 c3   **a6**
17 ♕d2   **♖e8**

18 ♖ae1   **♕d7**
19 ♕f4   **♕d8**

Very odd! Evidently Black is not yet too worried about what White is up to, and it is as though he is asking White to give him his best shot. Alternatively Black has had a rethink with regards to where his pieces should be, and he can afford to swallow his pride and admit that his previous move didn't fit in. One immediate problem was where his bishop would go after 20 g4.

20 ♕g3   **♗d7**
21 ♗e3   **♕c7**
22 ♗d4   **b5**
23 ♗d3   **♖f8**
24 ♗e4   **♗e8**
25 ♕e3

On the face of it, it really does look as though neither side has been doing much, bar White's failed probing on the kingside. However Black has now secured his king position, and in the next few moves we see a remarkable turnaround.

25 ...   **f5!**
26 ♗f3   **♗f7**

Black has started to push forward and now he focuses his attention on White's vulnerable d5-pawn.

27 h3   **♔h7**
28 ♖e2   **♗f6**
29 ♖fe1   **♔g7**

A cleverly played manoeuvre, sidestepping the possibility of the annoying ♕h6.

30 ♔g1   **♖h8**
31 ♗b6   **♕c4**

Black has slowly improved all of his pieces, the space-gaining 25...f5 being the key. Now (though it was inevitable) the d5-pawn is about to drop off, which is completely disastrous for White.

32 ♘a5	♘xf3+
33 ♕xf3	♕xd5
34 ♕g3	e5 *(178)*

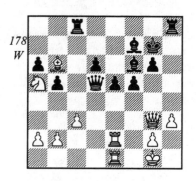

178
W

The floodgates are open. Not a pretty sight for White, whose h-pawn is unlikely to figure prominently!

35 ♗f2	f4
36 ♕f3	♕xf3
37 gxf3	♖xh3
38 ♘b7	♗d5
39 ♘xd6	♗xf3
0-1	

The final game of this chapter covers ideas in which White is uncharacteristically (for the Classical Variation) aggressive. At the very least White delays castling (often other developing moves as well), in order to launch his g- and f-pawns rapidly. Rooks start in the corner,

and as we have already seen them take a vital role in attacking the Dragon structure (see the Yugoslav Attack), it must be that the quickest route to the black king is down the h-file. Therefore Black does have a bit more time than usual before checkmate will arrive, but he must be on the ball. White's plan is to squash Black into complete passivity, before bringing in the deadly major pieces. If Black's pieces are based around his own back rank then the white king will be safe on the kingside, the queenside, or even in the middle.

Game 38
Grabarczyk-Fedorov
Katowice 1991

1 e4	c5
2 ♘f3	d6
3 d4	cxd4
4 ♘xd4	♘f6
5 ♘c3	g6
6 ♗e3	

It is unusual for a Classical player to play this so soon (though the move order is not relevant), but in Lupu-Ward (Mont St Michel 1992), White left the move out altogether. Instead in my opinion, White engaged in some premature attacking which never looked like succeeding and eventually backfired: 6 ♗e2 ♗g7 7 f4 0-0 8 ♘b3 ♘c6 9 g4 a5!? 10 g5 ♘e8 11 a4 e5!? 12 ♘d5 exf4 13 h4 ♘c7 14 ♘b6 ♖b8 15 ♘xc8 ♖xc8 16 ♗g4

♘e6 17 0-0 h5 18 ♗h3 ♕b6+ 19 ♔g2 ♘e5 20 ♗xe6 fxe6 21 ♘d4 f3+ 22 ♔h1 ♘g4 23 c3 ♗xd4 24 cxd4 ♕c6 0-1.

6 ...	♗g7
7 ♗e2	♘c6
8 ♘b3	0-0
9 f4	♗e6
10 g4 *(179)*	

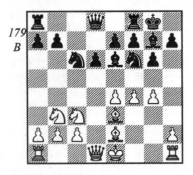

10 ...   ♘d7

Both 10...d5 and 10...♘a5 are playable here, and also possible is 10...♖c8!?, when I would like to give two practical examples:

a) 11 g5?! ♘d7 12 ♕d2 ♘b6 13 h4 d5 14 0-0-0 dxe4 15 ♕e1 ♕c7 16 ♘c5 ♘b4 (Hansson-McCambridge, Reykjavik 1984). White is a pawn down and his king is in far more danger than Black's.

b) 11 f5! ♗xb3 12 axb3 ♘e5 13 ♗d4 ♖xc3! 14 bxc3 ♘xe4 15 0-0 ♕c7 16 c4 (Yakovich-Ward, Copenhagen 1993). Because of the forced 11...♗xb3, the traditional exchange sacrifice has not shattered the white queenside pawns. However Black does have some

reasonable compensation based on White's exposed king and weak kingside pawns. Black continued with 16...♖d8, but 16...♕c6!? intending ...♘g5-h3 mate(!) certainly warrants consideration.

11 ♕d2

A couple of alternatives suggest themselves:

a) 11 ♘d4 ♕b6! (a familiar idea) 12 ♘xe6 ♕xe3 13 ♘xf8 ♗xc3+ 14 bxc3 ♖xf8 and White's dreadful pawns more than compensate Black for the exchange.

b) 11 f5 ♗xb3 12 axb3 ♘c5 with approximately equal chances.

11 ...	♘b6
12 h4	♘c4
13 ♗xc4	♗xc4
14 0-0-0	♖c8
15 h5	♘b4 *(180)*

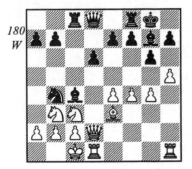

Both sides have been plugging away with their attacks and now things are really hotting up.

16 hxg6

Some may argue that White should have foregone 14 0-0-0 for 14 h5. Now he has castled, some may also argue that he should take time out to play 16 ♔b1. To be honest, nothing is completely clear.

16 ...   fxg6

In deciding which way to recapture, it is possible that Black overlooked the strength of 16...♗xb3! 17 axb3 ♕a5 18 ♕h2 h6.

17 ♕h2   h5
18 gxh5

In view of the rest of the game, again possibly 18 ♔b1 would have been wiser.

18 ...   ♘xa2+
19 ♘xa2   ♗xb3
20 ♘c3   ♖xc3
21 bxc3   ♕a5
22 e5?!

Attempting to block out the Dragon bishop. After 22 cxb3 ♕xc3+ 23 ♕c2 ♕xe3+, it is clear that Black has good compensation for the exchange. Nevertheless, perhaps he should try this or 22 ♗d4 ♗xd4 23 ♖xd4 ♖c8!?.

22 ...   ♖c8
23 ♗d4   dxe5
24 ♕h3   ♖c6
25 ♗xe5

If 25 fxe5 then 25...♗h6+ is terminal.

25 ...   ♗xe5
26 fxe5   ♖xc3 *(181)*

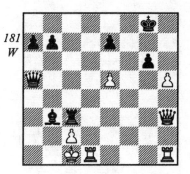

181
W

0-1

After 27 ♖d8+ ♔g7 28 h6+ ♔h7, there are no more checks, whilst the black pieces are poised to deliver checkmate.

9   6 ♗c4 and 6 h3

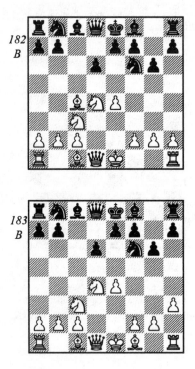

182
B

183
B

Although often regarded as a Classical variation, the move 6 ♗c4 is certainly worthy of a separate chapter in view of its recent popularity. White places his light-squared bishop on a very sensible diagonal, with quick development and kingside castling in mind. His plan is simply to try to keep control of the position, with rook centralization a common occurrence. As usual the d5-square is of key im-

portance and generally any White attack is fairly slow-moving.

White may choose to develop his dark-squared bishop on g5 to add weight to a later ♘d5 (due to surmounting pressure on f6 and e7), but this has the drawback of leaving the d4-knight short of protection. As the bishop tends to withdraw to safety on b3, this central knight has few available retreat squares. For this reason White may prefer ♗e3, but then of course he must guard against the very awkward ...♘g4. This, then, is where the cautious h3 comes into the picture (i.e. not just to stop a back rank mate!), with the bishop on c4 not performing the function that it would on e2. To be brutally honest, there is no very good reason for White to play 6 h3 unless he seriously intends the premature 7 g4?!. 6 h3 is most likely to transpose to the 6 ♗c4 lines unless White has in mind the aggressive, but little-seen and uninspiring set-up depicted in game 39.

As for 6 ♗c4, well, two very logical Black set-ups are covered. Games 40 and 41 see the traditional Dragon piece allocation with the common utilization of the c-file and particularly the occupation of the c4-square always in mind. As we have already seen, when White castles on the kingside, it is often playable for Black to fianchetto his queen's bishop after ...a6 and ...b5, and this idea is the subject of discussion in games 42 and 43.

Game 39
Hennigan-Ward
British Ch (Blackpool) 1988

1 e4	c5
2 ♘f3	d6
3 d4	cxd4
4 ♘xd4	♘f6
5 ♘c3	g6
6 ♗e3	

Again as a reminder, it is not necessary to prepare this with 6 h3 as now 6...♘g4?? loses material to 7 ♗b5+.

6 ...	♗g7
7 h3	0-0
8 ♕d2	♘c6
9 0-0-0 *(184)*	

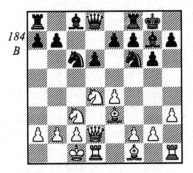

White has adopted a similar formation to that of the Yugoslav Attack. In exchanging f3 for h3, White is not so vulnerable to central breaks such as ...d5. However more important is that the h-file is the fastest route to the black king and so this alternative attacking plan (with f4) is much slower.

9 ...	♘xd4

A familiar idea. Black takes advantage of the fact that White has omitted ♗c4 by preparing to place his own bishop along this diagonal.

10 ♗xd4	♗e6
11 f4	

The most natural continuation. White gains a little space and starts his attack rolling with g4 and then f5 on the cards. The main problem with this move (the lack of protection for the e4-pawn) soon becomes apparent.

The slower but more solid 11 ♗d3 was played in Thomas-Gemmell, British Ch 1987 where White was really made to suffer: 11...♕a5 12 a3 ♖ab8 13 f4 b5! 14 g4 b4 15 ♘b1 d5! 16 axb4 ♕a2 17 e5 ♘e4 18 ♕e1 ♖fc8 19 ♖f1 ♖b7 20 ♖f3 ♖bc7 21 c3 ♖b7 22 ♗c2 a5 23 ♖dd3 ♗d7 24 ♕d1 e6 25 ♗b3 ♕a1 26 bxa5 ♕xa5 27 ♗c2 ♗f8 28 b4 ♕a6 29 ♖de3 ♖bc7 30 ♖e2 ♗b5 31 ♖h2 ♕a1 32 c4 ♕a2 33 cxb5 ♗xb4 34 b6 ♖c4 35 b7 ♖b8 36 ♕d3 ♖xb7 37 ♔d1 ♖bc7 38 ♗e3 ♘c3+ 39 ♘xc3 ♖xc3 40 ♕d2 ♖xc2 41 ♕xc2 ♖xc2 42 ♖xc2 ♕b3 0-1.

11 ...	♕a5
12 a3	

Not 12 ♔b1? ♘xe4!∓∓

12 ...	b5!? *(185)*

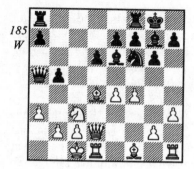

185
W

Highlighting the weakness of the e4-pawn, which in contrast to the Yugoslav Attack is not defended by a pawn on f3.

13 e5

White has no desire to trade his e-pawn for Black's b-pawn. 13 ♗xb5?! ♘xe4! 14 ♘xe4 ♕xb5 leaves Black with a bishop for a knight and some handy open lines against the white king.

13 ...   dxe5
14 fxe5

If 14 ♗xe5, then Black will simply continue his assault down the b-file and with 12 a3 a defensive concession, his task is easy. After the text, White obtains an isolated e-pawn. In many Sicilian variations this e5-pawn can be a useful attacking feature. Here, however, it is more of a weakness.

14 ...   ♘d5
15 ♘xd5   ♕xd2+
16 ♖xd2   ♗xd5
17 ♔b1

Not 17 ♗xb5? falling (and not for the first time!) for 17...♗h6.

17 ...   ♗h6
18 ♖f2   a6
19 ♗d3   ♖fd8
20 ♗c5   ♖d7

The most flexible move. Black avoids playing ...e6 just in case he is unable to round up the white e5-pawn.

21 h4   ♗g7
22 ♖e1   ♖c8
23 ♗b4   ♗e6

There is little doubt that it is Black who has won the opening argument. His endgame play isn't particularly great, but it is sufficient for a win.

24 ♗c3   h5
25 ♖ff1   ♖c6
26 ♗e4   ♖c4
27 g3   ♗h6
28 ♗d3   ♖g4

Black's pawn structure has always been the better, but he must always be careful of his queenside. Over there, his a- and b-pawns have held White's queenside majority at bay, but there is a danger that any carelessness could result in them dropping off!

29 ♖g1   ♗f5
30 ♗xf5   gxf5
31 e6

A necessary move, since if Black gets in ...e6, the e5-pawn will soon be easy prey.

31 ...   ♖d6
32 exf7+   ♔xf7
33 ♖gf1   ♖d5
34 ♗e5   e6
35 b3   ♗g7

36 ♗xg7   ♖xg7

Again one can't help feeling that Black has made a meal of this. Nevertheless his active rooks, combined with the backward g3-pawn, leads to the conclusion that he still has a clear plus.

37 ♖f3	♖g4
38 ♖fe3	♖d6
39 ♔b2	♖gd4
40 ♖c3	♔f6
41 ♖c8	♖d8
42 ♖c7	♖e4
43 ♖xe4	fxe4
44 ♖c5	♖d5
45 ♖c3	♔e5
46 ♖e3	♔d4
47 ♖e2	e3
48 c4	♖f5
49 ♖e1	♖f2+
50 ♔c1	bxc4
51 bxc4	♔d3
52 ♖d1+	♔c3 (186)

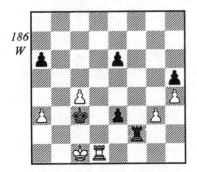

0-1

White can do nothing to prevent 53...e2 and 54...♖f1.

Game 40
Adams-Shirov
Biel 1991

1 e4	c5
2 ♘f3	d6
3 d4	cxd4
4 ♘xd4	♘f6
5 ♘c3	g6
6 ♗c4	♗g7
7 0-0	0-0
8 h3	♘c6
9 ♗e3 (187)	

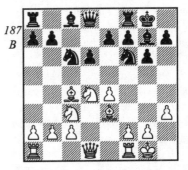

In view of the strength of the forthcoming combination, many White players now opt for the cautious ♗b3. This retreat may be traded in for 7 0-0 or 9 ♗e3 and either way, a direct transposition into game 41 is likely.

9 ...   ♘xe4!?

9...♗d7 is of course a reasonable alternative (see game 41).

10 ♗xf7+

The most critical. After 10 ♘xe4 d5 11 ♘xc6 bxc6, White must really preserve his bishop. However after 12 ♗d3 dxe4 13 ♗xe4 ♕c7, as we saw in chapter 8, the isolated queenside pawns are of little consequence, when weighed up against the potential b-file pressure and the power of Black's mobile kingside majority.

10 ...   ♔xf7!!

The sort of move that one could only discover with plenty of free time, whilst, say, languishing in a Latvian gaol. Interestingly enough, that's exactly where it *was* found, by a friend of Mr Shirov who, not being a Dragon player himself, decided to let the cat out of the bag. An absolutely brilliant move which supersedes the also playable 10...♖xf7.

11 ♘xe4   ♘xd4

Black of course does not mind ♘xc6, but the e6-square is a little moist, and so he prevents 12 ♘g5+ and ♘e6.

12 ♗xd4   e5!

This is what it's all about. The centre pawns move up, clearing space for the bishops behind them. Now the point of 10...♔xf7!! can be revealed. If the black rook were on f7 instead of f8, then White could now play 13 ♗c5 as the black queen is unguarded.

13 ♗e3   d5

Again consistent. Black is in control, but he must be careful (if possible) not to allow the white knight a permanent outpost.

14 ♘g3

Possibly more threatening is 14 ♗g5, but after 14...♕d7 15 ♘c3 h6

16 ♗h4 d4 17 ♘e4 ♕c6 18 ♖e1 ♗f5 19 f3 ♖ac8 20 c3 ♔g8 21 ♕b3+ ♔h7, Black still retained the upper hand, and went on to win in 41 moves in Jansa-Hellers, Herning 1991.

14 ...   ♔g8
15 c3   ♗e6
16 ♘e2

White wants to get the d4-square for his knight and so prepares 17 f4. The immediate 16 f4? is punished by 16...d4! 17 cxd4 exf4 with a tremendous endgame not far off.

16 ...   g5! (188)

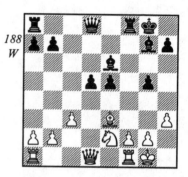

As White is missing his light-squared bishop, there is nothing weak about this aggressive and binding move.

17 ♕d2

White's knight could now head for h5 via 17 ♘g3, but even when it gets there, Black can comfortably preserve his bishop with ...♗h8.

17 ...   h6
18 h4!

The only challenging move. Although his own king position ultimately gets weakened by this, White's alternative is to sit back and wait to be squashed.

18 ...	**gxh4**
19 ♗xh6	**♕f6!**
20 ♗g5	

Up until now White would have been only too pleased to exchange off a pair of bishops. However in view of the problems that might be set down the h-, g- and f-files, White decides that his best bet lies with accepting the offered h-pawn.

20 ...	**♕g6**
21 ♗xh4	**♖f5**

Black prepares to double rooks or to switch his rook over to h5. White's correct reaction is to hit the panic button.

22 f4	**♕g4!**
23 ♗g5?!	

23 g3 is met by 23...♖h5 and hence probably White's last chance is 23 ♗e7!?. However then both 23...♔f7 and 23...♖e8, leave Black in a good position to continue his attack.

23 ...	**♖af8**
24 ♖f2	**d4!**

Preparing to let his light-squared bishop in on the action.

25 cxd4	**exf4**
26 ♗xf4	**♗c4**

Devastating. Now White must lose a piece.

27 ♗e3	**♖xf2**
28 ♗xf2	**♗xe2**
	0-1

The following beautiful game is very instructive. A lot of ideas already discussed are encompassed, and Black appears to win with consummate ease.

Game 41
Hector-Tiviakov
Haninge 1992

1 e4	**c5**
2 ♘c3	**♘c6**
3 ♘f3	**g6**
4 d4	**cxd4**
5 ♘xd4	**♗g7**
6 ♗e3	**♘f6**
7 ♗c4	**0-0**
8 ♗b3	**d6**
9 h3	**♗d7**
10 0-0	**a6**

Black prepares 11...b5, safe in the knowledge that White will not want to weaken his queenside with 11 a4?!. Clearly in such an instance, 10...a6 (preventing a piece coming to b5) is far more useful to Black than 11 a4 is to White. In addition the b3-bishop would be slightly more loose and the a4-pawn could be an eventual target.

11 f4

Having rejected 11 a4?!, White's main alternative is 11 ♖e1. The point behind this move is to add support to the e4-pawn, but with ultimate aim of pressurizing Black's e7-pawn. In Chandler-Watson (British Ch 1988) play continued with 11...b5!? 12 ♘d5

♘a5 13 ♕d3 ♖c8 14 ♖ad1 ♘c4 15
♗c1 ♖e8 16 c3 ♖c5 *(189)*.

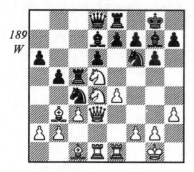

At this stage the players agreed a
draw, although it was generally accepted that Black has done far
more than equalize. White has
failed in his attempt to get Black to
play ...♘xd5, which after exd5
would have allowed White his
pressure on the e7-pawn, as well as
a potential outpost for his knight on
c6. Whilst White appears to have
maximized his position, his knight
is being pushed out of the d5-
square, after which Black can improve some piece placings and then
press forward on the queenside.

11 ...   b5
12 a3

Guarding against the simple
threat of 12...b4 and 13...♘xe4.

12 ...   ♖c8
13 ♕f3   ♘a5
14 ♖ad1   ♘c4!

Black's play has been fairly
straightforward so far and I find it
incredible that this very natural

continuation has not previously
been taken for granted.
14...♘xb3?! may gain a bishop for
a knight, but after 15 cxb3, White
has few problems and is able to
carry on with such moves as g4 and
e5. It should be noted by the reader,
that doubling White's b-pawn(s) is
often not such a good idea. White
regains control of the c4-square,
and any exchange sacrifice on c3
will no longer shatter the white
pawn structure.

15 ♗c1   ♕c7

The black queen removes herself
from the same file as the d1-rook
and gives White ...♘xa3 to think
about.

16 ♔h1   e5!

The standard treatment. The e5-
square will soon be back under
Black's control and, although temporarily blocked in, the Dragon
bishop will certainly surface again.

17 ♘de2   ♗c6

Eyeing up both the e4-pawn and
the d5-square.

18 f5

This is critical. If White can get
in g4 and g5, then Black (whilst
losing control of d5) is in danger of
being steamrollered. Therefore
Black takes steps to intercept this
plan.

18 ...   h6
19 ♗xc4

White was hoping to avoid this
move, but he can think of nothing
else constructive to do.

19 ...   bxc4

20	♘d5	♗xd5
21	exd5	e4!

Hassling the white queen, re-opening the a1-h8 diagonal, and as we will soon see, vacating a vital square.

| 22 | ♕e3 | g5! |

Again excellent play. This time removing the f4-square from White's options.

| 23 | h4 | g4 |

White regains the f4-square, but now has holes around his own king and zero play down the f-file.

24	♕g3	♖fe8
25	♗e3	h5
26	♘f4	♖e5
27	♗d4	♖ce8! *(190)*

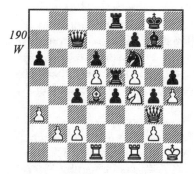

190
W

A lovely positional sacrifice. Black resists the tempting 27...♖xf5? when after 28 ♗xf6 and 29 ♘xh5 White is very much back in the game.

28 ♖de1

As nothing is doing for White, he should probably accept the offerings with 28 ♗xd4!?. Then Black can choose between 28...dxe5, which is similar to, but not as good as the line in the game, or 28...♖xe5!?. The latter would therefore be a simple exchange sacrifice. We know that a Dragon bishop is often considered to be as good or even better than a white rook. Well, here there are no open files and the Dragon bishop will dominate the dark squares. In addition White's d5- and f5-pawns may eventually drop off and, as in the notes to White's 30th move, Black has available the ultimate plan of ...e3 and ...♘e4.

28	...	e3
29	♗xe5	dxe5
30	♘xh5	

The lack of squares for the white queen now becomes apparent. If now 30 ♘e2 then 30...♗h6. Black defends the e3-pawn and threatens 31...♘e4, whilst if 32 ♘c3 then 32 ...♗f4 is very embarrassing.

However, the text is of course no better. Black obtains two perfectly good minor pieces for a rook and still with passed e-pawn(s), is never in danger of failing to win!

30	...	♘xh5
31	♕xg4	♘f6
32	♕g3	♕c5
33	♖xe3	♕xd5
34	♕f3	e4
35	♕e2	♗h6
36	♖g3+	♔h7
37	♖c3	e3
38	♖xc4	♘e4
39	♖f3	♘d2

40	Ёa4	♘xf3
41	gxf3	♕d2

0-1

Game 42
Jansa-Kir.Georgiev
Malmö 1986/87

1	e4	c5
2	♘f3	d6
3	d4	cxd4
4	♘xd4	♘f6
5	♘c3	g6
6	&c4	&g7
7	h3	0-0
8	0-0	

Instead of 8 0-0, the prophylactic 8 &b3 would not be a surprise as generally speaking, lines will transpose. However in S.B.Hansen-Ward, Gausdal 1992, after 8 &b3 a6, White continued with the over-cautious 9 a4. This move cannot be recommended, as rather than trying to prevent ...b5, White should probably allow it and then later make the ultimate timely challenge of a4. Indeed after 9 a4, Black could (as mentioned in game 41) play 9...♘c6 favourably, but things also turned out very well with 9...b6 10 0-0 &b7 11 Ёe1 ♘bd7 12 ♘d5 e6 13 ♘xf6+ ♘xf6 14 &g5 ♕c7 15 &xf6 &xf6 16 c3 Ёad8 17 ♕g4 d5.

Another ineffective try is 8 ♘f3?!. This move really seems out of place before f4 has been played. 8...♘c6 is a sensible reply, but 8...♘bd7!? 9 0-0 a6 10 a4 b6 11

♕e2 &b7 12 &f4 ♕c7 13 Ёfe1 e6! 14 Ёad1 ♘e5 15 &b3 ♘fd7 16 ♘d2 ♘c5 17 &e3 Ёad8 was also good for Black in Benjamin-Gufeld, New York 1989.

8	...	a6
9	&b3	b5 *(191)*

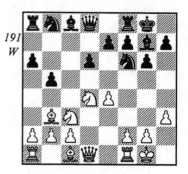

Black has been holding back on ...♘c6 because he intends to develop this knight to d7. From there it adds extra support to the f6-knight, and may then attack the e4-pawn with ...♘c5 or aim for the c4-square via e5 or b6.

10 ♘d5

For White's 10th move alternatives, see game 43. Here 10...♘xe4? can be met by 11 ♕f3 which sets up a discovered attack on the a8-rook. In this case White would be winning. However in Myrvold-Ward, Gausdal 1992, White played 10 ♘d5 in a position where 8 0-0 had been replaced by 8 &e3. As we have seen, &e3 loses much of its point if Black doesn't intend ...♘c6 (pressurizing the d4-knight). White does better to leave it on c1 until the time is right for, say, ♗g5, and in the above game Black decided to take up the gauntlet with 10...♘xe4!?. Notice here the key point is that White has not yet castled and due to this Black was able to sail through the complications and shortly to victory after 11 ♕f3 ♘c5 12 ♗g5 ♗b7 13 ♕e3 ♖e8 14 0-0-0 ♘xb3+ 15 ♕xb3 ♘c6 16 ♘xc6 ♗xc6 17 h4 ♖c8 18 h5 ♗xd5 19 ♖xd5 ♕c7 20 hxg6 hxg6 21 ♖d3 ♕c4.

10 ...	♗b7
11 ♘xf6+	♗xf6
12 ♗h6	♖e8
13 ♖e1	♘d7
14 c3	

White lends support to the centre, but also creates a potential target.

14 ...	♘c5
15 ♗d5	♕d7
16 ♕f3	b4!

Black immediately begins his minority attack.

| 17 ♖ad1 | bxc3 |
| 18 bxc3 | ♖ac8 |

White's queenside pawns are his only weakness, but Dragon expert Kiril Georgiev proceeds to exploit them exquisitely. An excellent example of why the Dragon isn't only about checkmate!

19 ♖b1	♖c7
20 ♖b6	♖ec8
21 ♗d2	♔g7
22 ♖eb1	♗xd5!

This exchange has been timed to perfection. There is now no pressure down the e-file and the c6-square is of little consequence once the black queen goes on the rampage.

23 exd5	♕a4
24 ♖1b2	♕c4
25 ♖6b4	♕d3
26 ♕f4	

With his vulnerable pawns, White will be reluctant to swap queens at the best of times. Here is no exception with 26 ♕xd3?? ♘xd3 netting Black the exchange.

| 26 ... | ♘e4 |

Now White's c3-pawn is certainly doomed.

27 ♘c6	♘xc3
28 ♕h6+	♔g8
29 ♖2b3	♘e2+
30 ♔h2	♕xd5
31 ♘b8	

A really sad move to have to see, let alone play!

31 ...	♗e5+
32 g3	♖c1!
33 ♗xc1	♖xc1
34 f3	♗xg3+ (192)

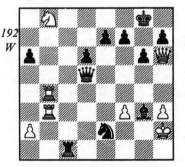

192
W

0-1

Just what we like to see! White has made no glaring errors in this game, but he will be mated after 35 ♔g2 ♖g1.

Game 43
Klundt-Watson
Kecskemet 1988

1	e4	c5
2	♘f3	d6
3	d4	cxd4
4	♘xd4	♘f6
5	♘c3	g6
6	♗c4	♗g7
7	h3	0-0
8	0-0	a6
9	♖e1	

Although on move nine, this cleverly disguised move is effectively a 10th move alternative as 9 ♗b3 and 9...b5 is yet to happen. Forgetting 9 ♖e1 for the moment and interpolating 9 ♗b3 b5 leaves us with one other major consideration in 10 a4. This aggressive thrust intends proving that 9...b5 was premature and is best met by 10...♗b7 (as Black is happy to trade wing for centre pawns). Then after 11 ♗g5 (see text for 11 ♖e1) both sides have their tricks. Firstly 11...♘xe4? is a mistake due to 12 ♘xe4 ♗xe4 13 ♖e1, with tremendous pressure on e7. But then if 11...b4 12 ♘d5 ♘bd7!?, the greedy 13 ♘xb4?! (eyeing up the c6-square), is refuted by 13...♕b6!, when Black is clearly better. Thus 13 a5 *(193)* has been suggested,

arriving at the tense position illustrated below.

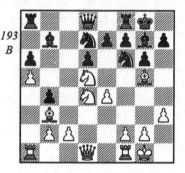

The b4-pawn is very much out on a limb, but the e4-pawn is still a problem for White, who will never want to play the hole-creating f3. **Here Black should consider** 13...♖c8 and 13...♘c5 as well as 13...h6, attempting to unpin on e7, and hence really throwing the cat amongst the pigeons!

9	...	b5
10	♗b3	♗b7
11	♗g5	

Again White can try the immediate 11 a4. Here though Black has three satisfactory replies in 11...♘bd7, 11...♘c6 and 11...bxa4. To give a couple of practical examples with the latter, we have:

a) 12 ♖xa4?! ♘bd7 13 ♗d5 ♘xd5 14 exd5 ♘b6 15 ♖b4 ♕c7∓ Nicholson-Watson, British Ch 1986. Black has the bishop pair, the d5-pawn is weak, and the white rook on b4 is misplaced.

b) 12 ♗xa4 ♛c7 13 ♗g5 e6 14 ♛d2 ♘bd7 15 ♗xd7 ♘xd7 16 ♗h6 ♗xh6 17 ♛xh6 ♘c5 18 ♖e3 e5 19 ♘f5 f6 20 ♘g3 ♘e6∓ Nicholson-Hodgson, British Ch 1986. For the second time in the same tournament, Nicholson had nothing to show for his venture into this variation.

11 ... ♘bd7
12 ♘d5 ♖e8

A common preparatory move. Black defends his e7-pawn so that his queen is free to move and so that taking on d5 won't be so disastrous.

13 c3 ♘xd5!?

An interesting decision which is by no means forced. Indeed many might choose to reject this move in view of 14 exd5. However evidently White doesn't fancy this recapture, which restricts his light-squared bishop. Possibly this is because of 14...♘c5.

14 ♗xd5 ♛c7

Obviously 14...♗xd5 really would be foolhardy as then White has the crucial c6-square.

15 a4 bxa4
16 ♖xa4 ♘c5
17 ♖a2?!

It is quite natural for White to defend his b-pawn, with the idea that when it moves, his rooks can double. Nevertheless he soon regrets this decision as the rook later has to buy its way back into the game.

17 ... e6

18 ♗xb7 ♛xb7
19 ♛e2 a5

Preventing 20 b4 and threatening a timely ...a4 to fix the pawns still further.

20 ♛b5 ♛c7
21 ♛c4 d5!

Again preventing 22 b4 and forcing the opening up of the e-file.

22 exd5 exd5
23 ♛f1 *(194)*

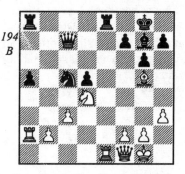

23 ... ♗xd4!

Showing great judgement. With the a2-rook out of the game, White will never be able to exploit the dark-squared weaknesses around the black king.

24 ♖xe8+ ♖xe8
25 cxd4 ♘b3
26 ♗e3 ♛c6
27 ♛d3 a4
28 ♖a3 ♖b8
29 ♗f4 ♖b4
30 ♗h6 f6

A useful precaution. Black has White's queenside tied up and will soon nobble the d4-pawn.

31 ♛e3 ♔f7

32	h4	♕e6		
33	♕f4	♘xd4		
34	♕c7+	♕e7		
35	♕c8	♘f5		
36	♗d2	♖xb2		
37	♖c3	♖b1+		
38	♔h2	♖b7		

43	♔g3	g5
44	♗e3	♖b3
45	♖c7+	♔g6
46	♖d7	♖d3 (195)

White is on his way out, but with his rook finally free, he has a few cards left to play. 39 ♖c7 was his first try.

39 ♕h8

This is his second try and it appears his last. Now Black 'traps' the white queen, thus forcing an exchange into an easily winning ending.

39	...	♕f8
40	♕xh7+	♕g7
41	♕xg7+	♔xg7
42	g4	♘xh4

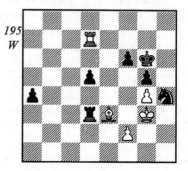

0-1

The white king is stuck and the two black passed pawns are too hot to handle.

10   g3 systems

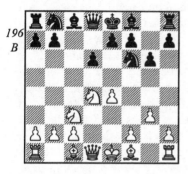

196
B

The scene was set. Garry Kasparov had just become the World Champion and was about to take on the so-called 'cream of English junior chess' in a much publicized simultaneous. Having been invited to take part, I was very excited at the prospect of possibly discovering what he would play against the Dragon. At that time, I hadn't even heard of chess databases, and my pre-match preparation of looking at his games, had provided me with nothing on my favourite variation. Kasparov announced that he was out for blood (the juniors were to make no draw offers!) and then set off like a train. Fortunately he opened 1 e4 on my board and as he whizzed around, it seemed like only seconds before

the critical Open Sicilian position had been reached. I bashed out 5...g6 and waited in eager anticipation for his reply. Then something intriguing happened. He stopped in his tracks and gave a very puzzled expression. Thoughts raced through my head. Could it really be that he had never seen the Dragon, or had it perhaps been long refuted in Russia? Everyone stared at him whilst he remained motionless and then looked up at the ceiling for a while. Then suddenly it came, ... 6 g3.

I can remember thinking, 'Is that it? Is that the best that the World Champion can come up with?'. Okay, a few players had played 6 g3 against me, but surely only because they considered "fianchettoing" to be trendy! With both 6 ♗e2 and 6 ♗c4 at White's disposal, why was there the need to take extra time to develop this bishop where it is obstructed by a pawn? Anyway, I continued confidently and with Kasparov constantly struggling to find a good plan, it was observed (by impartials!) that he had been outplayed. Then disaster struck in the following position.

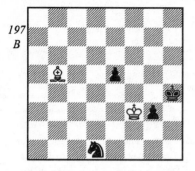

197
B

This had long been the only remaining game and unsure of the rules regarding how much thinking time I was allowed, I was still responding instantly to his moves. Over-confident, I had even begun contemplating what I might say on *News at Ten*. This, combined with the constant camera flashes, etc, etc, (?!) led me to the awful 76...♘e3??. I must confess that in all the confusion, as my knight was swiped and my opponent started waffling, I thought I had won. Sadly I was brought back to Earth as I realized that I was being subjected to a lecture on how he might have drawn earlier. His king was in fact still close enough to catch my g3-pawn and so he was declaring the game a draw! Of course after 76...e4+, Black is completely winning. Nevertheless I was consoled when my victorious mate, Phil Morris was interviewed later that night on television, and he fluffed his lines. That might have been me!

The upshot of all of this, is that quite frankly I have never been impressed by 6 g3 (or 6 ♘de2 ♗g7 7 g3). White's light-squared bishop is invariably a problem for him, and there is no cover for the key c4-square. In its favour, White need not place his dark-squared bishop on e3 and can instead concentrate on pressurizing the f6- and e7-squares. This can be done with the usual moves ♗g5 and ♘d5.

Although 6 g3 does deserve attention, it is clear that it doesn't really pose a threat. Evidence supporting this is that Classical Sicilian players (i.e. those who opt for 5...♘c6 instead of 5...g6) often like to meet 6 g3 with 6...g6, thus transposing directly into a Dragon (and this chapter).

After 6 g3 ♘c6! *(198)*, the diagram below is the starting position for our investigations.

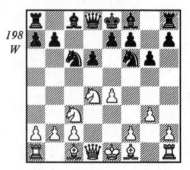

198
W

Now 7 ♗g2 ♘xd4 (see games 47 and 48) is considered to be harmless for Black, and so while others are briefly mentioned, 7 ♘de2 is our main line. This whole variation is generally fairly slow moving and so in order to bring in some fresh concepts, I am supplying three(!) lines of play for Black. Hopefully at least one of these will catch the readers fancy, and even a policy of 'chop and change' is not out of the question.

Game 44
Kagan-Smirin
Tel Aviv 1992

1 e4	c5
2 ♘f3	d6
3 d4	cxd4
4 ♘xd4	♘f6
5 ♘c3	♘c6
6 g3	g6

Transposing from a Classical Sicilian into the confines of this book.

7 ♘de2

Black was threatening to liquidate with 7...♘xd4 and so White retreats his knight to the most useful square. Elsewhere the white knight would be a bit out of it, and on 7 ♘b3?!, Black would do well to treat the position like a Classical Dragon (see chapter 8). One example runs:

7 ♘b3 ♗g7 8 ♗g2 0-0 9 0-0 ♗e6 10 h3 a5 11 a4 ♕d7 12 ♔h2 ♗c4 13 ♖e1 ♖fc8 14 ♗e3 ♘b4 15 f4 e5! 16 ♘d2 ♗e6 (Rajković-Marjanović, Vrnjačka Banja 1977). Black has the c-file under wraps and with a timely ...exf4, he may be able to expose the white king. Certainly the f4-pawn will then be vulnerable, and the g3-square will be ripe for invasion.

7 ...   b6 *(199)*

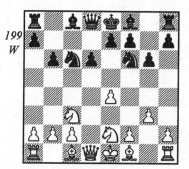

199
W

A new idea to this book, but there again 6 g3 is a different kettle of fish. This move must be played now if at all, as 7...♗g7 8 ♗g2 b6?? loses to 9 e5.

8 ♗g2   ♗a6

Slightly more active than the also playable 8...♗b7. If White now believes that Black has been tricked, then he is mistaken, as Black is the only one doing the tricking! 9 e5? may win the exchange, but after 9...♘xe5 10 f4 (10 ♗xa8? ♕xa8 leaves White so weak on the light-squares around his king, that he must be absolutely lost) 10...♘ed7 11 ♗xa8 ♕xa8 and Black has excellent compensation.

9 0-0

Delaying this obvious move is no improvement. 9 b3 ♗g7 10 ♗b2 0-0 11 ♕d2 ♖c8 12 0-0 ♕c7 13 ♖fd1 e6!? 14 ♖ac1 (if 14 ♕xd6?! then 14...♘xe4 and the complications favour Black) 14...♖fd8 15 a4 d5!? 16 exd5 exd5 17 ♘b5 ♗xb5 18 ♗xf6 ♗xf6 19 axb5 ♘e7 (Soltis-Yurtaev, Moscow GMA

1989). Pressure along the c-file and the better bishop more than compensate Black for his isolated pawn.

9 ...   ♗g7
10 a4

Once more 10 e5?! ♘xe5 is not advisable for White, but 10 b3, covering the c4-square is not silly. Then after 10...♖c8, the game Mokry-Lanc, Trnava 1986 saw 11 ♗b2 0-0 12 ♕d2 ♘d7 13 ♖ab1 ♘c5 14 ♘d1 ♗xb2 15 ♖xb2 ♘e6 16 ♘e3 ♘e5 17 f4 ♘d7 18 ♖f2 ♘f6 19 c4 b5! 20 cxb5 ♗xb5 21 ♘c3 ♗c6 22 ♘cd5 ♗xd5 23 ♘xd5 ♘xd5 24 exd5 ♘c5 25 ♕e3 a5 26 ♖fe2 ♕b6!. With a bind on the queenside and a knight preferable to the bad white bishop, Black eventually went on to win.

10 ...   ♖c8
11 ♘b5

The point behind 10 a4. White blocks out the black bishop, which will obviously not want to give itself up for a knight at this juncture.

11 ...   0-0
12 ♖a3

White removes his rook from the long a1-h8 diagonal, so as to be able to play b3 safely. Although it looks as though this rook may transfer across, it never does, which casts some doubt on the whole plan.

12 ...   ♗b7
13 ♖e1   a6
14 ♘bc3   ♘e5

Clearly White is well guarded against the c3 exchange sacrifice,

but Black has some other squares to probe.

15 ♘d5   ♘fd7

The good point behind ♘de2 for White, is that this knight is on the circuit (i.e. via c3 or f4) to d5. We know that d5 is an excellent square for a white knight. However seeing as only one knight can reside there, Black avoids a trade, with the intention of making the other one comparatively redundant. Certainly Black has plans for his own king's knight.

16 b3

Preventing ...♘c4 and hence freeing his dark-squared bishop from the defence of the b2-pawn. Nevertheless the price is dear. To say the a3-rook is now on the sidelines, would be a grave understatement.

16 ...   e6!

Pushing White back. Black's counterplay against the e4-pawn outweighs the weakness of his own d6-pawn.

17 ♘e3   ♘c5
18 f4   ♘ed7 (200)

200
W

19 f5

If White loses his e4-pawn (i.e. in a trade for the d6-pawn), then he will really regret having played 18 f4. Not only will his king be exposed, but the f4-pawn limits the scope of the dark-squared bishop and is present where the e2-knight might have ventured.

19 ...	**♗xe4**
20 fxe6	**fxe6**
21 ♕xd6	**♖c6**
22 ♕d1	

Black now has an isolated e-pawn, but this is irrelevant when compared to his (and White's lack of) piece play.

22 ...	**♗xg2**
23 ♘xg2	**♕f6**
24 ♗e3	**♘e5**
25 ♘d4	

Temporarily preventing 25...♘f3+, but allowing a very awkward pin.

25 ...	**♖d6**
26 ♖f1	**♕d8**
27 ♖xf8+	**♕xf8**
28 b4 *(201)*	

201
B

The threat was 28...♖xd4, followed by 29...♘f3+. If White thinks that with this move he has solved his problems, then he is in for a shock.

28 ...	**♘c4!**
29 bxc5	**bxc5**
30 ♖d3	**cxd4**
31 ♗c1	**♕f5**
32 ♖f3	**♕c5**
33 ♖d3	**♖b6**

It looks as though Black may roll his e-pawn or invade White's back rank, but he has an even more terminal line in mind.

34 ♕e2	**♘e5!**
0-1	

If the rook moves, then 35...d3+ doesn't bear thinking about.

When sifting through an enormous quantity of Dragon games, something I have observed is the surprisingly poor results that Dragon players obtain when they are White, and facing their own system. Below is such an example, with one of my childhood Dragon heroes venturing to the other side, and receiving a horrible drubbing!

Game 45
Kudrin-Rachels
USA Ch 1989

1 e4	**c5**
2 ♘f3	**♘c6**
3 d4	**cxd4**
4 ♘xd4	**♘f6**

5 ♘c3   d6
6 g3   g6
7 ♘de2   ♗d7

The start of another interesting idea. Though this is played here and now, it must be said that Black's moves seven to nine are often interchanged.

8 ♗g2   ♕c8 *(202)*

202
W

The point behind the curious 7...♗d7. For White now, harmonious development should go out of the window. As we shall see, White must soon decide whether to play h3. If he does, then obviously this pawn will be a target, and castling will become difficult. If he doesn't, then first of all, he will not be preventing a black piece from landing on g4. Also, Black will have the possibility of an attack by opening up the h-file with ...h5-h4, and ...♗h3 (to trade off the solitary defender).

9 ♘d5

After 9 h3 ♗g7 play might diverge in a number of ways. Some fascinating practical examples are:

a) 10 a4 0-0 11 ♗e3 ♖d8 12 ♘f4?! (if 12 ♕d2 then 12...♘b4 or 12...d5!?) 12...♘b4 13 ♘d3 (or 13 ♕d2 e5 14 ♘fe2 d5!) 13...a5 14 g4 ♗e6 15 ♘f4 d5! 16 exd5 (or 16 e5 d4!) 16...♘fxd5 17 ♘cxd5 ♘xd5 18 ♘xd5 ♗xd5 19 ♗xd5 e6 20 c3 ♖xd5 21 ♕b3 ♕c6 22 ♕b6 ♕d7 23 ♔e2?! ♖d8 24 ♕b3 ♖d2+! 25 ♗xd2 ♕d3+ 26 ♔e1 ♕e4+ 0-1 Trepp-Partos, Switzerland 1983.

b) 10 g4 ♖b8 11 g5?! (11 a4 a6 12 0-0 0-0 13 ♘g3 b5 14 axb5 axb5 15 ♗e3 b4 16 ♘d5 ♗e6 17 f4 ♘d7! 18 ♖b1 ♗xd5 19 exd5 ♘a5 was ∓ in Horvath-Hellers, Groningen 1984/85) 11...♘h5 12 ♘d5 f5!? 13 ♗f3 fxe4 14 ♗xh5 gxh5 15 ♘g3 ♘d4! 16 ♘f6+ ♗xf6 17 ♕xh5+ ♔d8 18 gxf6 ♕c4! 19 fxe7+ ♔c8 20 ♖b1 ♘xc2+ 21 ♔d1 ♘d4 22 ♔d2 ♕d3+ 23 ♔e1 ♘c2 mate (0-1) Mestel-Speelman, Hastings 1978/79.

c) 10 ♘f4?! 0-0 11 a4 ♘b4 12 ♗e3 ♖d8 transposing to (a) above. Even this is not the end of the story. Both 10 ♘d5 and 10 ♗g5 appear sensible and probably have been or will be tried.

9 ...   ♗g7
10 0-0

It is still not too late for 10 h3. With regards to my previous comments, the astute reader will note that in effect 9 h3 ♗g7 10 ♘d5 (or

9 ♘d5 ♗g7 10 h3) has been played (by whatever transposition) in Kagan-Speelman, Skara 1980:

10...0-0 11 a4 ♖e8 12 ♗e3 ♘a5 13 ♖a2 ♘c4 14 ♗c1 ♘xd5 15 exd5 e5 16 dxe6 ♗xe6 17 b3 ♘e5 18 ♔f1 d5 and Black, due to the poor position of the white king, was clearly better.

Indeed in these lines up to now, it can be seen that for White, messing about on the queenside achieves little. In addition, it appears that premature kingside attacking (with the king still in the centre) also has a habit of backfiring!

10 ...   ♘xd5

The reader has often been informed of the plus points of delaying or even completely avoiding this obvious exchange. Were White's light-squared bishop on e2, it would cover both g4 and c4. However it is not, and with the added weakness of f3, this is what makes implanting a knight on e5 so appealing.

11 exd5   ♘e5
12 a4

White gains a little space on the queenside, possibly with the idea of swinging the rook into play via a3. After 12 ♖b1, continuing as in the game with 12...♗h3 is logical, although 12...h5 13 h4 ♘g4 14 b3 ♕c5 15 ♗b2 ♗xb2 16 ♖xb2 0-0 17 c4 b5 (Kagan-Johannessen, Siegen 1970) also turned out a little better for Black.

12 ...   ♗h3
13 ♖a2   h5! (203)

Recalling the Yugoslav Attack chapters, here White is getting a taste of his own medicine. The difference is that he doesn't have the c-file counterplay that Black usually does.

14 ♗xh3   ♕xh3
15 f3

Preventing both 15...♘g4 and 15...♘f3+. 15 ♘f4 would only force a temporary retreat.

15 ...   g5!?

An interesting progression with the idea of a very timely ...g4 (i.e. not when ♘f4 would trap the black queen) in order to gain the f3-square for the black knight. Many might have prepared this advance with 15...♗f6, but with the text move, 16 ♗xg5 can be met by 16...h4 when 17 ♗xh4 ♖xh4! and 17 g4 ♘xg4! both look very good for Black.

16 ♔h1   ♗f6

| 17 | b3 | ♛f5 |
| 18 | ♘d4 | ♛g6 |

Black did not wish the queen to be incarcerated on h3. Therefore she has been withdrawn in preparation for the kingside onslaught.

| 19 | c4 | g4 |
| 20 | ♖g2 | |

If 20 f4?, then 20...♛e4+ when 21 ♖g2 is grim, but 21 ♔g1? loses material to 21...♛xd4+ 22 ♛xd4 ♘f3+.

| 20 | ... | h4 |

Simple chess. Black wants to open lines for the pieces behind.

21	gxh4	♖xh4
22	f4	♘d7
23	♘b5	

Threatening 24 ♘c7+ and hoping to dissuade 23...0-0-0.

| 23 | ... | 0-0-0 |

White is out of luck. The final force is on its way!

| 24 | ♘xa7+ | ♔b8 |
| 25 | ♗e3 | ♖dh8 |

There is no threat to Black, but meanwhile the dark clouds are gathering around the white king.

| 26 | ♛e1 | g3! |

The g2-rook is overloaded. It appears to cover both g3 and h2, but in reality it cannot perform these two vital functions.

| 27 | ♛a5 | |

Desperate, White throws his queen in the direction of the black king, hoping that a perpetual check might turn up.

| 27 | ... | ♖xh2+ *(204)* |

204
W

However Black doesn't intend letting White have another shake of the dice.

28	♖xh2	♛e4+!
29	♔g1	♛xe3+
	0-1	

These first two games have introduced a couple of particularly interesting ideas. The third and final game relating to the 7 ♘de2 lines is not as innovative. Nevertheless, it provides a solid and sensible alternative in tackling the matter at hand.

Game 46
A.Ivanov-Ernst
Gausdal 1991

1	e4	c5
2	♘f3	d6
3	d4	cxd4
4	♘xd4	♘f6
5	♘c3	g6
6	g3	♘c6
7	♘de2	♗g7
8	♗g2	0-0
9	0-0	♖b8 *(205)*

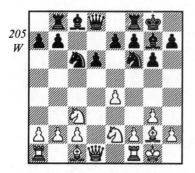

205
W

Black has developed in the usual Dragon fashion and now plays a fairly natural move. There is no need to commit the c8-bishop yet as Black at present is unsure of where it belongs. Instead he removes the rook from the h1-a8 diagonal (therefore avoiding any later e4-e5 tricks) and prepares to expand on the queenside.

10 a4

White wisely decides that if Black is going to get in ...b5, then he at least wants the a-file. I suppose 10 ♘d5 is playable, but 10 b3?! b5 11 ♖b1 b4 12 ♘d5 ♗a6 13 ♗b2 ♘d7 14 ♗xg7 ♔xg7 15 c4 bxc3 16 ♖e1 ♘c5 17 ♘exc3 ♘d3 18 ♖e2 e6 19 ♘e3 ♕a5 20 ♘a4 ♘c5 21 ♖c2 ♖fd8 (Condie-Kir.Georgiev, Dubai OL 1986) was certainly good for Black.

10 ...   **a6**

11 ♘d5

The most direct move, the main alternative being 11 h3. Then after 11...b5 12 axb5 axb5, both 13 ♗e3 b4 14 ♘d5 ♗b7, and 13 ♗g5 ♘d7!? 14 ♕c1 b4 give about equal chances.

11 ...   **b5**

12 axb5   **axb5**

13 ♗g5

Now 13 h3 is a little inconsistent. One continuation then is 13...♘d7!? 14 ♖a2 e6 15 ♘df4 ♕c7 16 ♗d2 ♘c5 17 ♘c1 ♗b7 18 ♘cd3 ♖a8 19 ♖xa8 ♖xa8 20 ♖e1 ♘a4 21 c3 ♘c5∓ Horvath-Kir.Georgiev, Lvov 1984.

13 ...   **♘d7**

The problem with exchanging knights on d5 now, is that there would then be an outpost on c6, and eventual pressure on the e7-pawn.

14 ♕c1   **♖e8!** *(206)*

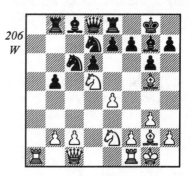

206
W

Black overprotects the e7-pawn and prevents the trade of bishops which 15 ♗h6 would have brought about.

15 ♖d1   **♘c5**

16 ♗h6   **♗h8**

17 b4?!

A miscalculation that effectively loses White the game. However things aren't exactly looking up for him. Black is threatening to increase his grip on the queenside with moves like ...b4 and ...♘e5-c4. Also the pride and joy of White's position, the knight on d5 will soon be forced back by ...e6.

17 ...	**♗xa1**
18 ♕xa1	**♘e6**

Saving the knight and stopping the mate on g7.

19 ♘df4

If 19 f4, then 19...f6 successfully closes off the diagonal, vital to White's existence.

19 ...	**♘e5!**
20 ♘xe6	**♗xe6**
21 f4	**♕b6+!**

The key move. Now White finds it impossible to keep his queen on the diagonal bearing down to g7.

22 ♔h1	**♖a8**
23 ♕c3	

If 23 ♕b2 then 23...♖a2 forces the white queen to move on.

23 ...   **♖ec8**

There is no peace for the wicked, and now the white number is up.

24 ♕d2   **♘g4**

Threatening the bishop on h6 and all sorts of horrors on f2. It looks as though White can resign, but he battles on bravely.

25 ♘d4!   **♖a2!**

Black correctly chooses to keep the initiative rather than go in for the not so clear 25...♘xh6 26 f5!.

26 f5	**♖cxc2**
27 ♘xc2	**♘f2+**
28 ♕xf2	**♕xf2**
29 ♘e3	**♗c4**
30 e5 *(207)*	

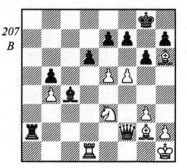

207
B

Black can't really be faulted for his businesslike finishing. Nevertheless he missed the beautiful 30...♗d5!, which cannot be taken by either of three white pieces and is therefore even more terminal.

30 ...	**gxf5**
31 exd6	**exd6**
32 ♖g1	**♖e2**
33 ♘d1	**0-1**

With this move White resigned, possibly in anticipation of 33...♕xg2+ 34 ♖xg2 ♗d5 35 ♘e3 ♖e1+ or 33...♕xg1+ 34 ♔xg1 ♖e1+.

Moving swiftly on to 7 ♗g2 (instead of 7 ♘de2), well, some texts even attach a '?!' to it. I find this a little harsh, although it is true that Black is fine after 7...♘xd4. The reader may wonder why it is that Black should choose now to volunteer this exchange, when it is rarely suggested elsewhere. The most obvious answer is that it drags the white queen into the centre (there is no bishop on e3 ready to recapture), where it may later be vulnerable to a discovered attack from the Dragon bishop. However more to the point is that 8 ♘xc6 bxc6 9 e5 is a threat which should be parried, and while 7...♗d7 is possible, 7...♘xd4 appears to be the simplest solution.

Game 47
Kirov-Speelman
Baku 1983

1 e4	c5
2 ♘f3	d6
3 d4	♘f6
4 ♘c3	cxd4
5 ♘xd4	♘c6
6 g3	g6
7 ♗g2	♘xd4
8 ♕xd4	♗g7

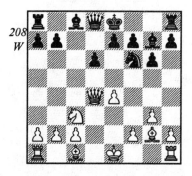

9 0-0

The only justification for delaying this move is if White wishes to fianchetto and/or castle on the queenside:

a) 9 b3 0-0 10 ♗b2 ♕a5 11 ♕d2 ♗e6 12 0-0-0 just doesn't look right. Black must avoid the usual 12...♖fc8 in view of 13 e5, but both

12...♖ac8, and 12...♖fe8 (reducing the force of ♘d5), are fine.

b) 9 ♗g5?! h6! 10 ♗e3 0-0 11 ♕d2 ♘g4 12 ♗d4 ♘e5∓. White must prevent 13...♘c4 and as 13 b3?! is met by 13...♗g4, he must concede his dark-squared bishop (for the h6-pawn) with 13 ♗xe5 ♗xe5.

| 9 ... | 0-0 |

10 h3

A useful move. There is no dangerous discovered attack, and so it is not necessary for White to move his queen yet. Nevertheless no less than four immediate queen moves are considered in Game 48. 10 b3?? loses a pawn to 10...♘xe4!, and the premature 10 ♘d5?! ♘xd5 11 ♕xd5 ♕c7, leaves Black with the c-file, and White with nothing much at all really!

| 10 ... | ♗d7!? |

This heralds a slightly different approach to the more usual 10...♗e6 (which has also scored quite well).

11 ♕d1   **♖c8**

Very natural. One good word to be said about this whole White kingside fianchetto plan, is that at least the bishop protects the e4-pawn. This means that the traditional exchange sacrifice on c3 is rarely on.

12 a4

Until this move, 12...b5 was certainly a consideration for Black, for example after the uninspiring but solid 12 ♖e1.

12 ...   ♖c4

Giving White more to think about and preparing to double, or even treble, on the c-file.

13 ♕d3

White appears unsure where his queen belongs and even Speelman suggested 13 ♕e2. The reason for this though is far from clear, and what White is really lacking is a plan.

13 ...   ♕c8!

Defending the rook and eyeing up White's h-pawn. Note 14...♗xh3 is a threat in view of 15 ♗xh3 ♕xh3 16 ♕xc4 ♘g4.

14 ♔h2   ♗e6

Due to the latent pressure against the c2-pawn, White has great difficulty in moving his c3-knight (e.g. to d5).

15 ♖a3?!   ♖c5!? (209)

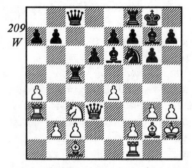

209
W

Black feels that White's last move puts the rook on a silly, rather than constructive square. Therefore he prepares to transfer the rook to h5 to drum up an attack. The text also threatens 16...♗c4, but

15...♘d7 with both ...♘c5 and ...♘e5 future options, is a sensible alternative.

16 ♖h1

An interesting way of meeting both threats, though now White's rooks aren't exactly what you might call coordinated!

16 ...   a6

17 g4

Played more to solve the h-pawn problem, than to start Black quaking in his boots.

17 ...   b5!

18 axb5   axb5

19 ♖a5

If 19 ♘xb5?, then both 19...♗c4 and 19...♖xc2 are excellent for Black.

19 ...   ♕c7

Sneakier than 19...b4.

20 ♖xb5? (210)

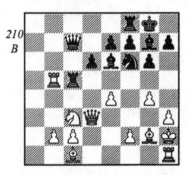

210
B

Falling for a clever trap, but there are no great alternatives as 20...d5+ will open up the position favourably for Black.

20 ...   ♖xc3!

21 bxc3

Not 21 ♕xc3? due to 21...♘xg4+.

21 ...   ♗c4
22 ♖b7   ♕c8!

Black is determined to win a whole rook, rather than the exchange. Now 23 ♕d4 again loses to 23...♘xg4+, and so White does his best to limit the material deficit.

23 e5   ♘xg4+
24 hxg4   ♗xd3
25 cxd3   ♕xg4

Piece-wise, White has a rook and a bishop for a queen. However these are scattered, and he is a pawn down with more to follow. To top it all, Black has an active queen and this just about wraps things up for him.

26 f4   dxe5
27 ♖f1   exf4
28 d4   ♕g3+
29 ♔h1   ♕xc3
30 ♖xe7   f3
31 ♗xf3   ♕xd4
32 ♖e4   ♕d3
33 ♗g2   h5
34 ♗g5   ♖b8
35 ♖e7?

With three connected passed pawns to deal with, White's cause is hopeless. Sadly the end coincides with his rook arriving on the seventh rank.

35 ...   ♕g3!
0-1

If 36 ♗f4 then 36...♕h4+ and if 36 ♖fxf7 then 36...♖b1+.

My final selection for this chapter may surprise the reader, as Black is hardly winning throughout. The more cynical of you may even suggest that I am even becoming (dare I say it) objective! No such fears (as if I haven't been really!). Anyway, the game features a second loss with White by Dragon player Sergei Kudrin. It is very instructive, particularly because White appears to make no glaring errors.

Game 48
Kudrin-Dlugy
USA Ch 1988

1 e4   c5
2 ♘f3   ♘c6
3 d4   cxd4
4 ♘xd4   ♘f6
5 ♘c3   d6
6 g3   g6
7 ♗g2   ♘xd4
8 ♕xd4   ♗g7
9 0-0   0-0
10 ♕b4

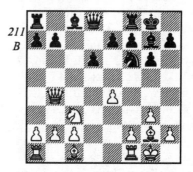

211
B

Some consider this to be dubious, but seeing as Garry Kasparov has played it (against me!), I am inclined to disagree. It certainly appears that there are no better queen moves:

a) 10 ♕d3 ♕a5!? (or 10...♗e6 11 e5?! ♘e8!) 11 ♗d2 ♕h5!? 12 f3 ♗e6 13 ♖ac1 ♖ac8 14 b3? ♘g4! 15 fxg4 ♕c5+ left Black with a significant structural advantage in Carstens-Polster, Bundesliga 1986/87.

b) 10 ♕d2 ♕c7 11 ♘d5 (11 b3? ♘xe4!; 11 ♖e1 ♗e6 12 ♘d5 ♗xd5! 13 exd5 ♖e8 14 a4 ♘d7∓) 11...♘xd5 12 exd5 b5 13 a4 b4! 14 ♕xb4 ♖b8 15 ♕h4 ♗xb2 16 ♗xb2 ♖xb2 Cuellar-Korchnoi, Stockholm 1962. Black has the better pieces and White has the worse pawns.

c) 10 ♕d1 ♗g4 11 f3 ♕b6+ 12 ♔h1 ♗e6 13 ♖e1 ♖ac8 and Black has no problems; Cabrilo-Kir.Georgiev, Varna 1983.

10 ...   ♕c7

For the sake of historical accuracy and completeness, etc, here are the moves of Kasparov-Ward, simul 1986: 10...♘d7 11 ♗g5 ♘e5 12 ♘d5 ♘c6 13 ♕a3 h6 14 ♗e3 ♗g4 15 h3 ♗e2 16 ♖fe1 ♗a6 17 ♖ad1 ♖c8 18 c3 ♖e8 19 h4 ♖a8 20 ♕a4 ♘e5 21 ♕c2 b6 22 b3 ♖c8 23 c4 ♕d7 24 ♕d2 ♔h7 25 ♗d4 ♕g4 26 ♕f4 ♕xf4 27 gxf4 ♘c6 28 ♗xg7 ♔xg7 29 e5 dxe5 30 fxe5 ♖ed8 31 f4 e6 32 ♘f6 ♘b4 33 ♘e4 ♘c2 34 ♖xd8 ♖xd8 35 ♖c1 ♘d4 36 ♔f2 ♘f5 37 ♗h3 ♘xh4 38 ♘d6 g5 39 c5 bxc5 40 ♖xc5 ♖d7 41

fxg5 hxg5 42 ♔e3 ♗b7 43 b4 f5 44 exf6+ ♔xf6 45 ♘xb7 ♖xb7 46 a3 ♘f5+ 47 ♔e4 ♘d6+ 48 ♔f3 ♘b5 49 ♔e3 ♘xa3 50 ♗f1 ♖xb4 51 ♗d3 ♖a4 52 ♖c6 a6 53 ♖xa6 ♘c2+ 54 ♔f3 ♖xa6 55 ♗xa6 ♘b4 56 ♗b7 ♘d5 57 ♔e4 ♘f4 58 ♗a6 ♘g6 59 ♗e2 e5 60 ♗g4 ♘e7 61 ♗d7 ♘g8 62 ♗g4 ♘h6 63 ♗e2 ♔e6 64 ♗c4+ ♔f6 65 ♗e2 ♘f5 66 ♗g4 ♘d6+ 67 ♔d5 ♘b5 68 ♔c5 ♘c3 69 ♔c4 ♘e4 70 ♗d7 ♘f2 71 ♔c3 g4 72 ♔d2 ♔g5 73 ♔e3 ♘d1+ 74 ♔e2 g3 75 ♔f3 ♔h4 76 ♗b5, arriving at diagram 197 in the introduction to this chapter.

11 a4   a5!?

I wasn't too sure about this move when I first saw it. My main concern was the outpost conceded on b5. However the white knight cannot be on both b5 and d5 at the same time, and the text does prevent the space-gaining push a4-a5 by White.

12 ♕b3   ♗e6
13 ♘d5   ♗xd5

It appears that in this chapter, Black often has a not unfamiliar decision to make: should it be his bishop or his knight which captures White's knight on d5? Here Black selects what is generally the more ambitious option. Nevertheless there is nothing wrong with 13...♘xd5 14 exd5 ♗f5.

14 exd5   ♖fc8
15 c3   ♘d7

This knight looks to be on course for c5, but Black has other ideas.

16 ♗h3   ♖cb8 (212)

17 ♖d1

My original thoughts on this game were that I should not include it. White has the two bishops and if he wants, he could redress the balance (materially speaking) with 17 ♗xd7. Then after 17...♕xd7 18 ♖e1, he had to be a little better. However a closer inspection indicates that this is not the case. If Black gets in ...b5, then White's b-, c-, and d-pawns all come under very close scrutiny. Therefore Black prepares this break with 18...♗f6 and on 19 c4, has the surprisingly powerful 19...h5! (or 19...♖c8 20 ♗e3 h5!). If White responds with 20 h4 then Black can lodge his queen on g4, but the alternative is to allow Black quite a nifty attack down the h-file with moves like ...h4, ...♔g7, and ...♖h8.

17 ...	♗f6
18 ♗e3	♘e5
19 ♖ac1	b5!
20 axb5	♕c4
21 ♕xc4	♘xc4

Bishops are particularly favourable to knights when the pawn structure is fluid. Ironically here it is Black who has gone for the pawn break (19...b5!). It is not difficult to see why. All of his pieces are now trained on White's queenside.

22 ♗d7

White must preserve his b5-pawn in order to deny the black rooks access to his position.

22 ...	♘xb2
23 ♖f1	a4
24 ♖c2	♘c4 (213)

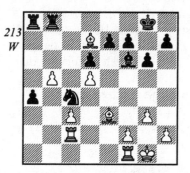

Black's knight is superb on this square. It is able to hold up White's b-pawn, help advance his own a-pawn, and inhibit the white rooks.

25 ♗c6	♖a5
26 ♖a1	a3
27 ♗d4	

A cheap shot at trying to dislodge the black knight. Hence Black avoids 27...♗xd4?? 28 cxd4 when he will lose his a-pawn and probably the game.

27 ...	♔g7
28 ♖b1	e5!?

Black decides that in order to make progress, he must make the white bishops less secure.

29 ♗e3

Evidently White didn't like 29 dxe6, but one suspects that he has over-estimated his drawing chances in the forthcoming endgame. There may be opposite-coloured bishops, but the presence of rooks means that Black has excellent winning chances.

| 29 ... | ♘xe3 |
| 30 fxe3 | ♗d8! |

It is abundantly clear whose bishop will be the better. White's bishop defends his b5-pawn and prevents the b8-rook from entering the game along the a-file. It would almost be easier to list the things that Black's bishop can't do!

31 e4	♖a4
32 ♖a2	♗b6+
33 ♔g2	♖xe4
34 ♖xa3	♖e2+
35 ♔h1	f5

White's queenside pawn majority is an annoyance. Black's kingside majority will become somewhat more.

36 ♖ab3	♖c2
37 h4	h6
38 ♖1b2	♖c1+
39 ♔g2	g5

These pawns will soon be able to control some important light squares. It is now also inevitable that Black will be able to create another open file, down which will come his currently inactive rook.

| 40 hxg5 | hxg5 *(214)* |

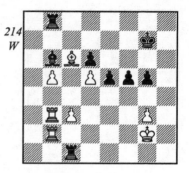

At first it looks as though this move is simply designed to lure away Black's bishop, so that the b-pawn can be advanced further. Then the truth comes home. Black was threatening checkmate with 41...♖g1+ 42 ♔h2 (42 ♔f3 g4 mate) 42...♖h8 and so the text is forced. The true power of Black's bishop has been exposed.

| 41 ... | ♗xf2 |
| 42 ♔xf2 | ♖h8! |

Cool as you like. Black has more mating nets up his sleeve.

43 b6	♖h2+
44 ♔e3	♖g1
45 ♔d3	

The only way to avoid mate.

45 ...	♖xg3+
46 ♔c4	♖h8
47 b7	♖b8

And he's back in time for tea!

| 48 ♗d7 | ♖f3 |
| 49 ♗c8 | g4 |

White may have incarcerated one black rook, but now there is that little matter of three connected passed pawns to deal with.

50	♖b1	g3
51	♖g1	♔f6
52	♔b4	e4
53	c4	♔e5
54	♔b5	♖c3 *(215)*

0-1

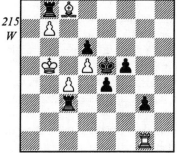

215
W

This is the first time that I have ever noticed a similarity between chess and 'Space Invaders'! There is of course no chance of the white rook destroying the black pawns as they come down. Meanwhile it is ironic that White's own pawns, even in the absence of Black's dark-squared bishop, are still fixed on light squares.

11 Levenfish Attack (6 f4)

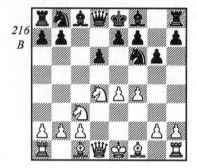

216
B

As I can vividly recall, my very first horror story with the Dragon came in what I later learnt was the Levenfish variation. It was the Lloyds Bank Under-10 England Championship and I remember I was the 'new kid on the block' playing against the 'top dog'. The game started as follows:

1 e4 c5 2 ♘f3 d6 3 d4 cxd4 4 ♘xd4 ♘f6 5 ♘c3 g6 6 f4 ♗g7 7 e5 dxe5? 8 fxe5 ♘g4 8 ♗b5+ *(217)*

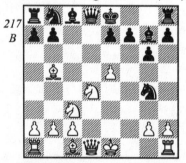

217
B

Blissfully unaware, I continued with 8...♗d7, only to be shocked by 9 ♕xg4!.

Actually after this major setback, I fought back rather well, only to blow it again later. Still, my opponent had words of consolation. He told me that in fact most of his opponents fell for this trap, with many walking into the even more terminal 8...♔f8?? 9 ♘e6+!.

Needless to say, I have never been tricked in this manner since, and hopefully, if the reader is on the ball, then for them there should never be this disastrous first time.

I was told that the mistake lay in the natural 6...♗g7, but truth be known that this is actually playable, only then 7 e5 must be met by 7...♘h5. However this is simply a bit of general knowledge as I am advocating two 6th move alternatives. I must confess that partly due to the above game, early on in my Dragon career, I developed a bit of a phobia about White's f4 and e4-e5 (and perhaps to e6) plan. Therefore I quite like the solid 6...♘bd7 (see games 52 and 53) which puts paid to this plan. Perhaps, though, more testing is 6...♘c6 (see games 49 to 51) which generally involves more complications.

Interesting in the Levenfish Variation is the connection with other Sicilian lines. After 1 e4 c5 ♘f3 d6 3 d4 cxd4 4 ♘xd4 ♘f6 5

♘c3 ♘c6 6 f4, Classical Sicilian players frequently play 6...g6, whist Sicilian Najdorf (5...a6) players also often meet 6 f4 with 6...g6 (or at least ...g6 commonly follows later).

Therefore if you like, they are abandoning their own variations, in favour of a Dragon formation. Their argument of course is that the Levenfish isn't a critical test of the Dragon and in fact this is true. Today the amount of top players who would wheel out 6 f4 against the Dragon is almost non-existent. This is hardly surprising though when you bear in mind that one of the alternatives is the even more aggressive, yet more controlled, Yugoslav Attack.

However at lower levels the Levenfish is actually quite popular. I believe that the reason for this, is that many club players appear to have a standard recipe for 'Sicilians' in 'razzing' their f-pawn up the board! Game 49 is unlikely to be of too much theoretical interest, but is fairly typical of the rather neanderthal treatment that the reader may come to expect.

Game 49
Revenu-Ward
Toulouse 1988

1 e4	c5
2 ♘f3	d6
3 d4	cxd4
4 ♘xd4	♘f6

| 5 ♘c3 | g6 |
| 6 f4 | ♘c6! |

218
W

7 ♗b5

The main alternative 7 ♘xc6 is examined in games 50 and 51. I suppose that White can now adopt a 'Classical' approach with 7 ♗e2, intending 8 ♗e3. The reader may recall that such a set-up was detailed in chapter 8 and should refer there, as a direct transposition would be likely. Note also game 53. The above may apply to 7 ♘b3, whilst 7 ♘f3 can be met adequately by 7...♗g7 or 7...♗g4!?.

| 7 ... | ♗d7 |
| 8 ♗xc6 | ♗xc6 |

I have never believed in this idea for White and consequently, before writing this book, did not bother looking up the theory on it. This may explain why three years later, upon reaching the same position, I forgot all about this highly satisfactory game and instead opted for the also appealing 8...bxc6. Similarly, though, White continued in a manner that wouldn't look out of place in *Jurassic Park*!: 9 e5 ♞d5 10 ♞xd5 (10 exd6 ♞xc3 11 bxc3 c5! 12 ♞f3 ♝g7 leaves Black with good compensation for the temporary pawn) 10...cxd5 11 exd6 (11 ♛f3 e6 also looks better for Black because of his two bishops and solid pawn structure) 11...e6 12 f5 (unbelievable!) 12...♛h4+!? 13 g3 ♛e4+ 14 ♚f2 ♝g7 15 c3 ♝xd4+ 16 ♛xd4 ♛xf5+ 17 ♚g2 ♛c2+ 18 ♛f2 ♛xf2+ 19 ♚xf2 f6 and with a rather effective kingside majority, Black went on to win the endgame in Allen-Ward, Maidstone Open 1991.

9 ♞xc6?!

Although this regains the bishop for the knight, it cannot be justified. I feel that the only consistent continuation is 9 e5, but after 9...dxe5 10 fxe5 ♞e4 11 ♞xe4 ♝xe4 12 0-0 ♝g7, I don't believe that White's piece activity (e.g. the f-file) properly compensates him for his positional weaknesses (such as the e5-pawn and his lack of light-squared control).

9 ...   **bxc6** *(219)*

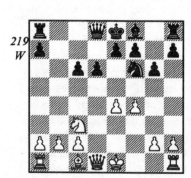

I have rambled on enough in this book about why ♞xc6 is generally a bad move. The hypothetical factors of the half-open b-file and the control over the key d5-square, have previously been put forward. Here these can be seen in action, where Black's pawn structure is definitely proven to be preferred.

10 ♛f3   d5!?

In such positions, this move doesn't always have to be played so early, if at all. Here though it deals with the threat of 11 e5. As the pawn now on d5 is bolstered by the c6-pawn, Black is not worried by 11 e5, as after 11...♞d7, White will never be able to get in f5. In contrast, Black may later opt to blast the centre open again with ...f6.

11 ♝e3   ♛a5!

Beginning the tussle over the e4-square and daring White to try the suicidal 12 0-0-0.

12 0-0   **♝g7**
13 f5   **0-0**
14 g4

Not hanging about. However as White is losing control of the centre, this over-ambitious wing play is always likely to rebound.

14 ...   **♛b4!**

Hitting b2, e4, and through to g4! Hence White's centre is about to be dissipated. Nevertheless, the caveman style continues.

15 g5   **dxe4**
16 ♛h3   **♞d5**
17 ♞xd5   **cxd5**

18 f6	exf6
19 gxf6	♗h8

A temporary retreat and a small price to pay. Black is already one good pawn up and the f6-pawn shouldn't be too long in dropping off.

20 ♖f5

Still, it's never over until it's over and White still has plans. Now not 20...gxf5?? leading to mate after 21 ♕g3+.

20 ...	d4
21 ♕h6	

By now all of the readers should know that after 21 ♖h5 dxe3 22 ♖xh7 ♗xf6, White has absolutely nothing.

21 ...	♗xf6!

Putting a stop to any funny business. Remarkably if 21...dxe3?? then Black is completely lost after 22 ♖h5!.

22 ♖h5

Desperation sets in. After 22 ♖xf6 dxe3, White is several passed pawns down, with an exposed king.

22 ...	gxh5
23 ♔h1	♕b6

The same treatment that would have been dished out to 23 ♕xf6.

0-1

There are no more tricks!

Game 50
Klinger-Tukmakov
Szirak 1985

1 e4	c5
2 ♘f3	d6
3 d4	cxd4
4 ♘xd4	♘f6
5 ♘c3	g6
6 f4	♘c6
7 ♘xc6	bxc6
8 e5	

Based on the premise that 8...dxe5 9 ♕xd8+ ♔xd8 10 fxe5 ♘g4 11 ♗f4 is a slightly better endgame for White, this is his only move.

8 ...	♘d7
9 exd6	

The main move. After 9 ♕f3, Black can happily play 9...d5. However he should resist the temptation to do so after 9 ♗c4 as it falls for 10 ♘xd5! cxd5 11 ♕xd5. Instead 9...♘b6 is probably best, avoiding any 'cheapoes' and leaving Black with no problems whatsoever.

9 ...	exd6

220 W

An interesting and critical position. Black's c- and d-pawns are potentially strong or potentially weak. Similarly White's f4-pawn may become a menace, but at present really gets in the way.

10 ♕d4

Played with the intention of castling long. 10 ♗e3 (with similar aspirations) is detailed in game 51, and that leaves two other sensible possibilities:

a) 10 ♗e2 ♘f6 11 ♗e3 ♗g7 12 ♗f3 0-0! 13 ♗xc6 ♖b8 and Black has excellent compensation. Note here, just like in many of these variations, White would really like to place the f4-pawn back on f2!

b) 10 ♕e2+ ♕e7 11 ♘e4 ♕e6 12 ♗d2 ♗e7 13 ♗c3 0-0 and in my (totally unbiased!) view, Black's position is preferable.

10 ...	♘f6
11 ♗e3	♗e7
12 ♗e2	0-0
13 ♗f3	d5
14 ♕d2	

Evidently White is afraid of a later ...c5 and ...d4.

14 ...   ♗g4!

Attempting to loosen still further White's grip on the light-squares g4 and e4.

| 15 0-0-0 | ♖e8 |
| 16 h3? | |

Allowing 15...♗xf3 was just about okay for White as at least his doubled pawns control some squares. However 16 h3? (also conceding the g3-square) is really taking too much of a liberty.

Nevertheless after 16 ♗xg4 ♘xg4, 17 ♗g1 ♖b8 is very uncomfortable, and the alternative of conceding the dark-squared bishop is even worse.

| 16 ... | ♗xf3 |
| 17 gxf3 | ♕d7! *(221)* |

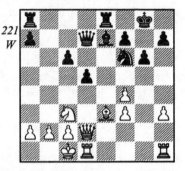

Fixing the f-pawns and connecting the rooks.

| 18 ♕d3 | ♘h5 |
| 19 ♖dg1 | ♗d6 |

Apart from the obvious 20...♗(or ♘)xf4, 20...♖xe3 is also a major threat.

20 ♔b1	♗xf4
21 ♗xf4	♘xf4
22 ♕d2	♕f5

Black is a pawn up and very much in control, whilst White is finding it difficult to get anything going.

| 23 ♕d4 | ♘e2?! |

Not really a bad move, but 23...c5! would have killed things off. For example 24 ♕xc5 ♖ac8 25 ♕d4 ♘e2 26 ♘xe2 ♕xc2+ 27 ♔a1 ♖xe2 and White is tied up in knots.

24 ♘xe2	♖xe2
25 ♕c5	♖ae8
26 h4	h5
27 ♖c1	

Defending c2 so as to be able to capture the c6-pawn without ...♖c8 being terminal.

27 ...	♕xf3
28 a4	♕e4
29 ♕xc6	♖b8
30 ♖h3	♕f5
31 ♖c3	d4
32 ♖f3	♕c8

Black is happy to trade queens, bearing in mind his strong kingside pawn majority.

33 ♕f6	♕d7
34 ♖cf1	♖b7
35 ♕g5?	

Black seems to have been going 'around the houses' somewhat in order to win this game, but now White obliges with the decisive mistake. 35 ♕a6 ♖e6 still leaves him clearly worse.

35 ...	♕xa4
36 ♕c5	

Presumably White had intended 36 ♕d8+ ♔g7, but then after 37 ♕f6+ ♔h7, there is no perpetual check.

36 ...	♖be7
37 b3	♖e1+
0-1	

38 ♖xe1 ♖xe1+ 39 ♔b2 ♕a1 is finally the end!

Game 51
Nunn-Miles
London 1982

1 e4	c5
2 ♘f3	d6
3 d4	cxd4
4 ♘xd4	♘f6
5 ♘c3	g6
6 f4	♘c6!
7 ♘xc6	bxc6
8 e5	♘d7
9 exd6	exd6
10 ♗e3	♘f6!?
11 ♕d2	♗g7
12 0-0-0	d5
13 ♗c5 (222)	

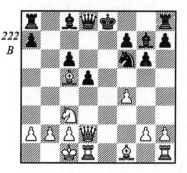

222
B

Black has a very solid central pawn structure and excellent chances for an attack down the b-file. 13 ♗c5 is absolutely necessary, as if Black is allowed to castle, he has everything going for him.

13 ...	♗e6
14 ♕d4	

Placing the queen in the Dragon bishop's line of fire seems like a strange decision. However, White is clearly worried about the problems that might arise on his queenside. If 14 ♗e2 then 14...♕a5 and the pressure is mounting. What soon becomes clear, though, is that the text move doesn't actually solve any problems.

14 ...	♕a5
15 ♗b4	♕c7

Threatening 16...♘h5 winning the f4-pawn.

16 g3	♖b8
17 ♗a3	♖g8! *(223)*

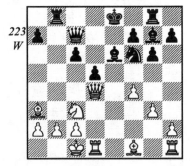

223
W

An incredible move and an incredible position! Black deploys a whole rook simply to defend the Dragon bishop. Now, however, the white queen is forced to move to prevent 18...♘e4.

18 ♕a4	♕b6
19 ♗g2	♘d7
20 ♖d3	♗f5!

Even now the bishop has moved, it appears that White cannot exploit the black king position. Mind you, it is very safe on d8, and the open e-file could be looked upon as an entry point for the g8-rook.

21 ♖e1+	♔d8
22 ♖f3	

The sacrifice 22 ♘xd5?! attempts to uncover the black king, but merely succeeds in uncovering White's own, e.g. 22...♗xb2+ 23

♔b1 cxd5 24 ♖b3 ♗xc2+ 25 ♔xc2 ♕f2+ and it's all over!

22 ...	♖e8
23 ♖xe8+	♔xe8

Black's king is still in the middle, but it is the white king that is in trouble. White's queenside is under a great deal of pressure and his kingside is also a little exposed.

24 ♘d1	♘c5
25 ♖e3+	♔d8
26 ♗xc5	

Reluctantly allowing Black the advantage of the bishop pair in favour of keeping the queen!

26 ...	♕xc5 *(224)*

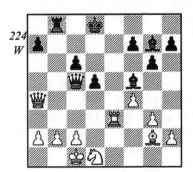

224
W

27 c3	d4!

Opening more lines toward the white king.

28 ♖f3	♗e4
29 ♖f2	dxc3
30 ♗xe4	cxb2+
31 ♔d2	b1♕
32 ♗xb1	♖xb1
33 ♖f3	

Black has lost one of his raking bishops, but cannot complain. I suppose White would like the queens off so as to avoid being checkmated, but if 33 ♕c2 then at the very least 33...♖b2 liquidates to a winning king and pawn ending.

33 ...	♖b4
34 ♖d3+	♔c7
35 ♕a3	a5
36 ♘c3	♗f8
37 ♕c1	♕f2+
38 ♔d1	♕g1+
39 ♔e2??	

Rather an incredible blunder. Still White has had a rough time and with pawns beginning to fall with check, there seems little sense in prolonging the agony.

39 ...	♕xc1

0-1

Game 52
Kenworthy-Ward
County Match 1993

1 e4	c5
2 ♘f3	d6
3 d4	cxd4
4 ♘xd4	♘f6
5 ♘c3	g6
6 f4	♘bd7 *(225)*

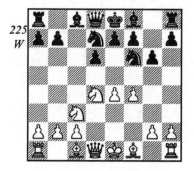

Preventing the annoying 7 e5, without 7 ♘xc6 being an option for White. As we have seen before, the knight is not badly placed on d7, as it can often spring to c4 via b6 or pressurize White's e4-pawn with ...♘c5. The drawbacks are that White's d4 knight is not troubled, and that Black's light-squared bishop is temporarily blocked, hence relinquishing some control over the g4-square.

7 ♘f3

Consistent. Once more preparing the e5-e6(or exf6!) push and taking advantage of the fact that Black can't play 7...♗g4. The quieter 7 ♗e2 crops up in game 53.

7 ...	♕a5!?

Again instead of 7...♗g7, I feel that it is a good idea to cover e5 immediately. Also logical is 7...♕c7!?. In many respects this is less aggressive, but it does prevent a white bishop from arriving on the active c4 post. After 8 ♗d3 ♗g7 9 0-0 a6, play will have transposed into a well known Sicilian Najdorf position. Black can delay castling if he so wishes, to take the sting out of White's attacking plan ♕e1-h4. He should pressurize the e4-pawn with ...b5 (or ...b6 if White opts for the restricting a4) and ...♗b7. The c-file should be utilized in the normal fashion and, as we saw in chapter 8, Black may do well to aim for a timely ...e5.

8 ♗d3

Removing the crafty threat of
8...♘xe4.

8 ...	♗g7
9 0-0	b5?! *(226)*

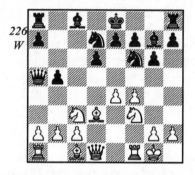

226
W

I feel that this is an instructive
game because of the two typical
mistakes made. Here playing
Black, I thought that I was repeating an idea which was successful in
the game Lanc-Perenyi, USSR
1982. In fact this game saw 9...0-0
10 ♔h1 and only then 10...b5!?.
The point is that after 11 ♗xb5?!,
Black has 11...♘xe4!. Therefore
play continued with 11 ♘xb5 ♖b8
12 ♘c3 ♘c5 13 a3 ♘xd3 14 cxd3
♗a6 15 ♖a2 ♖fc8 when the holes
in White's queenside and the open
lines, gave Black some very reasonable compensation for the
pawn.

10 e5?!

The second mistake is believing
without question Black's last
move. Probably White should grab
the (not so much hot as luke
warm!) pawn with 10 ♗xb5.
10...♘xe4?? then loses to 11

♗xd7+ and so I doubt that Black
has sufficient compensation.

It is not unnatural for White to
consider Black's wing play as premature, bearing in mind the king is
still on e8. Nevertheless in the
forthcoming complications, White
discovers his own king to be a little
exposed along the a7-g1 diagonal
and then open to a variety of tricks
on h1. Therefore it appears that
blasting through the middle is not
the solution.

10 ...	dxe5
11 fxe5	♘g4
12 ♗xb5	a6!

Avoiding the temptation of 12
...♕b6+? 13 ♔h1 ♘f2+? 14 ♖xf2
♕xf2 15 ♘d5!, when the threats of
16 ♘c7+ and 16 ♗e3 will prove to
be too much. The text, forcing the
bishop to retreat, gives the black
queen more freedom.

13 ♗a4

Conceding the bishop pair with
13 ♗xd7+ is pointless as Black
will eventually regain his pawn on
e5.

13 ...	0-0
14 ♗b3?!	

This move doesn't work out well
for White, but no alternatives ex-
cel. Perhaps 14 ♗xd7, but after
14...♖d8 15 e6 fxe6, Black's piece
activity compensates him very
adequately for his weak pawns,
e.g. 16 ♗xe6+ ♗xe6 17 ♕e2 ♕c5+
18 ♔h1 ♗c4 and that's the end of
that!

14 ...	♕c5+

Accepting the challenge.

    15 ♔h1   ♘f2+
    16 ♖xf2   ♕xf2
    17 ♘d5   ♘xe5!
    18 ♗e3 *(227)*

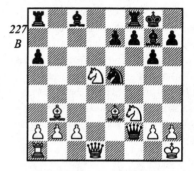

Is the black queen trapped?

    18 ...   ♘g4!

Yes, and No! The escape plan had to be seen when Black went in for winning the exchange.

    19 ♗b6   ♖b8

More accurate than 19...♕xb6 20 ♘xb6 ♘f2+ 21 ♔g1 ♘xd1 22 ♘xa8 which is also better for Black.

    20 ♘xe7+   ♔h8
    21 ♘xc8   ♖fxc8
    22 ♘g5   ♖xb6
    23 ♘xf7+??

An incredible oversight which makes you wonder what White thought Black was playing at, as 23...♔g8(??) is hardly appetizing! 23 ♕xg4 keeps him in the game, but after 23...♖c7, Black remains the clear favourite.

    23 ...   ♕xf7

            0-1

The queen has vacated the f2-square to make way for the knight.

In the next and final game of the book, a familiar theme is revisited. If you do not spot the key move, then please read over the book again. If on your second time around, you still don't get it, then I'm afraid that:

(a) You have a lousy memory! and

(b) I have failed in my task to make you a true Dragon player. Sorry about that!

However if as I suspect, your now natural response is correct, then you are there. The road ahead will not always be smooth, but you are now on that exciting path of discovery and your chess will never be quite the same.

Anyway, enough waffle and back to the game, featuring in the Black corner the (now) two-times British champion:

Game 53

Klundt-Hodgson

Cap d'Agde 1985

    1 e4   c5
    2 ♘f3   d6
    3 d4   cxd4
    4 ♘xd4   ♘f6
    5 ♘c3   g6
    6 f4   ♘bd7
    7 ♗e2   ♗g7
    8 ♗e3   0-0
    9 0-0

White has adopted a 'Classical' approach and can soon begin the unenviable task of storming the black fortress. Meanwhile Black can start movements on the queen-side, as usual targeting the e4-pawn via pressure on the c3-knight.

9 ...   **a6**
10 f5 *(228)*

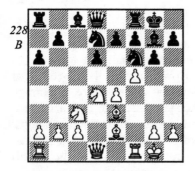

This aggressive-looking move puts a stop to any plans of the thematic ...e5 break that Black may have had. It also prepares a possible g4-g5, but has the very big drawback of conceding the e5-square.

10 ...   ♞**e5**
Never look a gift horse in the mouth!

11 a4
Preventing what would have been an awkward ...b5-b4. Nevertheless White appears to want a controlled attack, when all of the positional factors are in Black's favour. 11 g4 intending to meet 11...b5?! with 12 g5 is far more direct, but then Black has the usual antidote of 11...d5!. Then, all that

White will have to show for his early kingside pawn sortie, is some weaknesses and an exposed king (i.e. all his own!).

11 ...   **b6**
12 ♕e1
As we will see, vacating the d1-square for a rook, and preparing to swing into the attack on h4. One fault is that it relinquishes some control over g4. Therefore, 12 ...♞eg4 should now be a consideration, although evidently Black is plotting White's downfall in another way.

12 ...   ♝**b7**
13 ♕h4   ♜**c8**
14 ♖ad1 *(229)*
In the diagram below, what could it be that Black has in mind?

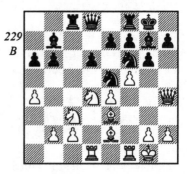

14 ...   ♜**xc3!**
That's right, business as usual. Now White's position comes apart at the seams.

15 bxc3   ♕**c7**
Well played. The e4-pawn will be taken later. For the time being,

Black prepares to wreak havoc with his queen.

16 &d3 &xc3
17 &e2

White has little constructive to do. Black is actually threatening the 17...&xe4 (hardly forced) and so White prevents this, in the vain hope of re-routing the knight to somewhere useful.

17 ... &c6
18 &b1

White singles out the only weakness in the black camp, but the response is very appropriate.

18 ... &c4!

Another of the key Dragon (though also other Sicilians) moves. Of course, White must preserve his dark-squared bishop, but here as well, should his light-squared bishop go, then all of his pawns will follow!

19 &d4 &xa4
20 &f2 &d2
21 &xb6

White has opted for the practical decision of returning the exchange for some counterplay. However this is minimal, and Black cleans up ruthlessly.

22 ... &xf1
23 &xb7 &d2

24 h3

24 &xe7 is not possible because of 24...&a1+.

24 ... &a1+
25 &h2 &fxe4!

Tieing up the loose ends with a nice combination.

26 &xe4 g5

The queen is deflected from the defence of the e4-bishop.

27 &xg5

If 27 &g4 then 27...&f1+ 28 &g1 &e3+ wins the white queen.

27 ... &xe4 (230)

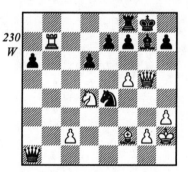

0-1

White is about to lose his knight and has no chances whatsoever. Therefore, coinciding with the end of this book, he calls it a day.

Goodbye and good luck!

Index of Variations